BRITISH INDUSTRIAL FICTIONS

British
Industrial
Fictions

edited by

H. GUSTAV KLAUS and STEPHEN KNIGHT

UNIVERSITY OF WALES PRESS
CARDIFF
2000

© The Contributors, 2000

British Library Cataloguing-in-Publication Data.
A catalogue record for this book is available from the British Library.

ISBN 0–7083–1597–6 paperback
     0–7083–1596–8 hardback

Typeset at University of Wales Press
Printed in Great Britain by Dinefwr Press, Llandybïe

Contents

Notes on Contributors

Ian A. Bell is Professor of English and Head of Department at the University of Wales Swansea. His publications include *Defoe's Fiction, Literature and Crime in Augustan England, Henry Fielding: Authorship and Authority* and *Peripheral Visions*, as well as many articles on eighteenth-century writing, crime fiction and Scottish literature.

Kathleen Bell is a Senior Lecturer in English at De Montfort University, Leicester, where she leads a course on working-class writing. Her publications are chiefly on twentieth-century poetry and popular fiction; she lives near Nottingham, the setting for *Saturday Night and Sunday Morning*.

Andy Croft lives in Middlesbrough, where he makes a living teaching poetry in local schools. His books include *Red Letter Days, A Weapon in the Struggle*, and three collections of poetry, *Nowhere Special, Gaps Between Hills* and *Headland*.

Valentine Cunningham is Professor of English Language and Literature at Oxford University and Fellow and Tutor in English at Corpus Christi College, Oxford. He has written extensively about Victorian literature, the thirties, Spanish Civil War writing, and theory. His most recent book is *The Victorians: An Anthology of Poetry and Poetics*.

James A. Davies is a part-time Senior Lecturer in English at the University of Wales Swansea. His many publications on Victorian literature and Welsh writing in English include *John Forster: A Literary Life, The Textual Life of Dickens's Characters, Leslie Norris* and *A Reference Companion to Dylan Thomas*.

Gary Day is Principal Lecturer in English at De Montfort University, Bedford. He is the author of *Re-reading Leavis: Culture and Literary Criticism* and a new introduction to *The Ragged Trousered Philanthropists*.

Simon Dentith is Reader in English at Cheltenham and Gloucester College of Higher Education. His most recent books are *Society and Cultural Forms in Nineteenth-Century England* and a volume on parody in the *New Critical Idiom* series.

John Fordham lectures in twentieth-century literature at Middlesex University, where he did a Ph.D. on 'James Hanley: modernism and the working class'. He has published articles on Hanley and is working on a full-length book on him.

Ian Haywood is Reader in English at the University of Surrey at Roehampton. His books include *The Literature of Struggle: An Anthology of Chartist Fiction* and *Working-Class Fiction: From Chartism to Trainspotting*.

H. Gustav Klaus is Professor of the Literature of the British Isles at the University of Rostock, Germany. His publications in the field of industrial writing include the edited essay collections *The Socialist Novel in Britain* and *The Rise of Socialist Fiction 1801–1914*, as well as the monographs *The Literature of Labour* and the recent *Factory Girl*.

Stephen Knight is Professor and Head of English Literature at the University of Wales, Cardiff. He has published essays on medieval and modern literature and his books include *Form and Ideology in Crime Fiction, Arthurian Literature and Society* and *Robin Hood: A Complete Study of the English Outlaw*.

Rolf Meyn is Professor of American Literature at the University of Rostock, Germany. He has published articles on nineteenth-century American fiction and a study of *Die 'Rote Dekade': Studien zur Literaturkritik und Romanliteratur der dreissiger Jahre in den USA*.

Mike Sanders is a lecturer in English at University College, Northampton, and one of the co-founders of the 'Radical Tradition' network. He is currently editing a four-volume anthology on 'Women and radicalism in the nineteenth century' and is also at work on a study of Chartist poetry.

Ingrid von Rosenberg is Professor of British Cultural Studies at the University of Dresden. She has published books and articles on English working-class and socialist novels, women's literature, the history of cultural studies, sexuality, German-English cultural relations and black British literature.

1

Introduction

H. GUSTAV KLAUS and STEPHEN KNIGHT

In 1958 a Welsh critic identified a batch of English works of fiction as 'The Industrial Novels', among them *Mary Barton, North and South* and *Hard Times*. The irony of this categorization dawned on Raymond Williams later, as he came to see the limitations of these novels, their exclusive northern English setting, their preoccupation with the textile industry, their middle-class perspective.[1]

But in one sense Williams's original identification was right. If Britain was internationally a leader in industrial fiction no less than in industry itself, it was England and English authors that pioneered and set the tone in that development. There is no significant industrial fiction in either Scotland or Wales until after the First World War, though when the industrial experience entered the writing of those two countries it became more sustained than in England and made a major contribution to the industrial fiction of Britain.

In travelling from Teesside to not just south but also north Wales, from Clydeside to the English South Coast (Robert Tressell's Hastings), *British Industrial Fictions* recognizes regional and national variation across the range of British industrial fiction. In dealing with shipbuilders, quarrymen, nailers, builders, needlewomen and bicycle-factory workers, it moves beyond the well-trodden path of the textiles and coal-mining novels. Not only in analysing what outside observers, however well-intentioned, made of the Industrial Revolution, but also in giving prominence to the cacophonous voices from within the world of labour, this essay collection claims to set the record straight.

This is also true in terms of the topics of the essays gathered here. While some duly reconsider the classics of English working-class fiction – *The Ragged Trousered Philanthropists*, *Love on the Dole*, *Saturday Night and Sunday Morning* – others cover dozens of lesser known and sometimes, unfortunately, hard-to-obtain works. The collection concludes with a look at the efforts of contemporary writers to come to terms with deindustrialization, the often enforced closure of coal-mines, shipyards and steel plants – in short, the 'post-industrial' experience.

This last term needs to be taken with some caution, as, although heavy industry and factory production of the traditional kind have indeed largely gone from Britain, they have not dematerialized, but literally gone elsewhere. They have vanished from the face of most European countries only to surface in other parts of the globe, which now set out on their own painful paths through industrialization. For ships still need to be built, coal and ores to be extracted, cotton to be spun, garments to be manufactured, indeed, industrial fictions to be written – and studied. A lament for lost industry runs the risk of weaving a universal truth out of a local phenomenon: the world of industry and industrial fiction is wider than Eurocentric angst.

Nor is there truth in the accompanying myth that the working class is dying, either in Britain or elsewhere, however consoling that view might be to various kinds of modern politicians. While this class has, by most definitions, certainly contracted in most OECD countries, there were never more industrial workers on this planet than in the second half of the twentieth century. Even today those employed in the new manufacturing industries or dirtying their hands in some form of manual labour still comprise a quarter of the working population in Britain, Germany and other Western countries. What have occurred are technical transformations in the productive sector, entailing shifts and cracks within the working class and leading to 'a crisis not of the class but of its consciousness'.[2] The international character of the working class remains a reality, and the nature of international working-class fictions remains a topic for future essays and collections.

Having said that, it is still true that in Britain at least a particular settled and self-conscious way of living and working, marked by both social cohesion and social segregation from other classes, has been eroded, and such British fictions as celebrate work these days are quite different from those in which past generations both realized and challenged their arduous environment. We have therefore reached an appropriate moment in which to take stock of the literary and – given its strength – especially the fictional inheritance of this British industrial world.

This book, part honorific obituary, part rescue archaeology, traces how writers responded imaginatively to the impact of industry upon human lives in Britain, how they saw people coping with and resisting the demands made upon them, how they detected at once human waste and slumbering potential beneath so much degradation, how the dream of a juster, healthier, more dignified life was never lost. A certain shape in the development of British industrial fiction over the ages is discernible, both with regard to authorship and thematic focus. We note a shift from the Captain of Industry novels of the early Victorian period, through the Capital and Labour genre of the following decades, to an emphatic concentration on the working-class environment, most successfully realized by writers born in working-class families. In its growing confidence, even militancy, this type of working-class novel becomes the dominant form in the first half of the twentieth century.

But, most remarkably, throughout this period we register, as in all other periods, a powerful attention to and valorization of work, a commitment to the importance of labour which is even present in a negative context as in the unemployment novels of the 1930s. The representation of the work of ordinary men and women and the analysis of its economic, social and political implications are the unique contributions of industrial fiction to the literature of the nineteenth and twentieth centuries; the hands of the writers have conveyed both the operations and the implications of labouring hands, and it is these processes that are explored by the contributors to this collection of essays.

The editors' thanks are due to the SOCRATES academic network and to the University of Wales, Cardiff, for providing funds to permit the 1998 conference on Industrial Fictions at which the themes explored in this collection were first raised; to Dawn Harrington for her expertise in handling the materials assembled in this collection, and at the University of Wales Press to Ned Thomas, Ceinwen Jones and Jane Robson for their care in creating this book.

Notes

[1] Raymond Williams, *Culture and Society 1780–1950* (London, 1958), part 1, chap. 5; also see 'Working-class, proletarian, socialist: problems in some Welsh novels', in H. Gustav Klaus (ed.), *The Socialist Novel in Britain* (Brighton, 1982), 113.

[2] Eric Hobsbawm, *Age of Extremes: The Short Twentieth Century 1914–1991* (London, 1994), 305.

2

'Graphic Narratives and Discoveries of Horror': the Feminization of Labour in Nineteenth-century Radical Fiction

IAN HAYWOOD

It has long been accepted that British 'industrial fiction' came to fruition in the 1840s with the appearance of the 'social problem' or 'industrial' novel: Disraeli's *Sybil* (1845), Gaskell's *Mary Barton* (1848) and *North and South* (1854–5), Kingsley's *Alton Locke* (1850), Dickens's *Hard Times* (1854) and George Eliot's *Felix Holt the Radical* (1866).[1] These novels represent the literary response to the 'condition of England', a term coined to reflect widespread anxiety in mid-Victorian society about the demoralized physical and moral condition of the urban working class. As Carlyle declaimed, 'the sum of their wretchedness merited and unmerited welters, huge, dark and baleful, like a Dantean Hell'.[2] Such fears were supported by a series of shocking parliamentary reports into the working, housing and sanitary conditions of the poor. In the words of the contemporary feminist Anna Jameson, the Blue Books were 'teeming with graphic narratives and discoveries of horror'.[3]

But novelists were not only attracted to this sensational material for reasons of artistic opportunity, moral duty or social sympathy. The middle classes feared that social misery was driving the working class towards Chartism and violence. The year 1842 saw the convergence of the second Chartist petition, the publication of two of the most important Blue Books (Chadwick's report on urban sanitation and the Employment Commission report into children's and women's employment) and a summer of major 'disturbances' in the industrial midlands and north. The most conspicuous generic feature of the industrial novel, as Raymond

'The needlewoman at home and abroad' from *Punch* Vol. 18 (1850).

Williams noted, is its aesthetic failure to identify with the cause of the working class.[4] In order to contain the threat of Chartism, the social experience of the unpropertied British proletariat is forced to conform to the dominant conventions of the bourgeois novel: individualism, romance and the property plot. Hence, Disraeli's lower-class heroine Sybil turns out to be of aristocratic birth, *Mary Barton* becomes a whodunnit, Alton Locke renounces Chartism for religion and Dickens finds more hope for social transformation in Sleary's circus than in industrial struggle.

The industrial novel is unrepresentative in another way. Far less critical attention has been given to the contribution made by popular and radical fiction to the 'condition of England' debate.[5] Yet it was at the level of popular culture, in the press, periodicals and didactic 'improving' fiction, that the earliest and most sustained engagement with the Blue Book 'discoveries' took place, and where most readers would get their first taste of 'graphic narratives', either in excerpts from the originals or in spin-off stories. Popular culture also responded more directly than mainstream novels to the Blue Books' investigations of female labour, and in particular the plight of the needlewoman. It was this figure more than any other which captured the mid-Victorian imagination and established itself as an icon of debased and brutalized capitalist labour.[6]

The plight of the needlewoman was exposed in two important documents: R. D. Grainger's report for the second Children's Employment Commission in 1843, and Henry Mayhew's survey of London labour in the *Morning Chronicle* (1849–50).[7] The Employment Commission had been established to investigate the labour of women and children in occupations and workplaces that lay beyond the regulatory reach of factory legislation. Mayhew shed light on the murky urban backwaters of 'dishonourable' slop-work. These inquiries unveiled an appalling picture of the extremes of poverty and exploitation: low pay, long hours, unhealthy working conditions, insecurity, ill health. In the words of a doctor, 'a mode of life more completely calculated to destroy human life could scarcely be contrived' (p. 232). Another of Grainger's informants described this 'mode of life' tersely:

> In the fashionable season, occupying about 4 months, thinks the average time allowed for sleep is about 6 hours, frequently less. Often the young persons sit up all night, sometimes for two nights in succession. The effects of this long labour are most painful; it causes great exhaustion, and often leads to a fatal result. (f. 204)

Such details would alone have been sufficient to establish the needlewoman as an archetype of proletarianization. But even more shocking to polite readers was the revelation that thousands of needlewomen topped up their deficient earnings from casual prostitution.[8] Many needlewomen had migrated to the cities to seek work; the more genteel or skilled journeywoman might find work in a fashionable show-shop serving the 'seasons' of fashionable leisure, but the less fortunate were left to do slop-work in their lodgings. If no work came in, the choices were stark: needlewomen, many of them widows with children, faced starvation, the workhouse or 'being obligated to go a bad way'. Some of the women interviewed by Mayhew were resigned to this cycle of existence: 'And then at last I found it impossible to get on; when a man lodging in the house was anxious to get a partner, and made offers to me, I thought it better to accept them than to do worse.'[9] But such worldiness was too subversive for Victorian sexual morality. It was easier to see the needlewoman as a species of fallen woman whose sexual transgressions conformed to the sentimental- ized and moralized conventions of romance: lost pastoral innocence, urban corruption and temptation, and tragic demise. In this mythical narrative, the heroine is 'exposed in a peculiar degree to the temptations of the metropolis' (p. 236).

The more melodramatic versions of the myth absolved the heroine from any collusion and made her a saintly martyr, a passive victim of circumstance. The needlewoman problem was therefore shifted discursively onto the more manageable grounds of sexual morality and away from the failures of political economy. The mythical solution to the needlewoman's plight lay in the regulation of femininity rather than state intervention: the women workers needed protection against vice, and the fashionable ladies who demanded new garments at short notice were asked to moderate their vanity and excessive tastes. The historian Helen Rogers concludes that the cultural effect of this paternalism, which she traces across the political spectrum from Tories to radicals and feminists, was further to disempower the needlewoman and to weaken the first tentative steps taken towards economic regulation.[10] However, a rather different conclusion can be drawn from a reading of needlewoman stories. It is here that we can find a more resistant and subversive tone and can read against the grain of the needlewoman myth. In particular, I want to focus on periodical fiction and the achievements of two Chartist writers, George W. M. Reynolds and Ernest Jones.

Within months of the publication of Grainger's report, Thomas Hood's famous 'Song of the Shirt' was published in *Punch* (1843) and became the 'anthem of the reformers'.[11] Hood created an icon of the toiling, isolated, downtrodden seamstress:

> With fingers weary and worn,
> With eyelids heavy and red,
> A woman sat in unwomanly rags,
> Plying her needle and thread —
> Stitch! stitch! stitch!
> In poverty, hunger, and dirt.

Though the lyric is genuinely indignant at this injustice, it was the romantic ingredients of the poem, the lonely, 'unwomanly' suffering, which pricked the conscience and captured the imagination of the Victorian public. The poem lent itself to visualization, and within a year Richard Redgrave's influential painting *The Sempstress* (1844) gave the needlewoman a place in high culture.[12] Redgrave showed the needlewoman working through the night in a run-down garret room with only the light of the moon and a single spluttering candle. The expression on her face is deeply spiritual. In Bakhtinian terms, the social force of the image comes from the contrast between her 'classical' body and the 'grotesque realism' of her surroundings.[13] The garret scene captured the essence of the sentimental representation of the needlewoman, and was widely imitated in different media.

As Martin Meisel has shown, this process of 'realization' across visual, literary and theatrical media was a hallmark of mid-Victorian culture, and enabled controversial social themes to be circulated quickly and effectively at all social levels.[14] Mark Lemon's melodrama *The Sempstress* (1844) was based on the scene, and it figured with minor adjustments in many needlewoman stories and their illustrations.[15] However, it is important to note that the image of the isolated, nocturnal needlewoman did not completely dominate the iconographic field. Two other types of scene were also popular: the workshop scene and the diptych or contrast scene. The first scene shows a group of women working under a supervisor; the second scene counterpoints needlework (either solitary or collective) with fashionable life. These images operate within a more realistic tradition, depicting social relations and class forces, though the scenes can still utilize populist tropes: the diptych, for example, relies on the emotional force of melodrama. Some artists abandoned realism altogether and opted for satirical or Gothic effects in which the 'unwomanly' body is transformed into an image of death.[16] This range of 'realizations' shows that writers and artists taking up the cause of the needlewoman were not restricted solely to the conventions of the sentimentalized heroine. In most needlewomen stories we see a blending of documentary, sentimental and melodramatic influences. Even the more conservative Evangelical authors pull no punches in exposing the needleworkers' misery and in condemning the social irresponsibility of the ruling class. The task of Reynolds and Jones was made easier by the fact that radical literary foundations had already been laid.

The first few years after Grainger's report formed a particularly fertile period, producing Elizabeth Stone's novel *The Young Milliner* (1843), Charlotte Tonna's *The Wrongs of Woman* (1843–4) and a series of tales by Camilla Toulmin in Douglas Jerrold's radical *Illuminated Magazine*.[17] Despite the fact that most of these stories are directed at a genteel female readership and defend *laissez-faire* economics, there are many 'unwomanly' subversive moments. In *The Young Milliner* the task of explaining the evils of the competitive system to the heroine is given to a prostitute (as we shall see, this is a motif which Reynolds uses to great effect).[18] Great play is made in several tales of the contrast between the employer's 'brilliantly lit showroom' and the 'dingy, cold, uncomfortable garret' of the workers.[19] Toulmin also attacks the lifestyle of 'pampered dames' as 'contemptible'.[20] But the most disturbing story is Toulmin's 'The Shawl Buyer. An Incident of 1843'. The tale is about the moral dilemma of a seamstress who has sold a smallpox-infected shawl to a genteel customer, a scenario later reworked by Kingsley in *Alton Locke*.[21] She decides to confess the error and is rewarded with further well-paid work. However, she is opposed by an insalubrious colleague who seethes with class hatred: 'Let them sicken and die . . . Don't they grind us down to what we are?'[22] For this woman, contagion is a weapon in the class war. Her presence in the story is a chilling reminder of the class antagonism beneath the 'polite' surface of needlework.

The presence of the needlewoman in a large number of radical and 'improving' stories in the 1840s and early 1850s contrasts sharply with her virtual absence from the mainstream realistic novel. Dickens's *Nicholas Nickleby* (1838–9) is exceptional in its focus on the plight of Kate Nickleby at the hands of the dressmaker Madame Mantalini. Dickens took up the theme again in his Christmas fable *The Chimes* (1844), clearly under the influence of the first wave of fictionalizations. But the Meg Veck garret scene appears as a nightmarish prophecy rather than established social reality. In Gaskell's *Mary Barton* (1848) the eponymous heroine is a 'beautiful little milliner' who narrowly avoids being seduced by the local factory owner's son. There are a few chilling reminders of the health risks involved in such work, such as Margaret Legh's blindness, but the novel's moral focus is on the seduction plot and its catastrophic consequences.[23] Gaskell's novel *Ruth* (1854) is concerned with redeeming the fallen heroine from her needlewoman

THE ORPHAN MILLINERS.

A STORY OF THE WEST END.

BY MISS CAMILLA TOULMIN.

" Work—work—work !
Till the brain begins to swim !
Work—work—work !
Till the eyes are heavy and dim !"—Hood.

There is a certain spot in one of the midland counties, which, for the sake of preserving its incognito, I will call Willow-dale. It is really but three or four miles from a market town, yet lying away from the high road, and being still further removed from any rail-road, it is about as secluded a place as the imagination can picture. Yet beautiful exceedingly is its rich meadow land ; and pleasant to view the varied beauty of its flowering, fruitful orchards ; and pure the health-giving breezes that come from the neighbouring hills. Above all, to my heart has it the exquisite charm of silence,—that profound silence which is felt as a delicious sensation ! The few cottages which are scattered over about a quarter of a mile of the Dale, are called—by the dwellers therein—a village ; though by malicious detractors they have been said to comprise only—a hamlet. Narrow the distinction, I grant ;
Vol. II.

but measure two little persons together, and see if they do not stand upright, to say nothing of getting on tiptoe if they dare.

In one of the prettiest of these cottages lived for some years a widow and her two daughters. A small life annuity secured to Mrs. Sandford, was their only dependence ; and Willow-dale had been chosen as a residence, because house rent was low, and the little income would go farther in such a neighbourhood than elsewhere. It does not seem to have occurred to the mother, that it was possible to *add* to their narrow means by any exertions of her own, and so provide against casualties. No ; she was one of those characters in whom feminine softness borders very decidedly on feminine weakness. Of placid, unaspiring temper, she thought little of the future, and was easily contented with the present. The little she did think
Y

'The Orphan Milliners' from Douglas Jerrold's *Illuminated Magazine*, Vol. II (1843–4). Illustration by Hine.

past.[24] So the theme is either chronologically or narratively distanced, and this displacement reminds us that an important original feature of needlewomen stories was their contemporary setting, a major departure from the backdating strategies of most Victorian novels. It is also worth noting that most of the stories were written by women journalists, and merit attention as an important if minor contribution to women's literary and cultural history. It is with a certain irony, therefore, that I now turn to two male writers for the most radical representations of the needlewoman.

George W. M. Reynolds's *The Seamstress* appeared in his own periodical *Reynolds's Miscellany* in 1850.[25] Unlike the authors mentioned so far, Reynolds commanded a massive following both as an author and radical leader.[26] The title illustration for *The Seamstress* indicates Reynolds's mode of intervention into the needlewoman myth. A diptych shows the contrast between a garretted needlewoman (the 'midnight toiler') on the left and a fashionable ball on the right. Between the two scenes stands a huge, erect, forbidding pair of scissors surrounded by needles and cotton bobbins. The use of counterpointed images of social injustice was in common usage in popular journals such as *Punch*, and Reynolds used several diptychs of this kind on the front covers of his publications. These images depicted the melodramatic contrast between rich and poor: on the left side, the suffering victims of poverty; on the right side, the decadent rich.[27] However, in the woodcut from *The Seamstress* it is clear that the 'midnight toiler' is not only poor; she is also a worker, producing the luxury items which are consumed by and which legitimate the lifestyle of the ruling classes. The correct way to read the image is therefore as an expression of a class relationship.

This dynamic replaces the more familiar trope of Old Corruption: rich against poor, enfranchised against disenfranchised. Reynolds imputes a class consciousness to the conventional melodramatic conflict. Moreover, in the tale this consciousness is also imparted to the heroine Virginia Mordaunt, who is not merely a passive victim of her appalling circumstances. Though she undergoes the conventional misfortunes of starvation wages and seduction, she gains an insight into the economic injustice of her situation. This revelation exposes the invidious 'middlewoman' system which mediates between her proletarianized production and upper-class consumption. So the class consciousness of the diptych supplies the bourgeois economics which are formally absent from

'Needle Money', 'Pin Money' from *Punch*, Vol. 17 (1849).
Illustration by John Leech.

the melodramatic antithesis of the high and the low (what Peter Brooks calls the 'excluded middle'[28]). In the story we also see the role of villain transfer from the libertine nobleman to the workplace overseer, a dramatization of the new balance of class forces.

The story commences with a 'realization' of the famous garret scene. In order to squeeze maximum pathos out of Virginia's suffering, Reynolds makes her into an idealized and stereotypical figure of beauty, purity and saintly virtue. She is the 'classical' body in 'grotesque' surroundings. The male gaze of the narrator anticipates uneasily the rapacious designs of the story's villains: 'Her dress, of a dark stuff, ascended to the throat, thus concealing the charms of that bust whose virgin contours the close-fitting corsage nevertheless developed' (p. 5). But the point is that Virginia is doubly exploitable as sexual and economic commodity. Her goodness is exaggerated so that she can 'pass uncontaminated through the ordeal' (p. 6) of privation, isolation and sexual intrigue. Despite all the temptations put in her way, she never succumbs to a life of even casual prostitution. But although Virginia's exploited body is textually foregrounded, the narrative emphasis in the opening scenes is equally on her growing understanding of the competitive system that oppresses her: the 'middle-women' who are the petty-bourgeois intermediaries between Virginia and her aristocratic consumers.

There are no fewer than five steps on this ladder of increasing surplus value. For the 'superb velvet dress' (p. 6) she stays up all night to make Virginia earns 3*s*. 6*d*.; her employer Mrs Jackson gets 7*s*.; her client Mrs Pembroke gets 14*s*.; at the summit is Madame Duplessy, who touts for business in fashionable circles: she gets £4. 4*s*., a clear profit for her of £3. 10*s*. Virginia seeks further enlightenment from her fellow lodger Miss Barnett, whose elegantly furnished room is a sign of immoral earnings. But, though 'her charms were wholly of a physical nature' (p. 19), she explains to Virginia why it is impossible ' "for the poor seamstress to obtain the real value of her labour" ' (p. 20). The middle-women system is a mechanism of economic control designed to keep down wages and protect the propertied élite from having to engage directly with labour: ' "were Madame Duplessy left to fight the battle of labour's value direct with *you* who did the labour, she would be pretty well at your mercy" ' (p. 20). It is characteristic of Reynolds's literary audacity that a prostitute should be the most radical character in the story.

But when Virginia manages later in the story to cut out the middlewomen and obtain work 'direct' from Aaron and Sons' emporium, she is still at the mercy of a brutal cash nexus and a supervisor who tries to rape her. The emporium is 'a colossal proof of the grinding tyranny which capital wields over labour'. The description of this grand building is a satirical debunking of the pleasures of consumerism: 'the towering edifice, so grand without and so superb within . . . with its magnificent windows, its plate glass and its brilliant illuminations . . . is a mighty monument which capital has raised in honour of the Genius of Competition' (p. 77). In the next sentence Reynolds rereads the building 'morally':

> its foundations are built with the bones of the white slaves of England, male and female: the skeletons of journeymen tailors and poor seamstresses, all starved to death, constitute the door-posts and the window-frames: – the walls are made of skulls – the architectural devices are cross-bones – and the whole is cemented firmly and solidly by the blood, pith and marrow of the miserable wretches who are forced to sell themselves in the Slave-Market of British Labour.

This emporium is a Castle of Despair, a Gothic travesty of the body politic. Reynolds likens capitalism to a contagion of vampires, cannibals and plagues 'spreading an awful demoraliza-tion throughout the country' (p. 80). The sensationalist imagery of popular culture is mobilized for a critique of commercialism.

As a passionate republican, Reynolds uses the needlewoman story to launch salvoes of anti-aristocratic invective against the traditional melodramatic enemy. He concentrates on the ruling class's moral and cultural deficiencies rather than their political illegitimacy, as this focus allows him to make a running comparison between the lifestyles of the aristocracy and the poor:

> it is a diabolical, a scandalous, and an atrocious insult to denounce the immorality of the 'lower orders', while they have neither the power nor the inducement to be virtuous . . . yet the British Aristocracy, male and female, is the most loathsomely corrupt, demoralized, and profligate class of persons that ever scandalized a country. (pp. 80, 86)

The clearest proof of the moral superiority of the working class occurs in a scene where Virginia is cared for by another needle-woman:

> Thus it is that the poor assist each other in the hour of need . . . for though poverty and the extremes to which it drove them had destroyed their delicate notions of morality, yet their feelings were not blunted by the same influences: on the contrary, they who were so cruelly oppressed, scourged, persecuted, tortured, and trampled upon by their task-masters, were full of the milk of human kindness towards a fellow-creature! (p. 84)

Reynolds seizes triumphantly on this discovery of a residual benevolence, as it shows both Virginia and himself the 'sublime disposition of the working classes'. While Virginia dreams about 'just government, an honest legislature, and a good social system in this country', Reynolds 'swears by all that is sacred never to desert [the] cause' of the working classes 'so long as he has the power to wield a pen or to raise a voice to proclaim their wrongs and assert their rights' (p. 84). This is more than sentimental bluster, as Reynolds was by this time a leading Chartist activist. His trans-formation from narrator to tribune carries the authority of his political agitation outside the text. Radical fiction was not predicated on the bourgeois aesthetics of transcendency but on the republican aesthetics of the unmasking of power. Reynolds speaks directly to his mass readership and Chartist following: 'Let not the *immorality*, but the *wages* of needlewomen first absorb attention' (p. 80). The way forward is not protectionism or domestication but economic justice.[29] This cannot be achieved without a 'just government' prepared to take on both the bourgeoisie and the aristocracy: 'capitalists, competitors and monopolists . . . pensioners, placemen and sinecurists' (p. 78).

But until the wider problem of the general exploitation of labour is solved, it is business as usual for Aaron and Son. In another radical departure, Reynolds refuses the reader the consolation of full narrative closure: 'That establishment still exists, and the system whereon it is based flourishes more than ever' (p. 112). It still flourishes today.

Ernest Jones's *Woman's Wrongs* was first published in his periodical *Notes to the People* in 1852.[30] The work does not qualify as a conventional novel as it comprises four tales linked by the titular theme of the social oppression of contemporary women: 'The Working-Man's Wife', 'The Young Milliner', 'The Trades-man's Daughter' and 'The Lady of Title'. Jones explains his methodology in an Introduction: 'I purpose, therefore, to lift the veil from before the wrongs of woman – to shew her what she suffers at her own home hearth – how society receives her – what society does for her – where society leaves her' (p. 515). Unlike Tonna's *Wrongs of Woman*, to which it clearly owes a debt, Jones's portfolio of stories is not organized according to different female trades or professions but instead reflects the class hierarchy: his aim is to show injustice 'upward, downward, through all the social grades'. This totalizing aesthetic means that female labour is only one focus of the narratives, and Jones can interrogate other central aspects of the feminine sphere (romance, family relations) within their respective class position. Indeed, the fourth story by defini-tion takes place in the leisured world, though the elite society it unmasks is shot through with the malign influence of property. In order to expose the contradictions of the capitalist construction of femininity, Jones gives the reader of *Woman's Wrongs* two axes of interpretation. The vertical axis foregrounds gender identity and the common victimization of women by 'the vile mechanism of our system'. The horizontal axis emphasizes class ('social grades') and the relativity of suffering. This dialectical structure is also operative within the tales where the overlapping forces of gender and class determine the heroines' tragic destinies.

This process is particularly acute in 'The Young Milliner'. As we have seen, a striking ideological feature of the needlewoman story was its feminization of the discourse of class, relocating production and consumption (and hero and villain) within the feminine sphere. This displacement posed a perplexing alternative to the male agency of classical political economy but also contained that challenge within the dominant cultural traditions of romance and melodrama (evoking the tropes of martyrdom, seduced innocence and aristocratic decadence). Like Reynolds, Jones radicalizes the fallen-woman plot through narrative commentary, the consciousness of the heroine, and the aiming of his story at a radical and (in a later move) popular readership. His heroine Anna is in the 'distressed needlewoman' mould. She is a respectable farmer's daughter, but the death of her parents has left her a 'friendless orphan' (p. 630) and she has moved to London to take up slopwork. The story begins with the well-known garret scene including the customary references to isolation, beauty and spiritual pining. There are a few, predictable details about her work, but the narrative focus is on the shallowness, hypocrisy and malice of bourgeois sexual morality. Anna's progress from proletarianized saint to tragic sinner follows some of the well-trodden steps of her fictional predecessors, but also involves several new departures. At the core of the tale's radicalism is the configuring of Anna's body as a commodity.

The familiar 'extenuating circumstances' (p. 690) of her fall are economic (poverty, insecurity), social (isolation, urban alienation) and sexual (beauty, predatory males). Anna is in love with the faint-hearted medical student Charles Trelawney. This romance is socially precarious, but she has little hope once she spurns the amorous advances of a jealous fellow lodger, Frederick Treadstone, a downwardly mobile footman. His revenge is to ruin Anna by spreading salacious rumours about her relationship with Trelawney and getting her sacked. Anna has no one else to turn to but Trelawney, whereupon he seduces her in a moment of drunken passion. To make matters worse, Treadstone immediately exposes the affair. This scandal means that Anna's reputation is lost and she becomes even more dependent on Trelawney. They live together for a while, but inevitably his love cools and after his mother intervenes he returns to the bosom of the family and abandons the pregnant Anna. A narrative jump then takes us to the tale's macabre conclusion. After giving birth to a stillborn son, Anna dies in the same hospital (University College London) in which Charles is being trained. Her body is then used for an anatomy lecture which Charles attends. When he recognizes her features on the slab he faints with horror and guilt.

This denouement is not only memorable as the most horrific ending of all the needlewoman stories. Anna's defiled body signifies the destructiveness of the luxury economy and the male gaze which supports it: ' "your body has ministered to the *amusement* and *instruction* of the favoured few" ', says one of Trelawney's more humane fellow students (p. 712). As the Blue Books demonstrated only too well, the working woman's body was an object of voyeuristic revulsion. The anatomy lecture is presented as a cheap thrill. The rowdy students only quieten down when 'the professor raised the cloth from a part of the body . . . the words "young woman" had rivetted attention' (p. 712). This 'unnatural' exposure of breasts, reminiscent of scandalous images of female miners, functions as a key signifier of class identity. Jones's achievement is to weave together the oppressiveness of female labour and the oppressiveness of bourgeois romantic love: both are systems based on the exploitation of women and the perversion of healthy social and erotic relations. Jones refers to the values of 'gay' life as a 'contagion' (p. 629). This metaphorical disease is passed from high to low, an apposite inversion of the bourgeois fear that clothes had become a means of transmission of smallpox from the poor to the rich.[31] Ironically, the hospital is a site where the 'contagion' of class domination flourishes.

Significantly, Anna's strongest flourish of class consciousness arises from an awareness of the contrast between her proletarian-ized body and the pampered polite women whose clothes (and therefore beauty) she manufactures. The most telling comparison is between the condition of hands: the 'small white hands' of the 'gay things' are protected by 'soft gloves'; Anna's 'poor hands' are 'worn and bleeding with premature toil' (p. 632). This moment is another striking example of the feminization of the discourse of class, as the word 'hand' was commonly used to refer to the unskilled male worker. Yet Anna feels 'as good and beautiful' as these other women.[32] Anna's passions are also class signifiers, as

Jones refuses to make his heroine meek and passive. In the opening garret scene her 'dreamy reverie' is broken by 'a momentary eagerness'. The narrative shields her from equal culpability in her fall, as she is only semi-conscious when she first has sex with Charles, but once 'restored to animation' she 'gave herself up, after a passing coyness . . . to the full torrent of her generous, ardent, enthusiastic love' (p. 671). Jones does not condone her actions, but he chivalrously defends her virtue relative to her accusers. Over forty years before *Tess of the d'Urbervilles*, Jones throws down the gauntlet to Victorian sexual morality:

> we do say this, – broadly, boldly, in the face of society and all its power, its prejudice, its ignorance, its cruelty, do we fling down the assertion; that young girl was better, more virtuous, more good – aye! more *pure* – than ninety-nine out of every hundred of the sanctimonious tyrants who, in their self-righteous morality, would trample that appealing spirit down into the street. (p. 690)

Jones denaturalizes the discourse of romantic love. Anna may have been wrong to have sex before marriage but while she is living with Charles as a wife 'the treasures of her intellect opened forth' (p. 690). It is his faithlessness, not her sin, which disrupts this progress. But social mobility is a mixed blessing: 'as her delicate hand grew softer and more white, so her nature grew less capable of tolerating the harsh, rough surface of society'. Jones inverts the conventional emblematic connotations of the colours red and white.

When Jones republished *Woman's Wrongs* in 1855 in penny issue form, he added a fifth story based entirely on this motif.[33] 'The Girl with the Red Hands' is another tale about a decent, industrious milliner who falls for a fickle, weak-hearted dandy. In her desperation to please him, she works even longer hours than normal so that she can purchase cosmetics to whiten the skin of her hands (she fails to see the irony of this endeavour). When this tactic fails, she tries to regain his love by making him a beautiful silk purse (clearly, a sexual and monetary symbol) but it is intercepted by her rival, a woman with whiter hands. The lover and rival resort to crime to maintain their foppish, dissipated lifestyle. In flight from the police, they coincidentally take refuge in the dying heroine's room. As in 'The Young Milliner', the male lover is confronted with the body of his victim. Her expiring hands are indeed now white, a point she makes 'with an hysterical laugh' (p. 63). By Jones's standards 'The Girl with the Red Hands' is an inferior piece of writing, but it shows that the needlewoman continued as a folk-heroine well into the 1850s. Her revival is long overdue.

Notes

[1] Louis Cazamian, *The Social Novel in England: Dickens, Disraeli, Mrs Gaskell, Kingsley* (London, 1973 [1903]); Kathleen Tillotson, *Novels of the 1840s* (London, 1954); Raymond Williams, 'The industrial novels', chapter 5 of *Culture and Society 1780–1850* (London, 1958); Arnold Kettle, 'The early Victorian social problem novel', in Boris Ford (ed.), *The Pelican Guide to English Literature*, vol. 6 (London, 1958); John Goode and John Lucas (eds.), *Tradition and Tolerance* (London, 1966); Sheila M. Smith, *The Other Nation: The Poor in English Novels of the 1840s and 1850s* (Oxford, 1980); Catherine Gallagher, *The Industrial Reformation of English Fiction: Social Discourse and Narrative Form 1832–1867* (Chicago and London, 1988); Kate Flint, *The Victorian Novelist: Social Problems and Social Change* (London, 1987); Josephine M. Guy, *The Victorian Social-Problem Novel: The Market, the Individual and Communal Life* (Basingstoke, 1996).

[2] Thomas Carlyle, 'Chartism' (1839), in *Selected Writings* (London, 1988), 176.

[3] Anna Jameson, *The Athenaeum*, 4 March 1843, reprinted in Susan Hamilton (ed.), *'Criminals, Idiots, Women and Minors': Victorian Writing by Women on Women* (Ontario, 1995), 21–6, 21. Other relevant works by Jameson include 'Woman's Mission and Woman's Position', in *Memoirs and Essays Illustrative of Art, Literature and Social Morals* (London, 1846), and *The Communion of Labour: A Second Lecture on the Social Employment of Women* (London, 1856). Kate Flint notes that the Blue Books unearthed a world so foreign to most polite readers that only the discourse of romance could encompass this sense of strangeness and social remoteness. See Flint, *The Victorian Novelist*, 7.

[4] Williams, 'The industrial novels'.

[5] See Wanda Neff, *Victorian Working Women: An Historical and Literary Study of Women in British Industries and Professions 1832–1850* (London, 1929), chapter 4; Elizabeth K. Helsinger, Robin Lauterbach Sleets and William Veeder, *The Woman Question: Social Issues, 1837–1883* (Manchester, 1983), chapter 3; Joseph Kestner, *Protest and Reform: The British Social Narrative by Women 1827–1867* (London, 1985), 144–50, 160–64; Gallagher, *The Industrial Reformation of English Fiction*, chapter 6; Flint, *The Victorian Novelist*, 172–99; Richard D. Altick, *Punch: The Lively Youth of a British Institution 1841–1851* (New York, 1997), chapter 7. For discussions of the patriarchal attitudes of radical authors see Jutta Schwarzkopf, *Women in the Chartist Movement* (Basingstoke, 1991), chapter 2, and Anna Clark, *The Struggle for the Breeches: Gender and the Making of the British Working Class* (Berkeley and London: 1995), chapter 14. For an interesting discussion of the figure of the needlewoman in the Romantic period see Sonia Hofkosh, *Sexual Politics and the Romantic Author* (Cambridge, 1998), chapter 3.

[6] Helen Rogers, 'The good are not always powerful, nor the powerful always

good: the politics of needlework in mid-Victorian London', *Victorian Studies*, 40, No. 4 (1997), 589–624. Rogers has a substantial bibliography, to which can be added Leonore Davidoff and Catherine Hall, *Family Fortunes: Men and Women of the English Middle Class, 1780–1850* (Chicago and London, 1987); Deborah Valenze, *The First Industrial Woman* (Oxford, 1995); and Pamela Sharpe, *Adapting to Capitalism: Working Women in the English Economy, 1700–1850* (Basingstoke, 1996). The place of needlework within the nineteenth-century artisan economy is discussed briefly by Iorwerth Prothero in *Radical Artisans in England and France 1830–1870* (Cambridge, 1997), 11–16. The governess and the factory girl were also iconic figures. See Helsinger et al., *The Woman Question*, 113–15.

[7] R. D. Grainger, *Report on the Employment of Children and Young Persons in the Manufactures and Trades of Nottingham, Derby, Leicester, Birmingham and London*, in *Children's Employment Commission. Appendix to the Second Report of the Commissioners (Trades and Manufactures) Part 1: Reports and Evidence from Sub-Commissioners* (London, 1843), 1–307. Further page references are inserted in the text. For Mayhew see E. P. Thompson and Eileen Yeo (eds.), *The Unknown Mayhew* (London, 1971).

[8] According to E. P. Thompson, Mayhew's discovery of widespread prostitution amongst needlewomen was the 'most sensational moment' of all his investigations. See Thompson and Yeo, *The Unknown Mayhew*, 24, 32. There is only one overt reference to the trend in Grainger (Mr Devonald's evidence, 236) but it is clear from the literary responses that needlewomen like other women workers were commonly thought to be promiscuous. Mayhew's 'sensational' impact may have been less to do with the actual transgression than its authentication in first-hand testimony.

[9] Thompson and Yeo, *The Unknown Mayhew*, 148, 174.

[10] See Rogers, 'The good are not always powerful', 594–5. The Society for the Aid and Benefit of Dressmakers and the Society for the Relief of Distressed Needlewomen were attempts at voluntary regulation. The Tory reformer Lord Ashley was a patron of the latter. On his involvement with Mayhew, see Thompson and Yeo, *The Unknown Mayhew*, 21–30. Several reforming organizations favoured emigration, a Malthusian and imperialist solution which is dramatized in Camilla Toulmin's story 'Lucy Dean: The Noble Needlewoman' mentioned below.

[11] Rogers, 'The good are not always powerful', 598.

[12] T. J. Edelstein, 'They sang "The Song of the Shirt": the visual iconology of the seamstress', *Victorian Studies*, 14 (1980), 183–210; Deborah Cherry, *Painting Women: Victorian Women Artists* (London and New York, 1993), chapter 8.

[13] See Peter Stallybrass and Allon White, *The Politics and Poetics of Transgression* (London, 1986), 21–3.

[14] Martin Meisel, *Realizations: Narrative, Pictorial and Theatrical Arts in Nineteenth-Century England* (Princeton, 1983).

[15] Mark Lemon's *The Sempstress: A Drama in Two Acts* was first performed in May 1844. It was published by John Dicks in his voluminous Standard Plays series, no. 759 (London, n.d.).

[16] For example, see Kenny Meadows's brilliant title illustration for an article called 'Death and the Drawing Room' in the *Illustrated Magazine*, volume 1 (1843), 97. The image shows a skeleton in the place of the respectable dressmaker's body.

[17] Mrs [Elizabeth] Stone, 'The Young Milliner' (London, 1843); Charlotte Elizabeth [Tonna], *The Wrongs of Woman*, 4 vols. (London, 1843–44). Camilla Toulmin's stories were published in Douglas Jerrold's *Illuminated Magazine*: 'The

Shawl Buyer. An Incident of 1843' and 'The Orphan Milliners: A Story of the West End' appeared in volume 2 (1843–4), 217–21, 279–85; 'Life Behind the Counter' (written to support the Early Closing Movement) appeared in volume 3 (1844), 27–33. Jerrold satirized the sentimental treatment of the needlewoman problem, see 'The Novelist and the Milliner', in *Douglas Jerrold's Shilling Magazine*, 1 (1845), 160–7. Mayhew's revelations inspired another wave of fictionalizations including several articles and stories by 'Silverpen' (Eliza Meteyard) in *Eliza Cook's Journal*, see 'The Early Closing Movement' (no. 10, 7 July 1849, 154–6), 'Employment of Young Women' (no. 36, 5 January 1850, 145–7), 'On the Best Means of Relieving the Needlewomen' (no. 116, 19 July 1851, 189–91) and the serialized story 'Lucy Dean: The Noble Needlewoman' which appeared March–April 1850 (nos. 46–51). Reynolds's *The Seamstress* (1850) and Jones's *Woman's Wrongs* (1852) can also be seen as belonging to this second wave of literary treatments. I included several needlewoman short stories in my anthology *The Literature of Struggle: An Anthology of Chartist Fiction* (Aldershot, 1995). See also Sharon A. Winn and Lynn M. Alexander (eds.), *The Slaughter-House of Mammon: An Anthology of Victorian Social Protest Literature* (West Cornwall, 1992).

[18] Several of the needlewomen interviewed by Mayhew protested at their condition and blamed the government and employers. See Thompson and Yeo, *The Unknown Mayhew*, 121, 176.

[19] Toulmin, 'The Orphan Milliners', 281.

[20] Ibid., 282.

[21] In *Cheap Clothes and Nasty* (London, 1850), a short tract written for the Christian Socialists under the pseudonym 'Parson Lot', Kingsley warned the aristocracy that some of their fine clothes were 'tainted – yes, tainted indeed' (13). The Christian Socialists supported the establishment of co-operative workplaces similar to those set up after the French Revolution of 1848. See also Stallybrass and White, *The Poetics and Politics of Transgression*, chapter 3.

[22] Toulmin, 'The Shawl Buyer', 217.

[23] Elizabeth Gaskell, *Mary Barton: A Tale of Manchester Life* (Harmondsworth, 1970 [1848]), 121. It is clear from the outset that Mary is fatally attracted to the glamorous image of dressmaking, which places her in a precarious moral and sexual predicament.

[24] In Gaskell's short story 'The Three Eras of Libbie Marsh' (1847) the heroine's slop-work is barely mentioned as we witness Libbie turn into a social missionary.

[25] The story was serialized in *Reynolds's Miscellany of Romance, General Literature, Science and Art* between March and August 1850 (nos. 89 to 109). The original title was *The Slaves of England. No. 1* but this was soon changed to *The Seamstress: A Domestic Tale*. Page references are inserted in the text.

[26] For an overview of Reynolds's career see my article 'George W. M. Reynolds and the radicalization of Victorian serial fiction', *Media History*, vol. 4, no. 2 (1998), 121–40.

[27] Louis James discusses popular uses of 'analytic iconography' in *Print and the People 1819–1851* (London 1976), 80.

[28] Peter Brooks, *The Melodramatic Imagination: Balzac, Henry James, Melodrama, and the Mode of Excess* (New Haven and London, 1995 [1976]), 36.

[29] In one of his 'Letters to the industrious classes' Reynolds claims that a strike by needlewomen would disrupt the world cotton trade. See *Reynolds's Miscellany*, no. 16 (20 February 1847), 250–1.

[30] Ernest Jones, *Notes to the People*, 2 vols. (London, 1967 [1851–2]). *Woman's Wrongs* appeared in the second volume (1852). Pagination is continuous across the two volumes and is given in parentheses. For an overview of Jones's career see 'Ernest Jones' in G. D. H. Cole, *Chartist Portraits* (London, 1941).

[31] See above, note 21.

[32] Her awareness does not extend to a realization that these women are merely more elevated commodities, a theme Jones explores in 'The Lady of Title', though Anna does conclude on her death-bed that 'Men are by far the happier in this world' (711).

[33] This edition is dated 1855 in the British Library catalogue. The text was accompanied by cheap woodcut illustrations. Page references are given in parentheses.

3

Accidents of Production: Industrialism and the Worker's Body in Early Victorian Fiction

MIKE SANDERS

In 1818, before a Parliamentary Commission, Dr Edward Holme of the Manchester Infirmary was not prepared to concede that twenty-three hours' continuous labour was necessarily harmful.[1] In 1832 Harriet Martineau, in *The Hill and The Valley* (a tale from her series *Illustrations of Political Economy*), offers the following: 'It soon after happened, most unfortunately, that a boy who had in charge the management of some part of the new machinery, was careless, and put himself in the way of receiving a blow on the head, which killed him on the spot.'[2] Holme's barefaced denial and Martineau's tortured syntax suggest the difficulties which the facts of industrial injury caused the champions of the nineteenth-century industrial bourgeoisie. Awareness of industrial injury and occupational illness was profoundly unsettling to the bourgeois conscience, as it threatened to destabilize what Laqueur has termed the 'humanitarian narrative' which provided the social order with one of its most important narratives of legitimation.[3]

In this chapter I wish to trace the emergence of the 'accident', as both concept and fictional trope, and as a response to and resolution of this particular ideological crisis. Put simply, my contention is that 'accident' and its correlate 'accidental' made possible a compromise formula which allowed industrial capitalism to accept the fact that there were bound to be casualties, without having to admit its responsibility in producing those casualties. Furthermore, I will be arguing that 'accident' achieves this by confounding those questions of causation and intention which lay at the heart of the debate over working-class injury in this period. In order to understand how this was achieved it is necessary to consider the semantic evolution of 'accident' in the nineteenth century. By the start of the century, 'accident' had shed its earlier sense of 'event' or 'incident' and come instead to signify a *specific type* of event.[4] More accurately, 'accident' comes to signify a paradoxical kind of event, as Karl Figlio observes: 'The idea of an accident seems straightforward. It is an unforeseen event which is also expected . . . the moment of any one accident remains unknown, although it is often retrospectively "predictable".'[5]

In addition, as Robert Campbell notes, this term presumes a very particular form of agency: 'Accidents are caused but unexpected events (or the repercussions of events) involving human agency.'[6] Yet this agency must also be unintentional or unmotivated, 'the deliberately brought about is, by definition, non-accidental'.[7] From the notion of 'unintentional' it is but a small semantic step (or slip) to the notion of 'unwished for' or 'undesired'. The consequences of this slippage become apparent if we consider the difference between the following statements: 'industrial injuries are an unforeseen aspect of factory production' and 'industrial injuries are an undesirable aspect of factory production'. In the case of the latter, the 'facts' of intention effectively negate those of causation. Alternatively, the notion of the 'accident' permits the reverse of this. Figlio argues that 'accident' may establish 'a field of neutralized intention; [where] in place of actions come events which just happened'.[8]

It is clear then that 'accident' is a complex, multi-accented, overdetermined figure. An indication of its complexity is suggested by Judith Green's observation that 'accidents have become very specifically constructed as preventable events, which should not ever, in an ideal world, have happened'.[9] Similarly, Campbell notes that when either 'accident' or 'accidental' is used, claims are made 'simultaneously, about agency, epistemology and value'.[10] In addition, I would suggest that the simultaneity of these claims also permits their 'transcoding', allowing (epistemic) questions of causation to be judged according to standards appropriate to questions of intention (agency). An important consequence of this is the suspension of questions of culpability as either irrelevant or inappropriate. This allows the bourgeoisie to admit the harmful consequences of industrialization (accidents are caused events) without conceding its own responsibility (accidents are undesired events).

In a manner which resembles the statistical societies' decoupling of 'economic' and 'social' problems, 'accident' effectively decouples causation and intention. In doing this it legitimates the principle of 'accountability without culpability',[11] through the creation of an 'as-if' situation, in which neither party is blamed, or held to be at fault, but one of the parties agrees to behave *as if* they were responsible. The Workmen's Compensation Act 1897 can be seen as a formal ratification of this principle, stating that 'an injury could occur which was nobody's responsibility, but which fell to the employer to compensate, because it arose "out of and [in] the course of employment". The injury – or the disease – became an accident.'[12]

The fiction of the 'accident' makes it possible simultaneously to acknowledge the fact of working-class injury, to deny culpability, and yet to assume responsibility for such events. I wish now to consider the ways in which notions of the 'accident' are deployed in three mid-century novels, Charlotte Yonge's *Heartsease* (1854),[13] Charles Dickens's *Hard Times* (1854)[14] and Elizabeth Gaskell's *North and South* (1854–5).[15] These novels, all of which were published, or began publication, in 1854, illustrate the ways in which the 'accident' figured in the 'practical consciousness' of the period, and offer three distinctly different inflections of this figure, ranging from the conservative and blatantly 'ideological' use of this trope in *Heartsease*, through the hostile attitude manifest in *Hard Times*, to its 'orthodox' deployment in *North and South*.

One of the subplots of *Heartsease* concerns the awakening of a young aristocrat, Lord St Erme, to a sense of his social duties. St Erme inherits a recalcitrant and insubordinate workforce when he decides to assume full responsibility for a colliery which had previously been leased. Upon receiving reports that the lessee had compromised safety standards, he insists on inspecting the pit himself. In the course of this inspection a shaft collapses, trapping him and fourteen colliers. The situation appears hopeless but St Erme inspires and supervises the efforts of the trapped miners to rescue themselves, while his sister, Lady Lucy, similarly encourages the rescue work occurring above ground. After five days, not only are all the men rescued but class reconciliation has also been effected, with Lord St Erme firmly established as 'King of [the colliers'] hearts!' (p. 371).

On one level this text repeats the fantasy, shared by Disraeli and Kingsley, of a new generation of aristocrats conscious of, and anxious to fulfil, its social responsibilities. Moreover, it replays the fantasy wherein aristocratic leadership naturally calls forth an appropriate working-class response. Retelling the events St Erme remarks:

> I would not but have had it happen! One seldom has such a chance of seeing the Englishman's gallant heart of obedient submission. Some were men who would not for worlds have touched their hats to me above ground; yet, as soon as I tried to take the lead, and make them think what could yet be done, they obeyed instantly, though I knew almost nothing compared to them, and while they worked like giants, I could hardly move. (p. 405)

It is noticeable that this accident is used by Yonge to develop a situation in which the shared experience of bodily danger justifies and naturalizes, rather than obliterates, social hierarchy. The accident, therefore, functions dialectically as an image of both social disaster and social ideal.

In *Heartsease* 'accident' is intended to persuade the reader of a fundamental truth of the social order, as imagined by Yonge – namely the extent to which the maintenance of life literally depends on an active, aristocratic 'intelligence'. It is St Erme alone who remains calm when the roof-fall occurs and who encourages and directs the miners' attempts to save themselves whilst simultaneously 'supporting the head of the man who was hurt' (p. 369). Indeed, St Erme heroically maintains consciousness until the moment of rescue when the men 'no longer depended on him for encouragement, [and] he sank' (p. 370). The accident provides Yonge with a basis to imagine social reconciliation, harmony, mutuality and reciprocity which none the less respects and re-inforces existing class boundaries. The physicality of the miners is balanced by St Erme's intellect. St Erme's support of the wounded collier is reciprocated by the miner who supports the unconscious nobleman: '[St Erme] was drawn up perfectly insensible, together with a great brawny-armed hewer, a vehement Chartist, and hitherto his great enemy, but who now held him in his arms like a baby, so tenderly and anxiously' (p. 370).

The maternal inflection given to this image of proletarian strength must have provided both relief and reassurance to a middle-class audience more used to monstrous images of working-class power. The extent to which the miners have now fully identified their own interests with those of their social superiors is evidenced by this particular collier's refusal to return to his own home until he is certain that St Erme is still alive. For his part, St Erme considers that the physical suffering undergone as a result of the accident has facilitated the necessary empathy with the poor, 'Well, I know I shall never turn indifferently away again when I hear, "We are starving" . . . A man feels little for what he has not experienced' (p. 406).

This episode, a mining accident accompanied by frantic rescue activity above ground which is inspired by a near angelic woman, inevitably invites comparisons with *Hard Times*. Dickens also provides a maternalized image of proletarian strength: two of the rescuers emerge from the shaft 'tenderly supporting between them . . . the figure of a poor, crushed, human creature' (p. 289). There are, however, significant differences between *Hard Times* and *Heartsease*. The latter maintains an almost exclusively aristocratic focus, which leads to the non-realization of both the mine and the rescue-work. *Hard Times*, by contrast, attends to the technical difficulties of the rescue effort. These differing focuses not only betray the very different political concerns of their respective authors but, remembering that the 'accident' functions dialectically as an image of social disaster and of social ideal, provide two very different visions of the ideal society. *Heartsease* envisages an authoritarian paternalism in which benign aristocrats dictate orders which are instinctively obeyed by happily submissive workers. *Hard Times* offers a striking contrast with its vision of collective, unalienated, self-regulated labour within which work becomes a literally humanizing activity.

Another major difference between the two novels is that in *Hard Times* it is the retrieval of a broken working-class body which provides the narrative focus and it is around this same body that the waiting crowd assembles. Unlike *Heartsease*, it is obvious here that the rescued body is going to die rather than recover and, as a result, Stephen Blackpool's speech is invested with that authority traditionally ascribed to 'last words'. Stephen insists on three things: the reality of working-class sufferings, the need for a better understanding between the classes and the ubiquity of 'muddle'. 'Fro first to last, a muddle!' (p. 289) is how Stephen prefaces his catalogue of working-class suffering and death. 'See how we die an no need, one way an another – in a muddle – every day!' (p. 290). At first sight 'muddle', with its suggestion of unnecessary yet unintended and non-malicious deaths, appears to perform similar ideological work to that of 'accident'. In particular, 'muddle', like 'accident', appears to suspend any question of culpability. However, both of the proffered instances of 'muddle' resolve themselves, on a moment's reflection, into instances of neglected responsibility. Stephen refers to miners petitioning 'the lawmakers for Christ's sake not to let their work be murder to 'em', and describes Rachael's sister's fatal illness as a result 'o' sickly air as had'n no need to be' (p. 290). The use of 'murder' in the first instance and the emphasis on preventability in the second foregrounds precisely those questions of culpability and responsibility which it is the task of 'accident' to obscure.

Immediately after Stephen's first speech (which invokes 'murder') the narrator comments: 'He faintly said it, without any anger against any one. Merely as the truth' (p. 90). A little while later when Stephen asks Gradgrind to vindicate his reputation, he prefaces his request with the words, 'I mak no charges' (p. 291). Dickens is careful not to make Stephen a figure who accuses his middle-class audience (both within and beyond the text) directly. However, the text invites the reader to recognize the truth beyond his analysis of 'muddle'. This process is doubled within the narrative as Stephen's injunction to Gradgrind requires the latter to discover the extent of his son's responsibility for the events which led up to Stephen's death. Although 'muddle' recurs frequently in Stephen's dying oration, the subsequent narrative remains hostile to the notion of 'accident'. In particular, Dickens refuses to allow intention to negate the fact of causation and, again through the character of Gradgrind, insists on determining responsibility and allocating culpability for the witnessed events.

Dickens's hostility to the notion of 'accident' extends beyond *Hard Times* and would appear to be conditioned by his awareness of the (in his view) mendacious uses to which it was being put. In 1855, as editor of *Household Words*, he commissioned and published a series of articles on industrial 'accidents' as part of the ongoing campaign to extend the scope of factory legislation. The main thrust of these articles, made clear by titles such as 'Fencing with Humanity' and 'Deadly Shafts', was to insist that employers were responsible for preventable 'accidents' which occurred in their workplaces.

Paradoxically then, Dickens both preserves and abandons the humanitarian narrative. He stresses the 'causal chains' connecting sufferer and observer and insists on our moral duty to undertake ameliorative action. Yet he remains pessimistic about the possibility of ever expunging physical pain from human society. *Hard Times* suggests that working-class suffering is an essential and permanent feature of the social order, as Stephen observes of the mine: 'When it were in work, it killed wi'out need; when 'tis let alone it kills wi'out need' (p. 290). *Hard Times* recuperates the fact of physical suffering through its consecration, invoking Christian frames of reference at the end of the chapter. This represents an abandonment of the humanitarian narrative's emphasis on the secularized body in favour of a return to the much older tradition of Christian mercy which identifies Christ as the ultimate recipient of the merciful act performed.[16]

Consistent with the higher rate of mortality which prevails in her earlier novels, Elizabeth Gaskell in *North and South* presents the reader with three significant 'accidental' working-class deaths, those of Bessy Higgins, Leonards and John Boucher. Taken together these deaths constitute a textual sequence in the course of which notions of agency and responsibility concerning working-class injury are refined and redistributed. The following discussion will demonstrate the extent to which these redistributions depend on the (overdetermined) flexibility of the notion of the 'accident'.

The sequence begins with Bessy's death from byssinosis contracted as a direct consequence of her employment. Although Bessy is dying from an occupational illness which could be remedied by unilateral action on the part of her employer, the text is careful to apportion responsibility equally between employer and employee. The reader learns that there is a ventilation system which will carry away the cotton fluff, thereby preventing it from filling operatives' lungs, but its installation is apparently opposed by workers who value cotton fluff as an appetite suppressor: 'I've heerd tell o' men who didn't like working in places where there was a wheel, because they said as how it made 'em hungry, at after they'd been long used to swallowing fluff, to go without it' (p. 146). If anything, the suggestion is that Bessy is more of a victim of narrow-minded working-class attitudes than of her employers' cupidity.

The next death in the sequence occurs when Frederick Hale wrestles with and throws a railway porter named Leonards, who dies within a few days of this fall. This raises the possibility that Frederick might be responsible, albeit inadvertently and therefore accidentally, for Leonards's death. Indeed, Watson, the police inspector charged with investigating the death, refers to 'a pretty distinct chain of evidence, inculpating [Frederick]' (p. 350). This would appear to leave Frederick in a position analogous to that of Tom in *Hard Times*, held responsible for the unforeseen consequences of his actions. However, *North and South* seeks to minimize, and ultimately dissolve, Frederick's responsibility. The reader is informed that Leonards's fall 'was rendered fatal, the doctors say, by the process of some internal complaint, and the man's own habit of drinking' (p. 343). Mr Thornton uses this medical evidence to 'close the case', (ab)using his powers as a magistrate to prevent an inquest and consequently the public exposure of Margaret and Frederick.

Although Thornton is able to provide this official closure of the case there is a sense in which the narrative as a whole is unable to exorcize the memory of Leonards. Indeed, the narrative of his death is given on five separate occasions within the novel: by the narrator (chapter 32), by Watson the police inspector (chapter 34), again by him in chapter 35, where it is supplemented by Thornton's ruminations on the medical evidence; Thornton repeats his account in chapter 38, and finally Margaret offers her version of events to Mr Bell in chapter 46. What is remarkable is the consistency of these repetitions – it is as if the text has decided on an 'official' version of the events in which all the characters, in spite of misgivings, support each other's testimony. The hope is that if the tale is repeated often enough then it will finally convince us of its truth. Yet both of the retellings involving Thornton (which is when the 'official' version is established) are compromised by his wish to preserve Margaret's reputation. As a result of this, the circumstances surrounding Leonards's death are always figured textually as a 'guilty secret' shared by Margaret and Thornton. There is a sense in which the text seeks to assuage its 'guilty conscience' regarding Leonards through its handling of the deaths of Mr Hale and Mr Bell. Mr Hale's death is sudden (although not unexpected) and Mr Bell is contemptuous of the need for a coroner's inquest, as if to reassure us that there really was nothing untoward or unusual in the earlier denial of one (p. 432). Later, Mr Bell himself dies suddenly, and this time there is no reference whatsoever to an inquest. The third instance of sudden death without inquest is intended, I think, to dispel any lingering unease on the part of the reader regarding the circumstances surrounding the first.

The convoluted process by which the text seeks to absolve Frederick of any responsibility for Leonards's death is in marked contrast to the treatment of responsibility in the case of the final death in the sequence, that of John Boucher. Boucher's reluctant support for the union and the strike becomes a desperate desire to end the strike as quickly as possible. In pursuit of this aim Boucher leads the riot outside Thornton's factory and then, fearing prosecution, goes into hiding. When he emerges from hiding he offers his services as a strike-breaker to another employer, who publicly repudiates his offer. Realizing the hopelessness of his situation – unwanted by either union or employers – Boucher drowns himself. The discovery of Boucher's body is preceded in the narrative by an exchange between Nicholas Higgins (Bessy's father and one of the strike leaders) and Margaret, in which the latter insists that Higgins is responsible for Boucher's actions, 'You have made him what he is!' (p. 368). Clearly, very different tests for determining responsibility apply in the cases involving Higgins and Frederick. Frederick's immediate involvement in the events preceding Leonards's death is ultimately revealed to have had no direct effect on that death, whilst Higgins's heavily mediated involvement (he is, after all, only one of a number of local union leaders and at worst he is 'guilty' of sanctioning the use of communal pressure, that is the threat of 'sending to Coventry' anyone who is reluctant to join the union or who acts as a strike-breaker) in the circumstances surrounding Boucher's suicide renders him, according to both Margaret's and the narrative's logic, directly responsible for Boucher's death.

Indeed, the narrative affirms the validity of Margaret's charge, providing a scene which with savage literalism lays the body of Boucher at Higgins's door. In a powerfully realized, almost expressionistic episode, the narrative not only unfolds in 'slow motion' but, to extend the filmic analogy, also in 'close-up', as a crowd assembles itself around Boucher's body. This silent working-class body, narratable now only as a series of 'disfigurements' –

'glassy eyes . . . [face] swollen and discoloured . . . [skin] stained by the water' (pp. 368–9) – confronts Higgins. Ultimately Higgins, by accepting responsibility for Boucher's children, acknowledges his responsibility for Boucher's death. In order to discharge these responsibilities Higgins must secure a reconciliation with Thornton. Thus, in a stunning recuperation of what had previously been an almost exclusively anti-capitalist trope, the irretrievably damaged working-class body not only 'accuses' a fellow workman rather than a master, but also becomes a means of fostering class reconciliation rather than class antagonism.

The triad of working-class deaths in *North and South* collectively enacts an ideological move from the real to the ideal. The uncomfortable awareness of occupational disease is acknowledged, but represented as the joint responsibility of capital and labour. The second death transforms this into a situation where the appearance of middle-class co-responsibility is ultimately exposed as a fallacious assessment based on an inadequate understanding of the facts of the case. The third death mirrors the second insofar as 'expert' inquiry into the situation reveals previously hidden lines of causation, which this time inculpate rather than exculpate another character. This third death then represents the 'ideal' working-class death – caused not by the entrepreneur but the sole responsibility of the working class (this strengthened by Higgins's identification with the union), and an instrument of class reconciliation rather than antagonism.

The deaths of Stephen and Leonards share an underlying narrative configuration. In both cases, the son and heir of a significant middle-class character is in some way charged with responsibility for the death of a working-class character. In both cases the death occurs as an indirect and unforeseen consequence of the son's actions. Finally, in both cases the extent of the son's culpability is established by an unofficial enquiry conducted by a paternal figure whose purpose is to reassure the reader that justice has not been infringed in any way.

On one level this narrative configuration records violence perpetrated by the middle class on the working class, and this can be seen as an attempt to negotiate the profoundly unsettling insight that middle-class comforts depended on processes that maimed working-class lives. The narrative importance of the injured, dying or dead worker in the later 'Condition' novels testifies to the successful, if uneasy, recuperation of working-class injury within the 'practical consciousness' of the middle class. In its orthodox deployment, 'accident' is able to do this precisely because it confounds questions of intention and causation. The acknowledgement of injury is, therefore, always undercut by the insistence that such events were unintended (in the sense of being both unforeseen and undesired). Thus by mid-century the Victorian industrial bourgeoisie can acknowledge the fact of industrial injury by classifying such events as 'accidents' and ratifying them as 'accidental'. In short, 'accident' allows the middle class to absolve itself from any direct responsibility for working-class injury.

Notes

Earlier versions of this paper were given at the London Nineteenth Century Seminar (Birkbeck College) and the Northern Victorian Studies Colloquium (Trinity and All Saints College, Leeds). I should like to thank those who commented on and made suggestions concerning this paper. I am particularly indebted to Dr Catherine Cundy, whose critical acumen has greatly improved the rigour of both my argument and my prose.

[1] J. T. Ward, *The Factory Movement 1830–1855* (London, 1962), 25.
[2] Harriet Martineau, *The Hill and the Valley: Illustrations of Political Economy*, vol. 1 (London, 1834), 92.
[3] Thomas W. Laqueur, 'Bodies, details, and the humanitarian narrative', in Lynn Hunt (ed.), *The New Cultural History* (Berkeley, 1989), 176–8.
[4] Judith Green, 'Accidents and the risk society', in R. Bunton, S. Nettleton and R. Burrows (eds.), *Accidents in History: Injuries, Fatalities and Social Relations* (Amsterdam, 1997), 35–51.
[5] Karl Figlio, 'What is an accident?', in P. Weindling (ed.), *The Social History of Occupational Health* (London, 1985), 180.
[6] Robert Campbell, 'Philosophy and the accident', in Bunton et al., *Accidents in History*, 25–6.
[7] Ibid., 27.
[8] Figlio,'What is an accident?', 198.
[9] Green, 'Accidents and the risk society', 51.
[10] Campbell, 'Philosophy and the accident', 17.
[11] Roger Cooter and Bill Luckin, 'Accidents in history: an introduction', in Bunton et al., *Accidents in History*, 30.
[12] Figlio, 'What is an accident?', 182.
[13] Charlotte Yonge, *Heartsease* (London, 1895 [1854]). Page references are to the 1895 edition and are inserted in the text.
[14] Charles Dickens, *Hard Times* (London, 1985 [1854]). Page references are to the 1985 edition and are inserted in the text.

[15] Elizabeth Gaskell, *North and South* (Harmondsworth, 1985 [1854–5]). Page references are to the 1985 edition and are inserted in the text.

[16] Laqueur, 'Bodies, details', 177.

4

'In the Darg': Fiction Nails the Midlands Metal-worker

VALENTINE CUNNINGHAM

I want to praise *Sybil: or The Two Nations*, Disraeli's Condition-of-England novel of 1845. Not damn it with faint praise, or simply dish it with dispraise – which is what has mainly happened in the history of its reception. The various conventions of reading this novel are, I think, cause for great critical-historical concern. There is, for instance, the standard historicizing, research-led biblio-biographical kind of line, the Louis Cazamian–Sheila Smith–Martin Fido view of Disraeli as a more or less meretricious magpie, plundering his materials, lifting all his best lines, his most realist and also his most lurid stuff, from the parliamentary Blue Books, from other people's parliamentary speeches (especially those of the Young England supporter W. B. Farrand, MP for Bingley in Yorkshire) and from the crooked William Dodd's *Factory System Illustrated in a Series of Letters to Lord Ashley* (1842). On this view Dizzy is a lazy realist and a second-hand sensationalist but one also taking good care, at the same time, not to repeat in his novel the really shocking things that the government commissioners had dug up about, say, sex down coalmines, or the use of whores to lure the butties into using tommy-shops. Strongly undergirding this approach and framing it elegantly is the standard Raymond Williams kind of approach, which offers us Disraeli as a fearful, but also slick-dicky Tory, making high-handed Conservative ideology palatable with (Williams's memorable phrase) his novel's 'stucco elegance'.[1]

By contrast with such conventional goes at knocking Dizzy off his fictional perch, I want to take very seriously his passion to name, to possess the truth in words, in language, to do the voices, to get to the roots of the naming problematic. Who in England is in charge of the naming? Who christens? Who, indeed, is named aright? Who has the right title and entitlement? Who has rightful claims on being called English, on Englishness and England, on ownership, selfhood, the land, geography, place, property, on the nationalized form of Christianity known as Anglicanism? I want to take seriously, in other words, Disraeli's writerly passion to defy the accepted divisions of England – of which he, of course, is so wonderfully the namer – that is, the Two Nations, and especially the cruel divisions of English womankind. All of which, I would argue, *Sybil* puts to us and embraces – and does so finely – as the writer's proper sphere of contemporary engagement, as the novelist's imperative modern duty to reveal and reflect, as well as a most important set of preoccupations for the unmisguided English politician.

I want, though, to come at *Sybil* gradually, archaeologically in fact, in order to negotiate and register, as well, the way this novel's sense of its own difficulties in contemporary fictional naming, defining, truth-telling – the difficulty of telling what it calls the 'Terrible news from Birmingham' (bk. 5, chap. 1), and of doing so, again in the novel's own words, in a fashion which is not just 'a repetition' for the reader of facts from 'the blue books you have already read' (bk. 4, chap. 6); the difficulty in particular of the task of representing the role of women in nineteenth-century industrialism. I want to register the way Disraeli's particular difficulties are felt as an ongoing issue in nineteenth-century texts more widely, as a tricky matter for the whole nineteenth-century imagination. I would note, too, how these are, in fact, problems for writing that continue right down to the present.

So I begin, as one must with archaeological digs, at the modern end: with section xxv of Geoffrey Hill's long poem – or volume of poems – *Mercian Hymns* (1971). Geoffrey Hill, the poet born in Bromsgrove in the English West Midlands, gives us in *Mercian Hymns* a poetic meditation upon the archaeology of the West Midlands self. His verses offer a vision of late twentieth-century West Midlands selfhood and consciousness and language as being layered onto the deep underlying histories and roots of an ancient metal-working region. His poem keeps acknowledging the way traces of the region's long history of metal-working have a way of poking through the memory of the region and into the consciousness and experience of the Geoffrey-Hill-like boy who is the central subject of the poem. The West Midlands are, as it were, metallic all the way down. From King Offa on – 'he left behind coins', 'exemplary metal' – up through the manifestations of classic early English industrialism – the great iron bridge of Ironbridge – to the nail-making works of the mid-nineteenth century and the modern period of 'metalled' roads signified by the region's great M5 motorway, the workers of the region have bashed metal. And this metal-working haunts the poem's memory as it is offered as defining the region's consciousness and selfhood. The *I* of the poem – a kind of portmanteau self, whose voice blends with that of Offa – is given to encountering and remembering key aspects of this deeply layered metallic past. In section xxv he recalls his nail-making grandmother. He links the recollection with his reading of *Fors Clavigera*, that strange, mixed, rambling collection of circular letters sent by John Ruskin to the members of his anti-industrialist Guild of St George, and its Letter 80, in which Ruskin, for his part, meditates on West Midland metal-workers:

> Brooding on the eightieth letter of *Fors Clavigera*,
>> I speak this in memory of my grandmother, whose
>> childhood and prime womanhood were spent in the
>> nailer's darg.
>
> The nailshop stood back of the cottage, by the fold.
>> It reeked stale mineral sweat. Sparks had furred
>> its low roof. In dawn-light the troughed water
>> floated a damson-bloom of dust –
>
> not to be shaken by posthumous clamour. It is one
>> thing to celebrate the 'quick forge', another
>> to cradle a face hare-lipped by the searing wire.
>
> Brooding on the eightieth letter of *Flors Clavigera*,
>> I speak this in memory of my grandmother, whose
>> childhood and prime womanhood were spent in the
>> nailer's darg.[2]

Here, for the poet, is an irreducible set of memories, to do with family and locality. They're unshakable – at least, 'not to be shaken by posthumous clamour': no noise the poem or poet might make, this poet or any other writer, I take it, even a Ruskin and the swathe his writings might cut through these histories, can alter, or glamor-ize these recollections. Here is a history, a family history in a local history and a place in history for the recalling self, a position in a positioned family recollection of the female industrial home-worker who was grandma. What Hill's familiar recollection brings together is what the Children's Employment Commission of 1842 was particularly provoked by, namely the role of women and children, and not least female children, in Midlands industrialism. Grandmother spent her childhood and prime womanhood in nail-making. She was hurt in the work – her face 'hare-lipped by the searing wire' – the kind of deformation the government inspectors constantly noted. It is an uglification of the person perpetrated in an uglified landscape. The foulness of the location of Hill's family nailshop – reeking of 'stale mineral sweat', its attendant trough of water visibly polluted – is another constant theme of the inspectors, of R. H. Horne, it might be, writing of the stagnant pools around the houses of Wolverhampton metal-workers, the water 'the colour of dead porter . . . a disgusting mixture of gruel and soapsuds. After a day's rain many of them have a little pond in front, the size of a quilt, the colour of licorice tea.'[3] All of which is part of the day's work – of 'the nailer's darg'. *Darg dark dawark* is the word for a day's labour, task or job; the word too for the reward for the day's labour, the daily wage: *darg.*

This region, these working people, this. working woman had, and have, their own language, their own colloquialisms, their own idiolect, their own nicknames, for themselves and their doings: all alienating, different, estranged from the standard English viewpoint of the southerner, the visitor, the government inspector, the bourgeois politician and novelist. Noting these linguistic othernesses, the proletarian, regional, class lingo and dialect, was a constant activity of the Victorian inspectors and, of course, of the interloper novelist, the slumming reporter from another linguistic region or class, such as Dickens or Mrs Gaskell or Disraeli, as well as of the insider like Walter Greenwood, all of them anxious to make these strange other-lands known to the rest of the country. Their aim was familiarization by linguistic defamiliarization – the usual technical resort of the colonialist, the venturer into dark foreign fields. It is part of the mission of Hill's great regional poem.

Letter 80 of *Fors Clavigera* is dated 16 July 1877 and was written from Bellefield, Birmingham. Ruskin's host, the mayor of Birmingham, took him on a drive into Worcestershire nailing country, out 'towards Bewdley':

> . . . my host asked me if I would like to see 'nailing'. 'Yes, truly'. So he took me into a little cottage where were two women at work, one about seventeen or eighteen, the other perhaps four or five and thirty; this last intelligent of feature as well could be; and both, gentle and kind – each with hammer in right hand, pincers in left (heavier hammer poised over her anvil, and let fall at need by the touch of her foot on a treadle like that of a common grindstone). Between them, a small forge, fed to constant brightness by the draught through the cottage, above whose roof its chimney rose: – in front of it, on a little ledge, the glowing lengths of cut iron rod, to be dealt with at speed. Within easy reach of this, looking up at us in quietly silent question, – stood, each in my sight an ominous Fors, the two Clavigerae.
>
> At a word, they laboured, with ancient Vulcanian skill. Foot and hand in perfect time: no dance of the Muses on Parnassian mead in truer measure; – no sea fairies upon yellow sands more featly footed. Four strokes with the hammer in the hand: one ponderous and momentary blow ordered of the balanced mass by the touch of the foot; and the forged nail fell aside, finished, on its proper heap; – level-headed, wedge-pointed, a thousand lives soon to depend daily on its driven grip of the iron way.
>
> So wrought they, – the English Matron and Maid; – so was it their darg to labour from morning to evening, – seven to seven, – by the furnace side, – the winds of summer fanning the blast of it. The wages of the Matron Fors, I found, were eight shillings a week; – her husband, otherwise and variously employed, could make sixteen. Three shillings a week for rent and taxes, left, as I count, for the guerdon of their united labour, if constant, and its product providently saved, fifty-five pounds a year, on which they had to feed and clothe themselves and their six children; eight souls in their little Worcestershire ark . . .
>
> Yet it was not chiefly their labour in which I pitied them, but rather in that their forge-dress did not well set off their English beauty; nay, that the beauty itself was marred by the labour; so that to most persons, who could not have looked through such veil and shadow, they were as their Master, and had no form nor comeliness.

(The perceived ugliness, physical deformation and suffering of these women reminds Ruskin of the suffering servant of Isaiah 53, whose beauty was marred more than that of any man, and who had no form nor comeliness, nor any beauty that we should desire him: a messianic passage taken by Christian midrashics to refer to Christ on the Cross – another nailing whose analogous force Ruskin is no doubt feeling.) The immediate background of this meeting with the female nailers in Letter 80 is some provoked reflection of a Two Nations kind. Just before narrating the meeting Ruskin accuses his liberal Birmingham friends of an incapacity to imagine a good society which does not involve

> the main British modern idea that the master and his men should belong to two entirely different classes; perhaps loyally related to and assisting each other; but yet, – the one, on the whole living in hardship – the other in ease; – the one supported in its dishonourable condition by the hope of labouring through it to the higher one, – the other honourably distinguished by their success, and rejoicing in their escape from a life which must nevertheless be always (as they suppose) led by a thousand to one of the British people.

And such ingrained social contrasts are proven for Ruskin as he finds them signified in pronounced geographical and topographical oppositions which are, of course, also oppositions of class and culture. Ruskin had been taken in the mayor's carriage to the 'nailing' scene after driving 'by Shenstone's home, The Leasowes'. He had reached Bewdley's metal-workers by a kind of pastoral skewing. The editorial footnote in Cook and Wedderburn's great edition of Ruskin's works brings home the pastoral loveliness of the poet Shenstone's place, as described by Dr Johnson in his *Lives of the Poets* – 'rural pleasures . . . rural elegance . . . prospects . . . walks . . . waters . . .' – as well as the disfiguring encroachments of recent industrialization. According to Murray's *County Handbook*, a line of canal close to the place has interfered with its rural quiet, and brought the disagreeable accompaniment of rude traffic and vexatious depredation. Enough of their original appearance, however, remains to render these grounds highly interesting. The way of the nailer is hard, and the way to the nailer is down a path of pastoral disamenity and loss.

The sight of the two women nailers provokes in Ruskin a whole chain of reflections on a nation with two contrastive varieties of woman in it. All the while he was watching the nailers, he says, he was thinking of another pair of Englishwomen whom he had

recently observed in the new Grosvenor Gallery as he and they
looked at Burne-Jones's painting *The Mirror of Venus* (in which
Venus and a troupe of splendidly langorous women in a welter of
forget-me-nots inspect their reflections in a pool of water): 'Were
these then, here, – their sisters; who had only for Venus's mirror, a
heap of ashes; compassed about with no Forget-me-nots, but with
the Forgetfulness of all the world?' And immersion in this intricate
mesh of mirrorings of the female (the nailers mirrored in the
appalled regard of Ruskin's gaze and prose, reminding the gazer of
the two other women he had gazed at as they gazed at a painting of
Venus and her handmaidens gazing at their mirrored reflection in
water) launches Ruskin into a sequence of remembered encounters
with women who have from time to time upset him into social
critique. Some of them have been sweet little doll-like creatures, of
course, but there were also his companions at Furness Abbey, a
mother and two daughters, aesthetic admirers of the abbey, who
were offended by some ragged and drunken labourers, men quite
incapable of any aesthetic interest – an encounter which had set
Ruskin off in *Fors* Letter 11 (November 1871) on a tirade about a
nation divided into the unaesthetic peasants who dig for turnips
and the gentry, clergy, literary persons and so on, who need the
turnips those outcasts from beauty dig up. Aesthetic genteel
women, estranged from the world of labour, attractively beautiful
though they be, are the product of a society in the wrong, and
Ruskin is right to complain about them, and to draw adverse
comparisons with their wronged working-class sisters – and this
despite what Coventry Patmore, the exponent of the bourgeois
Angel in the House, has to say. Ruskin goes on (still in Letter 80) to
quote a letter he has received from Patmore objecting to the recent
tirade in *Fors* Letter 64 (April 1876) against some of his refined
friends for their being like biblical Egyptians, who relied on a
Hebrew slave class to make their bricks for them. These modern
Egyptians are deplorable for their eschewing of all useful manual
work, and in particular for allowing their dainty womenfolk to
delude themselves into thinking that their own daily tasks are part
of a 'trivial round' or a 'common task' worth the name, even
though they all like quoting John Keble's hymn with those phrases
in it and its allegation that those activities 'bring us daily nearer
God'. Letter 64 was savagely satirical (when Ruskin went to town
he really went to town):

'Oh, but my wife didn't mean *that* sort of "common task" at all!'

No; but your wife didn't know what she meant; neither did Mr Keble. Women and clergymen have so long been in the habit of using pretty words without ever troubling themselves to understand them, that they now revolt from the effort, as if it were an impiety. So far as your wife had any meaning at all, it was that until she was made an angel of, and had nothing to do but be happy, and sing her flattering opinions of God for evermore, – dressing herself and her children becomingly, and leaving cards on her acquaintances, were sufficiently acceptable services to Him, for which, trivial though they were, He would reward her with immediate dinner, and everlasting glory. That was your wife's real notion of the matter, and modern Christian women's generally, so far as they have got any notions at all under their bonnets, and the skins of the dead robins they have stuck in them, – the disgusting little savages. But that is by no means the way in which either your hands are to be delivered from making the pots, or her head from carrying them.

Patmore's reply, which Ruskin quotes with evident melancholy relish in Letter 80, only proves Ruskin's point about the gulf between the kind of women who spend their lives looking at lovely pictures of lovely Venus admiring herself, and unbeautiful women condemned to a heap of ashes for a mirror of their selfhood:

Poor lady! – and yet dressing becomingly and looking pleasant are a deal harder, and better worth doing, than brickmaking. You make no allowance for the many little labours and trials (the harder to do and bear, perhaps, because they are so little) which she must meet with, and have to perform in that 'trivial round' of visiting and dressing. As it is, she is at least no worse than a flower of the field. But what prigs would she and her husband become if they did actually take to dilettante (*ie*, non-compulsory) brickmaking! In their own way, almost all 'rich' people, as well as the so-called 'poor' – who, man, woman, and child, pay £5 each per annum in *taxes* on intoxicating drinks – do eat their bread in the sweat of their faces . . .

Small surprise that Ruskin should say that each time he read that letter his amazement deepened. He appeals to his 'fair friends' for their thoughts on it. His own mind, at any rate, had been long made up in the matter. In the run-up to the Patmore extract he had referred his readers back to 'Of queens' gardens', the second lecture of his *Sesame and Lilies* (1871), where he had talked of the perfect loveliness of woman being betrayed by idleness and the wrong kind of education. The education of bourgeois women, he had said there, was only an induction into ignorance: it was a kind of wrong baptism. For him, what was up with England was that there were indeed two kinds of English people, the rich and the poor, the busy and the idle, and that at the heart of this national dividedness was the gulf between two lots of womankind, the lovely idle aesthetic ones mirrored in that aesthetically pleasing painting of *The Mirror of Venus*, and the disfigured nail-making ones whose lack of their sisters' loveliness was mirrored in the ashes of the industrialized regions – women like Geoffrey Hill's grandmother, or like the proletarian women who feature so prominently in *Sybil*. In fact Ruskin's whole address to the nail-maker scene seems founded in the kind of work *Sybil* had done, the kind of fiction *Sybil* was, in fact in *Sybil* itself. Letter 80 of *Fors Clavigera* reads – as do whole chunks of *Fors* – like footnotes to *Sybil*.[4]

Sybil is notoriously about national – as one might say, Ruskinian – division and dividedness. Its very title is *Sybil: or, the Two Nations*. The title comes, of course, from that arresting encounter in bk. 2, chap. 5, in a momentously ruined monastery, between Egremont, the well-off Disraelian hero, and a couple of strangers, the younger of whom startlingly suggests that the new Queen reigns not over one nation, 'the greatest nation that ever existed', as Egremont put it, but two:

> 'Yes', resumed the younger stranger . . . 'Two nations; between whom there is no intercourse and no sympathy; who are as ignorant of each other's habits, thoughts, and feelings, as if they were dwellers in different zones, or inhabitants of different planets; who are formed by a different breeding, are fed by a different food, are ordered by different manners, and are not governed by the same laws'.
> 'You speak of – ' said Egremont, hesitatingly.
> 'THE RICH AND THE POOR'.

Disraeli has this two-ness run into every department of the novel, and makes it characterize every aspect of his depiction of England. In terms of class and economics, there is division between capital and labour, masters and servants, rich and poor. Within labour and the labour cause, represented by Chartism, there is further division: Morley's moral-force Chartists on the one hand, Gerard's physical-force Chartists on the other. The political and economic dividedness is, of course, mirrored in divisions of topography, geography, location and locale. It is a clash between utopia and dystopia. On the one hand there is the pastoral beauty of park and garden, of Gerard's cottage garden (a kind of allegorical Anglo-Catholic pastoral) and of the medieval past: the domains and demesnes of the owner, the gentry, the genteel, the aristocrat, of Old England and true religious (Anglo-Catholic) England. On the other, the hells of industrialism, the messed-up industrial towns, the slums, the novel's Hellhouse Yard, above all the home of the novel's metal-workers, the notorious Wodgate, 'the ugliest spot in England'. And at the heart of this opposition – this aesthetico-politico-economic dividedness – are two kinds of women (and two visions of women's role and 'Woman's mission').

Rich women, on the one side, are satirized, more or less, as victims of a culture gone wrong: Lady Firebrace and her set, the ennobled fixers and wheeler-dealers of the Tory Party; the scholarly, bookish Lady Joan who knows more about Aztec cities than the industrialized cities of England; and the good Lady Marney, with a sense of the good that infant schools might do, but utterly quenched in such ameliorative work through her bad marriage to the monstrous Marney ('no infant schools would ever be found in his neighbourhood'). On the other side are poor women whose condition is, of course, as much deplored as pitied. Girls coarsened by working in the mine,

> the mothers of England! But can we wonder at the hideous coarseness of their language, when we remember the savage rudeness of their lives? Naked to the waist, an iron chain fastened to a belt of leather runs between their legs clad in canvas trousers, while on hands and feet an English girl, for twelve, sometimes for sixteen hours a day, hauls and hurries tubs of coal up subterranean roads, dark, precipitous, and plashy; circumstances that seem to have escaped the notice of the Society for the Abolition of Negro Slavery. (bk. 2, chap. 1)

Daughters, like the novel's Harriet and Caroline, are condemned to live away from the family home, with all the temptations to sin and the low moral life which that brings. Women are plunged into a broken-up domesticity, forced to go out to work, with no energy or time, let alone the money, to run a home and look after husband and children. Women are married to men who have been emasculated by labour, so that they are 'the slaves of slaves', as Gerard puts it (bk. 2, chap. 16). Women are forced to shop at the company store, the rip-off tommy shop (the one in bk. 3, chap. 3 is a grotesquely Dickensian shop of horrors). No wonder a constant note of the radical social critics in the novel is that domestic life is smashed for these women beyond repair: 'what we call domestic life is a condition impossible to be realized for the people of this country'; 'the Home no longer exists'. And given central place in these awed meditations on the bad deal for women is the badness of their bodily condition. The proletarian female body is stunted and deformed by the conditions into which the metal-working woman is born and compelled to live, above all by the nature of the work she does. Like Sue, the metal-worker of Wodgate:

> Wodgate had the appearance of a vast squalid suburb. As you advanced, leaving behind you long lines of little dingy tenements, with infants lying about the road, you expected every moment to emerge into some streets, and encounter buildings bearing some correspondence, in their size and comfort, to the considerable population swarming and busied around you. Nothing of the kind. There were no public buildings of any sort; no churches, chapels, town-halls, institute, theatre; and the principal streets in the heart of the town in which were situate the coarse and grimy shops, though formed by houses of a greater elevation than the preceding, were equally narrow, and if possible more dirty. At every fourth or fifth house, alleys seldom above a yard wide, and streaming with filth, opened out of the street. These were crowded with dwellings of various size, while from the principal court often branched out a number of smaller alleys, or rather narrow passages, than which nothing can be conceived more close and squalid and obscure. Here, during the days of business, the sound of the hammer and the file never ceased, amid gutters of abomination, and piles of foulness, and stagnant pools of filth; reservoirs of leprosy and plague, whose exhalations were sufficient to taint the atmosphere of the whole kingdom, and fill the country with fever and pestilence.
> A lank and haggard youth, rickety and smoke-dried, and black with his craft, was sitting on the threshold of a miserable hovel, and working at the file. Behind him stood a stunted and meagre girl, with a back like a grasshopper; a deformity occasioned by the displacement of the bladebone, and prevalent among the girls of Wodgate from the cramping posture of their usual toil. (bk. 3, chap. 4)

Deformed place, deformed culture and economy and labour, deformed girl: Disraeli drew much of the detail of smashed-up domesticity from the reports for the Children's Employment Commission of Thomas Tancred from the South Staffordshire coalfield. The girl with the back like a grasshopper's comes, though, like so much else about the Wodgate metal-working region, from the testimony on Wolverhampton and Willenhall of Richard Henry (later on, Hengist) Horne, the ubiquitous Victorian man of letters, friend of Dickens and the great early encourager of Elizabeth Barrett Browning. So many of the workers Horne describes are scarred and otherwise physically distorted from their labour. *Stunted* is a frequently used word in Horne's reports. 'Filthy black with dirt, and deformed . . . utterly stunted, and her figure almost a square; her dress seemed to be a smutty old sack, out of which her head and limbs were thrust, like a tortoise': that was the seventeen-year-old Anne Preston from Wolverhampton, who thought Solomon was a disciple of Jesus, and did not know that the Queen's name was Victoria. Willenhall is full of youths with scarred hands and faces, many of whom are stunted. 'Nearly all those who sit, as they have to do so in one unvarying attitude the whole day, get a slight curve in the spine, with a projection of the blade-bones. The dress of the girls is sufficiently easy as to stays.' 'With some, this curve gradually becomes a positive distortion of the spine, just above the hips, together with a hump.' Middle-class children might miss a note in their piano-practice; in a metal factory a child misses a note and loses a finger or gets its head smashed in. Horne's touch for vivid metaphor and analogy of this sort is sure (he is the inspector who reported the fetid pond as being the colour of dead porter, or licorice tea, and the size of a quilt). Disraeli's horrified 'grasshopper's back' simile for Sue finds deep sanction in Horne's saddened poeticizings. But the metaphor is Disraeli's own. He is no merely slavish copyist of the commissioners' investigations; he is by no means simply taking down their dictation.[5]

The hump-backed Sue is Disraeli's representative proletarian woman. (There are are no humped backs in the other nation, except for Hump Chippendale, the gentlemen's bookie, who appears in the novel's second chapter.) She is a compound of Horne material, her physical deformation the bodily manifestation of the distorted bits and tags of Christian and biblical knowledge which,

Horne kept finding, were all she and her kind knew of Christianity and the Bible – the debris of a Christian country and civilization brought to ruin in the industrial areas. Strikingly, although Sue is said to be 'of the Baptist school religion', to have a clergyman of her own, and to have been baptized, and though she calls herself 'a reg'lar born Christian', she still manages to tell Morley that her husband, the metal-scarred Thomas, 'believes now in our Lord and Saviour Pontius Pilate, who was crucified to save our sins; and in Moses, Goliath, and the rest of the Apostles'. ('Ah! me', thinks Morley, much in the spirit of Dickens in *Bleak House*, 'and could they not spare one Missionary from Tahiti for their fellow-countrymen at Wodgate!') Horne found many such garbled versions of Christian practice and the Christian story in the metal-working Midlands. It was an apprentice padlock-maker he encountered in Willenhall who 'is of the Baptist school religion, whatever that is'.[6] Disraeli was clearly fascinated by these grotesquely skewed and ragged evidences of Christian teaching and practices gone hopelessly wrong, and he catches them up into what amounts in his novel to a protracted meditation on baptisms, and christenings, and namings gone awry – a concern clearly very close to his own deepest interests as a writer, a person whose business is with namings.

Wodgate is full of such pagan Christians as Sue and Thomas, people with only some of the proper and authenticated words, at least in Disraeli's conception of the matter, people with wrong names or only nicknames, people absolutely unchristened, un-baptized or only dubiously or uncomprehendingly baptized. The youth known as Devilsdust sums up some of this baptismal problematic. He never was baptized in a church. Abandoned by his mother to a carer after only a fortnight of life, he has no name 'baptismal or patrimonial'. He was simply 'the nameless one', until he got employment in the Wadding Hole, where cotton waste was 'worked up into counterpanes and coverlets'. 'The nameless one was preferred to the vacant post, received even a salary, more than that, a name; for as he had none, he was christened on the spot – DEVILSDUST': waste matter, a cast-off child, christened for the hellish waste-stuff he works with. Devilsdust; devilish baptism; hellish naming; the knowledge and naming of awfulness; the naming is a confirmation of an inheritance of industrial fallenness. And the character from the other nation called, with what turns out to be serious significance, Baptist Hatton is no less fallen. He is the brother of the so-called 'Bishop', the misnamed liberator of proletarian England, and he is a dubious inventor and maker of fake titles. An antiquary by profession, he trades in family names, providing bogus family trees, making up fictional claims on old nobility, plundering the records for ancient names for *nouveaux riches* – such as the waiter who becomes first Lord Fitz-Warene and then the earl de Mowbray of Mowbray Castle, thus robbing the good Gerard of his name, his title and his lands. It is a question, this one of old Christian, baptismal names and rightful inherit- ances, with obvious peculiar personal resonance for Disraeli, the Jew who became a baptized Christian, but who was never able to forget the Hebrew roots of Christianity, the consolation of the old Hebrew names, Sion, Bethel, Bethesda: 'names of a distant land, and the language of a persecuted and ancient race; yet such is the mysterious power of their divine quality, breathing consolation in the nineteenth century to the harassed forms and the narrowed souls of a Saxon peasantry' (bk. 2, chap. 3).

All these bad Baptists, as we might call them, the bad baptizers, the dubiously baptized and the downright unbaptized, focus, I suggest, *Sybil's* profoundest anxieties about the power of namings, of words, and about who has the right to name, who has got the namings right. The rhetoric of the novel is heavily invested in a war of namings. The dividedness of the nation is also about divided linguistic practices and powers. What is truly terrifying, as well as astonishing, to Disraeli the novelist and politician, as it was dismaying to the Parliamentary Commissioners and inspectors, is that there is a whole other world of namings, of discourse, in and of the industrialized areas, a proletarian lingo and dialect, existing alongside the official rhetorics of Church and State, a dilapidated language maybe, its signs and significations the signs and symptoms of a ruinous existence, but still a challenging alternative living language, if not a terribly well one. Out of it, and from its speakers, there are likely to come political challenges that would not just unsettle but might well overthrow the order the official namings manifest. The Chartist 'Bishop' talks terrifyingly, for instance, of his own and his movement's Lord Chancellor and Prime Minister. Political struggle is a struggle to own such titles and names. The Chartist revolution would be a verbal one. And quite clearly one great effort of Disraeli's novel is to try and wrest the power of naming away from such opponents of linguistic law and order, to prove that his namings, his way with the words, is the stronger, the more enduring, the more truthful.

In many ways *Sybil* is an undoubted linguistic *tour de force*. To a considerable extent, the linguistic force is, we might say, with Disraeli. As a satirist he is an ace namer. Thorough Base, Wriggle, Bombastic Rip, Mr Hoaxem: with names like these he is as sharp an allegorist as Bunyan or Dickens. And Disraeli the dandy, the Londoner, the parliamentarian, the club-man, has a wonderful way with the slang, the cant, of the gent, the cad, the bounder – as in the aristo political-racing talk of book 1, chapter 6: *no real go, dead beat, jockeying, shell out, swear till we are black in the face*. As a mere stylist Disraeli impresses no end with, say, his adjectival power. If ownership of the truth of experience and of the real depended on adjectives alone Disraeli would be more than home and dry. But in a way no doubt terrifying for him, when it comes to squaring up to the industrialized heartlands of linguistic otherness and to attempting to command linguistically the foreignness of proletarian and regional Englishness he is in a real sense more or less stuck for words. He tries his hardest, but time and again he is in fact outdone by the likes of R. H. Horne. For every vividly imagined grasshopper-back metaphor Disraeli comes up with, Horne has a dozen such. The regional and class idiolect, the workers' slang in the Saturday night shop scene of bk. 2, chap. 9, sounds wonderfully knowledgeable, a true inside job, full of intimate factory slang on the subject of *snicks* and *small cops* and *bad yarns*. But, as Martin Fido has nicely demonstrated, it is all lifted from William Dodd's *The Factory System Illustrated*.[7] Disraeli is not an insider here; his mastery and his knowledge are pilfered, his forceful naming is borrowed clothing. So the two linguistic nations remain two, for all Disraeli's efforts at crossing the linguistic border and breaking down the middle wall of linguistic – which is to say also political and class and regional – partition.

To observe which is, of course, by no means to crow over Disraeli. For the struggle for mastery over the names, and thus for the power of the one who knows, is indeed a very real one. Naming is indeed power. And we are compelled to admire Disraeli, I would suggest, for recognizing the fact. But in this contest for verbal mastery, and thus for analytical force, the novel, the fiction, is manifestly having to concede ground to the Blue Books – as Dickens would in the matter of *Hard Times*. For all Disraeli's worthy efforts to unlock, to be acknowledged as the one who unlocks the secrets of the shut-away, dark classes and regions of the Midlands lock-makers, and, of course, for all his desire to be acknowledged as an exposer and expositor, he does have to give place to the investigating and writing inspectors, the likes of R. H. Horne, who have preceded him.

This is, of course, a contest for acknowledged first writing place that Disraeli was perhaps doomed to lose. The documentarists of the Children's Employment Commission got there first, and insofar as the Condition-of-England novel is inevitably a bastard form, a miscegenated mode, in which documentary realism is married and perhaps subordinated to the demands and the modes of fiction, it is likely that we would feel that the writing force, as well as the political force, was rather with the commissioners. The literary union between document and fiction in a documentary fiction is always going to provoke potentially damaging questions of both sides of such a necessarily transgressive form. But then Disraeli and his novel are no strangers to transgressive unions. For Disraeli's main answer to the divisions of the Two Nations, especially of the two kinds of English womanhood, all he can come up with for his own and his readers' satisfaction, involves a certain ideological miscegenation worked out through a fantastic marriage plot. In what is only a fictionist's dream of a good story and a socially and politically happy ending, Egremont is finally married to Sybil, so that the aristocrat is brought together in a great symbolic union with the woman of the people, the Old Faith is united with the New, Land with Labour. But, of course, this a truly faked ending, for Sybil, the lovely proletarian, the wondrous, saintly daughter of a working man is actually no such thing, for her father turns out really to be an old landed aristocrat. For Disraeli, as of course for many another novelist, it is only in a fictional dream, the plot of fantasy, that the divides of Englishness can be bridged, healed, transcended.

But then, if we are thinking about rhetorics of healing, the projected bridgings of national and class and linguistic breaches that Victorian writers of all sorts are so busy in describing, we might remind ourselves that Ruskin's polemics were not all that much more successful in practical terms than Disraeli's plotted fantasies. The Guild of St George was a nicely moral idea for national redemption through labour, but hardly a practical way to political and cultural salvation. And Ruskin seemed to know it. Certainly in *Fors* it is by no means hard to detect the tone of exasperation as Ruskin shows himself sick and tired of having to keep on repeating himself, to keep making the same old criticisms again and again. Nothing much is changing out there. And as for Geoffrey Hill's most moving appropriation of Letter 80, that leaves him – and us – only *brooding* over the injustices Ruskin dwelt on. And while being made to brood may be the first step in incitement to action and change, it is by no means a guarantee of anything beyond itself taking place at all.

   This all said, however, there remains the fact – too little noticed, I think – that the dreamlike fictional restoration of Sybil to her ancestral title and lands, the bringing together of real and rightfully named Mowbrays with their rightful possessions and lands, does depend upon the riot with which the novel ends and upon the canniness of the Midlands metal-worker and lock-maker in being able to break into the unrightful earl de Mowbray's strong-room and strong-boxes. Disraeli, left to his own devices, might well be cack-handed, as well as second-handed, in unlocking the truths about lock-makers, but the Mowbray lads, Devilsdust and his unbaptized friends, the metal-working Hell-cats, the men from the metal trades and the lock-making crafts, have skills that come in mightily useful at the end – useful for the Disraelian plot and its fantasy resolutions, but useful also as a demonstration that these people can be, after all, really on the side of the principled moral-force radicalism of which Disraeli the politician dreams (amiably regarded thieves, they break into the strong-boxes where the necessary truth-telling documents about rights and names and inheritance are secreted). And, what is more, at the end of the novel Devilsdust and his friend Dandy Mick Radley are metamorphosed into small capitalists with the help of Egremont. Which, naturally enough in this novel, involves a new, authentic naming, a baptism which is a renaming and also a new placing.

   Devilsdust, having thus obtained a position in society, and become a capitalist, thought it but a due homage to the social decencies to assume a decorous appellation, and he called himself by the name of the town where he was born. The firm of Radley, Mowbray & Co., is a rising one; and will probably furnish in time a crop of Members of Parliament and Peers of the realm. (bk. 6, chap. 13)

The democratic future, youthful England, is on the side of the Midlands metal-worker, if he is properly allied with the real aristocracy of England. There is even a hope of redemption, in this general new baptism, for the women of Wodgate. One of the former refugees from a hopeless domesticity, the girl Caroline, marries Devilsdust, and not in any of the cod, proley fake marriages Wodgate once went in for – 'and Mrs Mowbray became a great favourite'. It is a conclusion which is comprised, of course, mostly of fantasy and wishful thinking about the healing of the nation, but at least it includes some of the metal-working proletarians, the people deemed at one time to be so absolutely dangerous in their nameless, unbaptized, otherness.

Notes

[1] Louis Cazamian, *Le Roman social en Angleterre (1830–1850): Dickens–Disraeli–Mrs Gaskell-Kingsley*, 2 vols. (Paris, 1935), vol. 2, chap. 2, pt 3, 'Disraeli – le Toryisme social', 75–103; Sheila M. Smith, 'Willenhall and Wodgate: Disraeli's use of Blue Book evidence', *Review of English Studies*, n.s. 12 (1962), 368–84; Sheila M. Smith, 'Blue Books and Victorian novelists', *Review of English Studies*, n.s. 21 (1970), 23–40; Martin Fido, ' "From his own observation": sources of working-class passages in Disraeli's *Sybil*', *Modern Languages Review* 72 (1977), 268–84; Raymond Williams, *Culture and Society 1780–1950* (Harmondsworth, 1961 [1958]), chap. 5, 'The industrial novels', 108.

[2] Geoffrey Hill, *Mercian Hymns* (London, 1971), xxv (unpaginated).

[3] *Appendix to the Second Report of the Commissioners. Trades and Manufactures. Part II. Reports and Evidence from the Sub-Commissioners* (London, 1843), Q6, 68.

[4] *Fors Clavigera*, vol. 7, Letter 80, 'The two clavigerae' (August 1877), *The Works of John Ruskin*, ed. E. T. Cook and Alexander Wedderburn (London, 1907), vol. 29, 170–80; *Fors*, vol. 6, Letter 64, 'The three sarcophagi' (April 1876), *Works*, vol. 28, 561–76.

[5] R. H. Horne, *Appendix to the Second Report of the Commissioners*, Q1–31 from Wolverhampton; Q38 ff. from Willenhall; Q24, 26, 27, evidence from Wolverhampton.

[6] Ibid., Q136, Willenhall evidence.

[7] Fido, 'Observation', 270–1.

5

The Shipbuilders' Story

H. GUSTAV KLAUS

'Greifet an, greifet an und rührt die Hände, baut des Schiffes stolze Wände': thus sings a disguised Peter I, Tsar of Russia, *allegro vivace* in Lortzing's comic opera *Zar und Zimmermann* (1837). The episode is well-known, if often blown out of proportion. The real historical potentate did try his hand at the trade of shipbuilding, though it is not reported whether he sang 'Tag für Tag, Schlag für Schlag! Handwerksmann hat seine Plagen, Lust zur Arbeit hilft sie tragen.'[1] For his apprenticeship of sorts the Tsar chose, first, the large shipyards of Zaandam (Saardam), where the opera is set but where, in fact, it turned out to be impossible to work incognito, and, second, Amsterdam, the greatest port in Europe. Here a cordoned-off wharf was found for him and his party on the premises of the Dutch East India Company, and, to loud complaints from his aristocratic entourage that they were not accustomed to such hard labour, he got ten 'volunteers' to work alongside him on a barque, and hence to have a stab at various shipbuilding skills in the space of two months.

Here is another famous carpenter at work:

> I felled a cedar tree: . . . It was not without infinite labour that I felled this tree. I was twenty days hacking and hewing at it at the bottom; I was fourteen more getting the branches and limbs, and the vast spreading head of it cut off, which I hacked and hewed through with axe and hatchet, and inexpressible labour. After this, it cost me a month to shape it and dub it to a proportion, and to something like the bottom of a boat, that it might swim upright as it ought to do. It cost me near

three months more to clear the inside, and work it so as to make an exact boat of it. This I did indeed, without fire, by mere mallet and chisel, and by the dint of hard labour, till I had brought it to be a very handsome *periagua* and big enough to have carried six and twenty men, and consequently big enough to have carried me and all my cargo.[2]

Such a poor shipwright, however, was Robinson Crusoe that he had forgotten to calculate the weight of the *periagua*, and consequently he never managed to float it. But through trial and error he achieves his aim on the next occasion, interestingly enough when he works no longer on his own but in collaboration with Friday.

Boatbuilding is an old craft, surely as old as mining, and there are references to it in world literature at least from Homer onward. A passage in the *Odyssey* (*c.*725 BC) displays a remarkable knowledge of shipwright's skills.

> Now toils the Heroe; trees on trees o'erthrown
> Fall crackling round him, and the forests groan:
> Sudden, full twenty on the plain are strow'd,
> And lopp'd, and lighten'd of their branchy load.
> At equal angles these dispos'd to join,
> He smooth'd, and squar'd 'em, by the rule and line.
> (The wimbles for the work *Calypso* found)
> With those he pierc'd 'em, and with clinchers bound.
> Long and capacious as a shipwright forms
> Some bark's broad bottom to out-ride the storms,
> So large he built the Raft: then ribb'd it strong
> From space to space, and nail'd the planks along;
> These form'd the sides: the deck he fashion'd last;
> Then o'er the vessel rais'd the taper mast,
> With crossing sail-yards dancing in the wind;
> And to the helm and guiding rudder join'd.
> (With yielding osiers fenc'd, to break the force
> Of surging waves, and steer the steady course)
> Thy loom, *Calypso*! for the future sails
> Supply'd the cloth, capacious of the gales,
> With stays and cordage last he rigg'd the ship,
> And roll'd on leavers, launch'd her in the deep.[3]

How is it, then, that when shipbuilding went industrial and became a prominent sector of the British economy, between the middle of the nineteenth century and the First World War, writing about it almost ceased? Why is there nothing to equal the amount and quality of coal-mining literature? Where are the Robert Tressells and Lewis Joneses of industrial shipbuilding?

At its zenith the industry in Britain employed something like 300,000 men – fewer, of course, than either coal-mining or engineering, but still an impressive number. They were a highly skilled, very specialized and hierarchical workforce, with each particular section watching anxiously over its demarcated area of work. They were also a relatively privileged labour force, coming at the top of Hobsbawm's list of the labour aristocracy.[4] On the Clyde they won the fifty-one-hour week as early as 1872 – though other areas continued to lag behind – and the engineers among them waged, though eventually lost, a struggle for the eight-hour day in 1897–8.[5] At the same time, the industry, more than any other economic sector, was subjected to constant periodic fluctuations in the trade, thus exposing shipbuilding workers to alternating periods of very intense work and enforced idleness.[6] But this is only to confirm that neither lack of education nor the absence of spare time can account for the scarcity of writing about the industry, heroic though it would be in any case to write in the evening after an exhausting day in the shipyard. Why did shipbuilders, contrary to the operatic tsar, remain mute even in song?[7]

It might be objected that I am asking the wrong sort of question, that it is unreasonable to expect every industry to throw up its minstrels and story-tellers, and that coal-mining and engineering form exceptions rather than the rule. But if we expect regions, cities, ethnic communities and subcultures to produce their literature, and we sometimes lament its absence, there is no reason to exempt an industry with its own sense of a community from such an expectation, especially when, just as in the case of mining, the shipbuilding community was close-knit, displaying a similar kind of trade continuity with son following father into the industry, and also extended to the tradesmen in the locality.

It is true that what fascinated writers about ships was never their actual production but their destiny. There are sea stories galore, narratives about journeys into dangerous or unknown worlds. And such voyages do bear a resemblance to the colliers' perilous explorations of the dark regions underground. It is a setting out without the certainty of return. Both sailors and miners are exposed to natural hazards: anchorages may be insecure, pit props yield; storms lead to shipwreck, roofs fall or explosions bring disaster; colliers are drowned in mines like seamen in the ocean. And, above all, both occupations are predominantly, though in the case of mining not exclusively, male universes, whose sequestered inhabitants work in claustrophobic conditions. James Hanley's short-story collection *Men in Darkness* refers to stokers and firemen, but the coal-mine is not so different from a stokehold.

However, stories of seafaring are really a world apart from an actual literature of shipbuilding. Among the few specimens I have come across, after an extensive search, there are from the heyday of the industry some poems by Ellen Johnston, among them 'Lines on Behalf of the Boatbuilders and Boilermakers of Great Britain and Ireland' (*c*.1860). The title says it all: it is written not by a ship-wright but a powerloom weaver. I am interested here in one stanza only, which describes the moment of the ship's launch:

> Which gave to each man joy and mirth
> The night when his well-finished work
> Was launched from the place of its birth,
> To brave both sea and shark.[8]

This picture of the craft pride belies the wholly negative view of the work-process in industrial society sometimes taken by nineteenth-century writers such as Ruskin, who thought that, owing to the division of labour, men can 'have no pleasure in the work by which they make their bread'.[9] Much as Ruskin admired the mystique of work, he saw joylessness and indifference reigning everywhere, shipbuilding included. In a little-known work, *The Harbours of England* (1856), published only a couple of years before Johnston's poem, he had this to say about the 'wonderful' art of shaping the boat's bow:

> The man who made it knew not he was making anything beautiful, as he bent its planks into those mysterious, ever-changing curves. It grows under his hand into the image of a sea-shell; the seal, as it were, of the flowing of the great tides and streams of ocean stamped on its delicate rounding. He leaves it when all is done, without a boast. It is simple work, but it will keep out water. And every plank thenceforward is a Fate, and has men's lives wreathed in the knots of it.[10]

Yet Johnston insists in another poem from the mid-1850s, 'Address to Napier's Dockyard', that the boatbuilders take as much pride in the fruits of their labour as the ship's owners:

> A thousand times I'd be a Factory Girl!
> To live near thee, and hear thy anvils clink,
> And with thy sons that hard-won pleasure drink.
> That joy that springs from wealth of daily toil,
> Than be a queen sprung forth from royal soil.[11]

Johnston writes from a sympathetic position inside the class and community, but outside the actual industry.[12]

It is not until the decline of shipbuilding in the interwar period that the first fictions are launched, notably on the Clyde, already the scene of Ellen Johnston's poems. But my first example, a historical novel by Storm Jameson, is taken from the north-east of England. *The Lovely Ship* (1927) is set during Ruskin's and Johnston's lifetime in a thinly disguised Whitby, the author's native town. It traces the changing fortunes of a strong-minded woman, from birth to an arranged marriage and motherhood at the age of fifteen, widowhood at seventeen, an ill-paid career in the family's shipyard office (extremely rare for a woman in the 1860s), to ownership of the yard and its shipping line. Jameson's novel is of relevance here for two reasons. First, it is a study of a shipbuilding company at the point of transition from sail to steam, wood to iron (and, subsequently, steel). What in hindsight appears as a foregone conclusion was to the contemporaries a fierce competition between the old technology and the new, and it took a keen-sighted entrepreneur such as the heroine to place all her confidence in steam and iron ships. With her characteristic obstinacy she overrules her cautious manager, on this occasion of decision-taking no less than during a strike over the victimization of a union man.

It is fascinating, and this is the second point of interest, how the author manages to divide her sympathies between the gender position of her protagonist, who mistresses her eventful life and the running of the firm, and the class position of the shipyard workers and the labour movement more generally (including a mildly ridiculed glimpse of the First International). To be sure, in this novel we never enter a shipwright's home, nor ever see a boiler-maker at work. We become aware of them only when they cause trouble and thus unavoidably enter the central figure's field of vision. Mary succeeds against the odds in a male world, but at the cost of internalizing that world's capitalist ethic. Driven by her obsession with ships, she becomes a shrewd, assertive, intransigent, even ruthless businesswoman who has 'ceased to bother about the human side of Garton's at all'.[13]

For a first abiding perspective on shipbuilding *workers* in fiction one has to turn to James Hanley's Merseyside novel *Ebb and Flood* (1932). This belongs with the early phase of the author, in which he engages with the dilemmas of adolescent boys, both on board ships and ashore. I have chosen this novel rather than the slightly earlier scandal-ridden *Boy* (1931) because it is consistently located in a port where the sixteen-year-old protagonist, introduced on the first page as 'a scaler and riveter', will regularly go about his work when he has not been laid idle. The book is not (or not yet?[14]) written in that sparse hammering style, characterized by clipped sentences, elided articles and occasionally missing predicates, that was to become the trademark of the author's string of working-class fictions in the first half of the 1930s. It is, in fact, a curious, arguably unintentional, hybrid of realist and expressionist modes, linking somewhat awkwardly the former's penchant for milieu description with the latter's neglect of probable incident, combining class and generational anguish with the nightmarish despair of the single consciousness. But *Ebb and Flood* also brings out Hanley's strengths: his sense of the confinement of working-class existences and of the drama involved in all attempts at escape. Here as elsewhere in his work one notices how the representation of the violence of ordinary life 'is clearly seeded by his experience and lingering vision of the First War'.[15] The young protagonist's father has died of the after-effects of gas-poisoning. His mate, also from a single-parent family, has lost his father in the slaughterhouse, that other epitome of violence in inter-war working-class fiction,[16] crushed by a dying bullock. This puny boy is at the mercy of a drunken mother, interested only in his earnings, and a brutal oversexed sister. In due time, after having gambled away his wage-packet and thereby his one dream of deliverance, the purchase of a chest expander, he will, like so many of Hanley's characters, commit suicide.

The author registers very perceptively how the sphere of production dominates the whole life of working people, penetrating their very homes:

Occasionally there came hurtling through this fog the steady rat-a-tat of the riveters working in the graving dock, and further north the rattling of the winches, carrying their sound far inland, over seas of roof, over battalions of brick, up every street, so that men returning home to bed took with them the song of the winch and the riveter, the rattle of the cranes. It was all a part of themselves. They were bound up in these things. Through the open windows came the sounds, so that for many the nights were sleepless, and for those who did sleep, a certain awareness robbed it of tranquillity and peace.[17]

The entire dock area is pictured as one

huge hulk that hung leech-like to the docks and the sea, bound to this world of sound, of darkness and machinery, a monstrous shadowy world, that seemed to harbour a stifled rage, a rage burnt in upon the brain. Each morning the boys went down to work in darkness, and each evening returned. Darkness drew them forth, and darkness drew them back.[18]

The three adolescent boys at the centre of this novel occupy a no man's land between childhood and adult age. They are no longer children. They are, in fact, proud of working like 'real men', in the company of 'riveters, carpenters, boiler-makers, fitters, joiners, scalers'. They take pride in the hard, dirty and dangerous job in the boiler of a ship. They celebrate proletarian masculinity, contrasting themselves favourably with those 'soft kites' of 'college boys [that are] being taken round a liner for inspection', and to the pen-pushers in offices:

The world in which they now dwelt seemed to clothe them with its own power, something far different from the drabness of their daily life. For there was darkness and they worked in it, by the white light of a blistering fire. This living fire passed from hand to hand. There was Condron taking the raw steel, and flinging it in, and later withdrawing it, alive with energy and power; so hour after hour the metal was heated, was flung down, was flung up, and so hammered home into the deckhead of the *Horsfall's* 'fridge'. It seemed to Condron that, working thus, they towered above office and shop boys, for they themselves worked in the night in which such innocents slept. They were men among men. A pride stirred itself in the youth's heart . . . [They] belonged to] this living, this pulsating energy, this demoniac fury, this power that made ships, and reddened the sky above them.[19]

Yet at the same time they experience the adult world as hostile. The novel is one long indictment of 'Them', but 'Them' includes not only the police, Corporation inspectors, priests and coroners, but also prying neighbours and bullying foremen, adults, that is, from the adolescent boys' own working-class environment.

Hanley's novel is set in the early 1920s, George Blake's *The Shipbuilders* (1935) at the height of the depression a decade later. It is a very different kind of fiction, making full use of the ambiguity of the word 'shipbuilder', which can denote both the man working in a shipyard and that yard's owner. In alternate chapters or sections the impact of the economic crisis on a family of each class is charted, and while the outcome is predictable in social terms, its individual colouring is not. Pagan's shipyard will close after the launch of the last ship, with not a single order even for a repair job in the books. It is the end of the road for three generations of entrepreneurs. But, the novel insinuates, far from this being solely an individual tragedy, a whole era of shipbuilding has run its course. During a trial journey downriver Leslie Pagan has the impression of looking at an industrial graveyard:

> It was in a sense a procession that he witnessed, the high, tragic pageant of the Clyde. Yard after yard passed by, the berths empty, the grass growing about the sinking keel-blocks. He remembered how, in the brave days, there would be scores of ships ready for the launching along this reach, their sterns hanging over the tide, and how the men at work on them on high stagings would turn from the job and tug off their caps and cheer the new ship setting out to sea. And now only the gaunt, dumb poles and groups of men, workless, watching in silence the mocking passage of the vessel. It was bitter to know that they knew – that almost every man among them was an artist in one of the arts that go to the building of a ship; that every feature of the *Estramadura* would come under an expert and loving scrutiny, that her passing would remind them of the joy of work and tell them how many among them would never work again. It appalled Leslie Pagan that not a cheer came from those watching groups. It was a tragedy beyond economics. It was not that so many thousands of homes lacked bread and butter. It was that a tradition, a skill, a glory, a passion, was visibly in decay and all the acquired and inherited loveliness of artistry rotting along the banks of the stream.[20]

Yet, when all is said and done, Pagan will be able to live as comfortably as before on the dividends from the enormous fortune made by his family over the ages. More perversely, his English wife actually welcomes the closing down of the yard, for it removes the last obstacle to her long-cherished wish to leave 'the inveterate grimness of the North', 'the squalor of Glasgow',[21] and settle in the pastoral rurality of the South Downs close to her aristocratic family.

By contrast, the riveter Danny Shields has not only to face unemployment but also a broken marriage. His is the real ordeal, involving a brief prison spell for public misdemeanour and a stay in hospital after having been beaten up by a rival firewood-seller, his own attempt at securing a precarious livelihood. But his stamina is never in doubt, and he doggedly refuses Pagan's offer of a gardening job in Surrey. His repeated 'I think I'll stick to my trade, sir' is as dour as it is heart-rending, for no riveter of the old school stands a chance of ever being taken on again:

> the monster men called Progress had overtaken such as Danny Shields and left them behind, rejects, on the deserts of industrialism. Now in the place of the riveter was the welder, joining the plates of ships with a melting jet of white flame . . . Now one man and a boy, working a machine, could do in the way of making hatches what it used to take fourteen craftsmen to do. Now boys manned piano punching machines, each halflin with his engine displacing twelve helpers. Another dozen helpers were out of work because a hydraulic machine, operated by a man and boy, could bend ships' frames. One man, commanding a single drill-punch, displaced six of his kind.

It is clear where the author's sympathies lie: Pagan's departure is seen as a 'desertion, betrayal, surrender'.[22] It may be no easy decision, but, contrary to the working man, Pagan can and will escape, and it is little excuse that he is pushed into withdrawal by his wife's intransigence.

This is another novel in which women are almost invariably painted black, though the English and the Jews are also strongly stereotyped. The other side of this misogyny is the male bonding between the two old soldiers, which is meant to account for the almost Dickensian relationship between master and man. Pagan is a capitalist with a human face and social conscience, guilt-ridden to the point of reflecting that his 'garage . . . was roomier and warmer than any house a riveter could ever hope to live in', or that a small party at his home 'in cash would keep for a week five of such families as must suffer through the closing down of Pagan's'.[23]

Blake's bleak pessimism and his well-meaning but condescending attitude to the unemployed met with an answer from the left within a year, in James Barke's massive *Major Operation* (1936). Barke retained the contrasting structure of the novel and the middle-class/working-class encounter, but gave it an unexpected twist. It speaks volumes for the confidence of the author that it is his proletarian representative, Jock MacKelvie, who is the intellectually superior person in what turns, in the end, into a showdown between 'The Two Worlds' (hence the subtitle of book 1 of this long novel). It is he who lends a helping hand to the bourgeois coal merchant George Anderson, when his business has gone bankrupt and his wife has run away.

Barke fights on several fronts at once. He is equally concerned to counter the gang warfare image of the Glasgow slum-dwellers delivered by the sensationalist novel *No Mean City* (1935). The portrait of MacKelvie does not yield one inch to the razor-slasher, wife-beater or drunkard image of the Glaswegian hard man. Thus whereas Shields in *The Shipbuilders*, although presented as a decent fellow undergoing a hard trial, on one occasion gets involved in a pub brawl and is promptly arrested, MacKelvie remains from start to finish a model worker, whose only confrontation with the police arises out of a march of the unemployed. This idealized conception of the working man is bound up with a moral contrasting of the two classes.

Yet actual descriptions of the men at work are rare in *Major Operation*, despite the author's first-hand knowledge of working conditions through his clerical job in a shipyard-cum-engineering firm. This may have to do with the political overdetermination of the novel. The scenes in the hospital ward, where Anderson, after prolonged intellectual bombardment by MacKenzie, is won over for the workers' cause, take up almost half the book. But *Major Operation* is also an unemployment novel. MacKelvie traverses seven lean years of steady or intermittent unemployment, in the course of which he is transformed from his trade as a red-leader to his calling as a red leader, a militant activist in the NUWM. It is thus only at the opening of the novel, before the onset of the Depression, that we are offered a glimpse of a repair yard in which MacKelvie and his workmates are watching the docking of a ship.

Perhaps the most revealing aspect of this scene is the authorial dig at the assembled body of foremen, here nicknamed 'hats':

> Of the small crowd that were gathered round the dockside there were only two hats in addition to Willie Donald. Foreman-joiner Simon Forbes, Foreman-electrician Sandy Bain. In the sun their bowler hats shone grey with dust. A foreman might dress much as he liked but his headgear had to be a bowler hat, symbol and survival of the Holy Victorian Empire and Scottish Presbyterianism . . . It was possible to spend a very pleasant life-time dodging about from one howff to another – if you were a foreman, a leading hand, a manager or a member of the staff. Having tea in one box, a smoke in another or a game of cards or a round of bawdy stories.[24]

Needless to say that MacKelvie, 'leading hand of the squad of red-leaders' – that is, casual workers and hence occupying a low rung on the social ladder of shipbuilding trades – does not belong to the caste of gaffers. Red-leading 'was the hardest, dirtiest and most uncertain job in the yard. It called for tough guys and tough guys it got.'[25]

With so few shipbuilders working in these fictions it comes as no surprise that we rarely get descriptions of industrial accidents. In the literature of coal-mining pit disasters bulk large, partly, I think, out of the pertinacious superstition that the Earth will take revenge for the violation of her bowels. But, while it is true that mining was an accident-prone occupation, the number of workers killed or maimed in the pit was not higher than those in the building or shipbuilding trades.[26]

There is a poem by Ronald Bottrall, 'Epitaph for a Riveter' (1934), which probably alludes to an industrial injury or an illness contracted at work:

> There need be no haste, slowly bear
> Him along by the tenements;
> He will never give heed to the Metro
> Crisply accelerating below the fence.
>
> Womb's entourage gave him small respite
> From the forensic bark of punctual steel:
> Expend no curses on the pathogen
> That stars him in his last newsreel.[27]

In any case, the references to the tenements and the underground suggest that we remain here on Glaswegian soil.

No doubts hang over the very narrow escape from an almost fatal winch-drop at the very opening of Hugh Munro's *The Clydesiders*:

> The winch-gear slipped and the pulley drum stopped revolving.
>
> Cursing, Big Mick grabbed at the motor switch-knob, forgetting he had only one cable turn round the drum. Like a ribbon of fire the steel hawser ripped through his fingers.
>
> Yelping, Mick let the cable go. His lift of staging planks leapt in mid-air and cascaded to the bottom of the drydock, the dervish-snaking cable and its free-falling ball-hook bouncing murderously with them.
>
> Under the tumbling load four riggers scattered desperately. The eldest, a stocky man in his forties, only just got clear. As the timber thundered and a plank cart-wheeled across the dock-floor slime to within inches of his ankles he looked up, his frozen, bellicose stance and spiky ginger moustache adding a walrus touch to his fury.[28]

This novel, while published in 1961, is once more set in the inter-war period. It is very much a domestic and street-life story, for as soon as the rigger who just got clear has been victimized after having sworn at Big Mick, the clumsy squad leader, we lose sight of the shipyard. Unemployment again dominates, though the tone is more relaxed than in any of the 1930s novels, and the shift of perspective from the adult married couple to the young generation, their concerns and especially entertainment, betrays the more confident mood of the late 1950s and early 1960s. The universe these youths inhabit is markedly different from that of Hanley's *Ebb and Flood*.

Someone who does not get away unharmed from the crash of a steel plate but ends up paralysed in a wheelchair is the charge-hand who is also the narrator's landlord in Tom Gallacher's *Apprentice* (1983). This purports to be the autobiographical account of a young Sussexman's five-year stint in a Greenock shipyard during which the 'I' is not only apprenticed to the secrets of marine engineering but also, and more importantly, to the mores and patois of the Clydeside working class. Hence the double meaning of the title. The figure of the middle-class stranger descending into the proletarian inferno is familiar in industrial fiction from Zola's *Germinal* (1885), Tressell's *The Ragged Trousered Philanthropists*

(1914) and Welsh's *The Morlocks* (1924) onward, the last probably itself indebted to Zola's novel. In *Apprentice* 'hell' has been softened to bed-bugs and the initiation rite of greasing the newcomer's genitals. Another difference is that the outsider figure is no longer an agitator. Indeed, Gallacher's work is a fiction with politics and trade unionism left out. Instead, the author's concern is with a number of striking characters taken from, or at least offered as exemplars of, real life. Of the five portraits, male and female, one for each year of the apprenticeship, only one is that of a 'shopmate', to use the title of an earlier collection of engineering stories.[29] As an industrial fiction the book's interest is thus limited, as the fictitious autobiographer, writing twenty-five years after the event, himself admits in the preface. The book is in part a journey of self-discovery, with the narrator almost compulsively meddling with the affairs of his proletarian environment, usually to no good effect at all.[30]

By the time *Apprentice* appeared, shipbuilding on the Clyde was almost extinct. But one could not glean from this celebratory retrospective view of the late 1950s that the industry would be in its death throes a decade later. A more seismographic view of the mood of the times can be found in Danny Kyle's industrial folk song 'The Great Iron Ship' from the 1960s:

> I'm working on deck of the great iron ship;
> Hell below zero, slung over the side.
> Riveter's guns play tattoos on the hull –
> We're the men that build ships on the Clyde.
>
> *Refrain*: With your hammering, your caulking,
> Your gouging and your burning,
> Snow in your face and tired inside.
> The conditions are bad, apprentice young fella,
> Don't hang around, get out with the tide.
>
> Look out down below, a hammer is falling –
> Beware, live cables lie on the wet decks;
> No smoking on board, say your safety precautions –
> And flames from the burner they blister your neck.
>
> (*Refrain*)

> Three men were sent down to the old double bottom;
> To protect them they wore safety hats on their heads.
> But gas got ignited in that small cramped department;
> One was dragged out, but the others lay dead.[31]

The song's pessimism resides not only in the bitter complaint against the working conditions but also in its sense of an ending, the advice to young men to leave the industry.[32] This is exactly what several young men contemplate doing in *Apprentice*. In the last stanza of 'The Great Iron Ship' even the launching day is revealed as an ambiguous occasion. The celebration in which the workers partake makes them forget their exploitation:

> A fur-coated lady swings a bottle of champagne,
> And breaks it against the iron ship's side.
> The workers stand cheering, their conditions forgotten;
> With their caps in the air, it's their launching-day pride.

This theme is age-old in plebeian and working-class writing. Already, 230 years earlier, Stephen Duck had exposed the harvest festival as a great delusion:

> Our master, joyful, at the pleasing Sight,
> Invites us all to feast with him at Night.
> A Table plentifully spread we find,
> And Jugs of humming Ale to chear the Mind;
> Which he, too gen'rous, pushes round so fast,
> We think no Toils to come, nor mind the past
> But the next morning soon reveals the Cheat,
> When the same Toils we must again repeat;
> To the same Barns must back again return.[33]

It is in music, too, though this time in pop, that two fine farewell anthems to the closed shipyards have been written in Elvis Costello's 'Shipbuilding' (1985) and Sting's elegy 'Island of Souls' (1991). The latter captures many essential aspects of a ship-builder's life, the growing up 'within sight of a shipyard', the 'son of a riveter's son' is expected, and dreads, to follow the father into the trade, the working 'like a slave' 'till the industry dies', the drowning in drink of the 'dream of a future', the crushing of the riveter in 'what they call an industrial accident' and the laughable compensation. 'And what else was there for a shipbuilder's son'? Perhaps the answer is the dream to be carried 'to a place far away from this town'. [34]

This survey ends as it began, with light music rather than weighty fiction. As has emerged, the narratives of industrial shipbuilding constitute less a full chapter in the history of the literature of labour than a lengthy footnote, in which large parts of the shipbuilders' story remain untold. A late arrival in the field, this fiction spans a mere half-century. Born during the industry's first convulsive and near-terminal crisis, its birthmarks are a defensiveness and nostalgia which it could never cast off. A craft in the process of devaluation, a workforce in redundancy, a community on the brink of disruption can become occasions for mourning and compassion but do not offer themselves for an apotheosis of human endeavour. Hence we look in vain for the celebratory militancy, the deep-seated anger, the class animosity, the radical edge so prevalent in other working-class and socialist novels. Even James Barke's *Major Operation*, a partial exception, is in the end geared to a political goal, the symbolic enactment of the Popular Front. The community in this work remains under-explored, the culture of the workplace untapped. But if no single work holds pride of place as the epitome of the industry at a particular moment in history we can at least fit together a few mosaic pieces. And we have a region, the West of Scotland, whose contribution outshines all the others.

Notes

[1] A. Lortzing, *Zar und Zimmerman: In Partitur*, ed. Gustav F. Kogel (Leipzig, 1900), 26–8 ('Get moving, get moving, get moving and lend a hand / To build the ship's proud sides'; 'Day for day, blow for blow / No artisan without his toil / But joy in work relieves the pain': my trans.).

[2] Daniel Defoe, *The Life and Adventures of Robinson Crusoe* (Oxford, 1926), 117–18.

[3] *Odyssey*, 5. 310–32, trans. Alexander Pope, *The Twickenham Edition of the Poems of Alexander Pope*, general editor John Butt, vol. 9 (London, 1967), 117–18.

[4] E. J. Hobsbawm, 'The labour aristocracy in nineteenth-century Britain', in his *Labouring Men* (London, 1967), 186–8.

[5] Sidney Pollard and Paul Robertson, *The British Shipbuilding Industry 1870–1914* (Cambridge, 1979), 159–60.

[6] Keith McLelland and Alastair Reed, 'Wood, iron and steel: technology, labour and trade union organisation in the shipbuilding industry, 1840–1914', in Royden

Harrison and Jonathan Zeitlin (eds.), *Divisions of Labour: Skilled Workers and Technological Change in Nineteenth-Century England* (Brighton, 1985), 156. For figures on the decline of the industry after the First World War, see Noreen Branson, *Britain in the Nineteen Twenties* (London, 1975), 148.

[7] 'Some huge, geographically concentrated industries such as the shipbuilding and engineering industries had few occupational songs.' Gerald Porter, *The English Occupational Song* (Umeå, Sweden, 1992), 15.

[8] Originally published in Ellen Johnston, *Autobiography, Poems and Songs* (Glasgow, 1867), 85; now reprinted in the appendix of my study *Factory Girl: Ellen Johnston and Working-Class Poetry in Victorian Scotland* (Frankfurt, 1998), 100–3.

[9] *The Stones of Venice*, vol. 2, chap. 6, quoted from *The Works of John Ruskin,* eds. E. T. Cook and Alexander Wedderburn, vol. 10 (London, 1904), 194.

[10] *The Works of John Ruskin*, vol. 13, 14. Ruskin's view is curiously echoed by James Hanley in his autobiography, *Broken Water* (London, 1937), 277–8:

> The worker's life is full of colour and drama and poetry. It is when they become articulate that this virgin essence is lost to them. That hand swinging the great hammer as the rivets swing home into the stout hull of the ship being born writes as fine a poem upon space and time as any poet ever wrote in his cloistered study . . . but if you tell your hammer-swinger he has just written a sonnet or a roulade on the air he will laugh at you, and then next time he remembers what you have told him. But the essence and the spirit have gone forever.

[11] Johnston, *Autobiography, Poems and Songs,* 12.

[12] The autobiographical sketch of the trade unionist and MP William Charles Steadman, 'How I Got On', published in *Pearson's Weekly* (8 February 1906), is no less atypical in that it comes from the pen of a London barge-builder rather than someone working in the heartland of the industry. In any case the account stops when the author is apprenticed to his trade.

[13] Storm Jameson, *The Lovely Ship* (London, 1927), 131. Entrepreneurial pride of a different sort is at work in a more recent historical novel, Barry Unsworth's Booker Prize-winning *Sacred Hunger* (1992), in which a merchant attentively and gleefully watches over the building of a ship (complete with a work accident, figurehead adornment and launch) destined for the slave trade between Africa and the West Indies.

[14] John Fordham, who has looked into the growth of the writer, has found evidence that during the years 1930–2, a 'period of furious productivity', Hanley worked simultaneously on several manuscripts and experimented with different styles. Cf. John Fordham, 'James Hanley: modernism and the working class' (University of Middlesex, PhD thesis, 1998).

[15] Valentine Cunningham, *British Writers of the Thirties* (Oxford, 1988), 56.

[16] Compare, for example, Ethel Carnie (Holdsworth), 'The Sheep' (1926) in *Tramps, Workmates and Revolutionaries*, ed. H. Gustav Klaus (London, 1993); Rhys Davies, 'The Fashion Plate', in his *Boy with a Trumpet* (London, 1949).

[17] James Hanley, *Ebb and Flood* (London, 1944), 18–19. This poorly produced and typo-infested 2nd edition was no. 2 in a projected Hanley Uniform Edition, published by Nicholson and Watson, which was, however, soon discontinued.

[18] Ibid., 19.

[19] Ibid., 192, 138, 103, 139–40.

[20] George Blake, *The Shipbuilders* (London, 1935), 173–4.

[21] Ibid., 250, 253.

[22] Ibid., 383, 383–4, 362.

[23] Ibid., 22, 63.

[24] James Barke, *Major Operation* (London, 1936), 31, 30. NUWM stands for the National Unemployed Workers' Movement.

[25] Ibid., 31, 40. For Barke also see my article 'James Barke: a great-hearted writer, a hater of oppression, a true Scot', in Andy Croft (ed.), *A Weapon in the Struggle* (London, 1998), 7–27.

[26] Regarding shipbuilding, John L. Williams notes in his historical survey *Accidents and Ill-Health at Work* (London, 1960), 169–70, that 'the fatality rate has remained the highest of all occupations under the Factory Acts'.

[27] *The Collected Poems of Ronald Bottrall* (London, 1961), 53; first published in *Festivals of Fire* (1934). Ships, harbours and the sea figure prominently in the poet's early work.

[28] Hugh Munro, *The Clydesiders* (London, 1961), 7.

[29] Stacey W. Hyde, *Shopmates* (London, 1924).

[30] I am obliged to Mike Sanders for drawing my attention to *Apprentice*, a title that recalls Edward Gaitens's earlier *Dance of the Apprentices* (1948) in which there are also faint echoes of the docks and shipyards of the Clyde.

[31] Nevis Records, Glasgow, NEV R007: II, 2; for a discussion of 'The Great Iron Ship' and the contemporaneous craft pride song 'The ballad of the Q4' by Matt McGinn, see Ian Watson, *Song and Democratic Culture in Britain* (London, 1983), 110–12, 102–5.

[32] Under the impact of the momentous Upper Clyde Shipbuilders' work-in of 1971 Kyle rewrote the final chorus: 'The conditions are bad, apprentice young fella / But please hang around, and fight from inside. / Please hang around and fight from inside.' But the new ending, with its emphasis on the right to work and the need to fight for jobs, sounds forced given the overwhelmingly negative attitude to the industry throughout the rest of the song.

[33] Stephen Duck, 'The Thresher's Labour' (1730), in his *Poems on Several Occasions* (London, 1736), 25.

[34] From the CD *The Soul Cages*. Sting's carefully chosen lyrics display his sensitiveness to the ideologically laden term 'accident': cf. Mike Sanders's discussion of this topic in chap. 3. Elvis Costello's 'Shipbuilding' picks up the 'rumour [that] was spread around town / . . . within weeks they'll be re-opening the shipyards', but immediately issues a sharp reminder 'that people get killed in / The result of this shipbuilding', suggesting in the process that people would better 'be diving for pearls'. See his CD *Punch the Clock*.

6

Highs and Lows:
the Problem of 'Culture' in
The Ragged Trousered Philanthropists

GARY DAY

Since Robert Tressell's *The Ragged Trousered Philanthropists*[1] deals with a group of jobbing builders and decorators instead of workers in a factory, it cannot strictly be described as an industrial fiction. This, however, is to take a somewhat narrow view of a novel which takes as its theme that of many 'industrial novels', namely the relation between physical workers and their employers. It examines this relation as a function of capitalism and questions why those who are its victims nevertheless show little interest in criticizing this system, and even less in changing it.

The lack of political interest of at least some sections of the English working class has attracted the attention of a number of commentators. Gareth Stedman Jones has argued that working-class radicalism declined as, from the middle of the eighteenth century, people no longer lived at their place of work. By the late nineteenth century, with the mechanization of heavy industry and the growth of the suburbs, a work-centred culture realized in trade feasts and a distinctive language and dress had been replaced by one centred on the home, the pub and sport.[2] Ross McKibbin makes a similar point when he argues that the small-scale nature of British industry in the early part of the twentieth century, together with divisions within the working class between 'respectable' and 'non respectable', militated against the development of a radical politics. Another factor in this process was the nature of working-class culture. Activities such as flower-growing, angling and pigeon-racing provided what McKibbin calls an 'associational structure' to urban life that was decidedly non-political.[3]

The relation of culture to a possible politics of change is a key element in *The Ragged Trousered Philanthropists*. This relation seems to be one of opposition. The 'philanthropists' (the ironic name given to the builders and decorators because of their willingness to defend the system that oppresses them) regard Frank Owen, the spokesman for socialism in the novel, 'as a bit of a crank' because he takes 'no interest in racing or football', preferring, as they see it, to talk 'a lot of rot about religion and politics' (p. 18). For his part, Owen despairs of the 'philanthropists' ever being able to understand the cause of poverty and how to remedy it because this is not an 'important' matter to them compared to 'a smutty story, a game of hooks and rings or shove-ha'penny . . . football or cricket, horse racing or the doings of some royal personage or aristocrat' (pp. 267–8).

The clear suggestion is that the 'popular' pastimes of the philanthropists prevent them from even being curious about the system under which they live. The same effect is achieved by one of the newspapers they read, the *Daily Chloroform*, while another, *The Daily Obscurer*, as its name implies, conceals the true nature of social reality. Tressell makes a similar point about 'popular' fiction which, with its captivating tales of such aristocratic characters as 'the Marquis of Lymejuice', blinds people to their surroundings. One passage describes how nurses and mothers are so absorbed in this kind of literature that they fail to see where they are going and thus bump their prams into builders' ladders (p. 400). Tressell stresses the potentially fatal consequences of this in order to link it to a later episode where one of the philanthropists, Philpot, is killed by a falling ladder (p. 511). Although his death is directly due to the failure to take safety precautions owing to the pressure to finish work quickly, the connection between the two passages is unmistakable and clearly implies that 'popular' fiction is allied with the destructive tendencies of unbridled capitalism. Thus, the novel intimates, not only does this kind of literature stifle curiosity but, by doing so, it constitutes a potential danger to life itself.

The distortions and distractions of 'popular' culture deny the philanthropists knowledge of their society. Its essentially escapist nature means that they never encounter representations of themselves or their lives which would enable them to make connections between the wretchedness of their condition and the structure of the social formation. Consequently, they have a passive attitude to life. Jack Linden, another of the philanthropists, sums this up when he says that things 'can't never be haltered . . . There's always been rich and poor in the world and there always will be' (p. 28). This passivity is reinforced by the visceral pleasures of 'popular' culture, its appeal being to the body rather than to the mind. The philanthropists prefer drinking beer to a lecture on politics, betting to an exposition of the laws of capitalism (p. 545). Their interest is in bodily processes not social policies. Hence they relish 'a dirty story' and delight in 'downward explosions of flatulence' (pp. 27, 220), while being supremely indifferent or else actively hostile to Owen's proposals for the elimination of poverty (p. 151).

Although the pleasures of the body are condemned because they prevent the development of a critical perspective on society, it is also the case that the body offers a site of potential resistance to the social order. This occurs when the philanthropists endeavour to 'get some of their own back' (p. 38), which takes the form of drinking, smoking and general horseplay instead of work. The most memorable example is when one of the employers, Rushton, sends a note to the philanthropists forbidding them to remove any materials or equipment from their place of work, and they return it to him smeared in human excrement (pp. 424–5). Such moments of defiance, however, are ineffective because they are not linked to a comprehensive analysis of society. This, the novel implies, can only be delivered by 'high' culture, because of its characteristic manner of discerning relationships between apparently discrete phenomena. The body, by contrast, endures or enjoys a series of separate sensations which sometimes appear to oppose the social order but which mostly reflect its subjection to it. Tressell's anxiety about bodily pleasures runs deeper than the late nineteenth-century socialist fear that an appetite for instant gratification threatened rational recreation, on whose foundation the new Jerusalem would be built. There is an almost Swiftian recoil from the flesh evident in such descriptions as that of Sweater's complexion having 'the colour and appearance of the fat of uncooked bacon' (p. 106). Whatever the source of Tressell's antipathy to the flesh, it obscures those moments where the body opposes the existing order and this represents a failure to recruit popular energies to the socialist cause. Tressell appears to believe that 'popular' culture deprives the philanthropists of their full humanity by reducing them to their bodies, but so too does he by his repudiation of the body, which finds no place in his Utopia of 'rational pleasures' (p. 494). Leisure is the time for 'self-culture', without which the philanthropists are no more than 'savages' and 'wild beasts'.

Although they would object to being characterized in this way, the philanthropists' frequent refrain that the 'good things' of life are not meant for 'the likes of us' (pp. 208, 451) shows that they hold themselves in low esteem. These 'good things' are 'the necessaries, comforts, pleasures, and refinements of life, leisure, books, theatres, pictures, music, holidays, travel, good and beautiful homes, good clothes, good and pleasant food' (p. 29). They represent 'civilization', defined by Owen as 'the accumulation of knowledge which has come down to us from our forefathers' and which is 'the common heritage of all' (pp. 29–30). As Owen remarks, anyone who 'cannot enjoy the advantages of civilization might just as well be a savage' (p. 29). Civilization is about knowledge not ignorance, change not stasis, and rounded development not sensationalism. Civilization, as 'the common heritage of all', is inclusive, whereas 'popular' culture, because of the part it plays in maintaining the divisions of capitalism, is exclusive. It is therefore implicated in the existence of poverty, the very opposite of a civilization whose 'benefits and pleasures will be enjoyed equally by all' (p. 485).

Tressell's claim is that capitalism is incompatible with civiliza- tion. The free market demands that everyone 'consider [their] own interests first . . . absolutely regardless of the well being of others' (p. 87). This leads to the abandonment of 'every thought and thing that tends to the elevation of humanity' (p. 459), a point graphic- ally illustrated in the case of the employers in the novel, Rushton, Sweater and Didlum, who had

> given up everything that makes life good and beautiful, in order to carry on a mad struggle to acquire money which they would never be sufficiently cultured to properly enjoy. Deaf and blind to every other consideration, to this end they had degraded their intellects by concentrating them upon the minutest details of expense and profit . . . Devoid of every ennobling thought or aspiration, they grovelled on the filthy ground, tearing up the flowers to get at the worms. (p. 459)

The alternative to this state of affairs is socialism, which will replace competition with co-operation and the chaos of the free market with the planned economy. More than that, as Barrington, who is from a wealthy family but who chooses to work as a labourer, declares '[w]hen we get Socialism . . . Everybody will be civilized' (p. 497).

This statement is an accurate reflection of the late nineteenth-century socialist belief that 'culture' could be a force for civilization. Robert Blatchford, James Blackwell and H. M. Hyndman were among the many socialists who argued that the recent increase in working-class leisure should be used for rational purposes such as education and self-improvement; for acquiring knowledge of the cultural heritage of the nation and for furthering the cause of socialism. Like Tressell, they despaired that the working class preferred the diversionary pleasures of the pub, the seaside excursion, gambling and the music hall to the elevating influences of the temperance cafe, the concert and the public lecture. However, as Chris Waters has argued, what this kind of socialist failed to understand was that 'workers had a rich cultural existence of their own',[4] including gardening, home improvement and sport, which they had no desire to exchange for a watered down middle-class one of rationality, health and morality. Throughout the nineteenth century the working class had struggled to rid themselves of middle-class interference in their affairs and, having freed themselves from such attempts at tutelage, they 'were reluctant to accept it again in the guise of socialism'.[5]

There are two contrary views of culture here. The first states that 'high' culture is superior to 'popular' culture, while the second asserts that working-class culture should not be judged by the standards of a middle-class one. The first assumes that cultures should be compared for the purpose of evaluation while the second adopts a more anthropological approach, seeking to understand cultures as particular ways of life, each valid in their own terms. However, this apparently 'democratic' anthropological approach conceals an element of conservatism to the extent that its respect for the internal logic of a culture can preclude it from criticizing it. Similarly, while there is an element of elitism in using 'high' culture as a form of evaluation, it can also be a spur to social change. Owen, for instance, upholds the ideal of 'high' culture or, as he calls it, 'civilization', in the hope of inspiring the philanthropists to work towards the dissolution of capitalism.

What is interesting about *The Ragged Trousered Philanthropists* is the way in which it combines the culture-as-evaluation approach with the culture-as-anthropology approach. It embraces the idea of culture as evaluation without completely abandoning the idea of culture as a particular way of life. A weakness in the novel is that it does not attempt to relate 'high' culture to the capitalist system, though it does argue that this is the way 'popular' culture should be understood. The novel analyses the function of 'popular' culture in the capitalist system but treats 'high' culture as if it transcended it. It is this occlusion of the relations between 'high' culture and the social formation that allows 'high culture' to be used as a form of evaluation. Ironically, however, it is precisely this use of 'high' culture which brings those relations to light.

Culture as a form of evaluation is used to criticize the quality of life in capitalist society. This means seeing people as more than economic units. Thus, when one of the philanthropists, Newman, is sacked because of the firm's need to cut production costs, Tressell is careful to bring out the human misery this causes:

> Newman stood in the darkening room feeling as if his heart had turned to lead. There rose before his mind the picture of his home and family. He could just see them as they were at this very moment, the wife probably just beginning to prepare the evening meal, and the children . . . setting the table . . . They had all been so happy lately because they knew that he had work that would last till nearly Christmas. And now *this* had happened, to plunge them back into the abyss of wretchedness. They still owed several weeks' rent, and were already so much in debt to the baker and the grocer that it was hopeless to expect any further credit. 'My God!' said Newman, realizing the almost utter hopelessness of the chance of obtaining another 'job' and unconsciously speaking aloud. 'How can I tell them? What *will* become of us?' (p. 162)

The Ragged Trousered Philanthropists identifies the human with 'high' culture, with 'civilization', but this same 'high' culture is, as we have seen, the standpoint from which the philanthropists are regarded as non-human, as 'savages' or 'wild beasts' (pp. 431, 541). The novel therefore has a contradictory relationship to capitalism condemning its inhumanity while itself labelling the philanthropists as inhuman (pp. 506, 543, 544). Furthermore, the description of the philanthropists as 'savages' is a reminder that one of the contexts of the novel was imperialism. A crowd of voters are dismissed as being 'intellectually on a level with the Hottentots' (p. 544), while Owen's whole approach to his fellow workers is that of a missionary endeavouring to bring civilization to the natives. The idea of the human is thus culturally specific and is not, as Owen had earlier implied (p. 30), the expression of universal civilization.

A further problem with culture as an evaluative category is that it bears little relation to the novel's social insights. From the point of view of 'high' culture, the philanthropists are 'despicable' and 'dirt' because they are not interested in improving their situation (p. 46). However, this is because right '[f]rom their infancy they had been trained to distrust their intelligence' and, even if this were not the case, '[t]hey were usually so tired when they got home at night that they never had any inclination for study or any kind of self improvement' (pp. 204, 394). Judgement and analysis do not so much complement as confront one another in this novel.

Nor does the establishment of a socialist society resolve the problems that cluster round the idea of high culture. The socialist Utopia is one where production should be geared to need not profit (p. 490). Culture too can be regarded as a surplus; in anthropological terms, because it is only when the means of life have been procured that culture can take place[6] and, in capitalist economic terms, because it cannot be justified according to the logic of profit and loss. 'High' culture asserts that value is a matter of quality, not quantity, and it is therefore always 'surplus' to a society in thrall to the balance sheet. It is also 'surplus' to the extent that it challenges established convention, refashions perception and extends the limits of experience. However, the novel's vision of socialism as a system where there is a consonance between production and need at every level undermines the very principle of 'high' culture which it otherwise ceaselessly invokes in its criticism of capitalism.

But although the idea of 'high' culture is deeply compromised – inevitably so – the fact remains that it is an image of a potentially more rounded and fulfilled existence than that found in capitalist society. It is a stimulus to change to the extent that it requires the philanthropists to imagine how things might be different – though that is precisely their objection to it. 'That's the worst of your arguments', sneers Crass, the foreman, '[y]ou can't never get very far without supposing some bloody ridiclus thing or other . . . let's 'ave facts and common sense' (p. 29). In order to deal with this and other objections, Owen is forced to reflect on how best he can communicate with the philanthropists. 'How was he to put it to them that they would have to understand whether they wished it or not' (p. 267). The answer is that he cannot because the difference between 'high' and 'popular' culture is too radical for there to be any common ground between them.

What Tressell shows is that the disjunction between 'high' and 'popular' culture is rooted in the division of labour – 'the men work with their hands and the masters work with their brains' (p. 138) – and it is this which accounts for the difference between the rather abstract and bloodless 'high' culture and the concrete full-blooded 'popular' culture. However, by opposing the one to the other, as Owen does, the division is not only maintained but perpetuated. The central contradiction of *The Ragged Trousered Philanthropists* is that the image of the new society is the means that reproduces the old: 'high' culture becomes the obstacle to the order of which it would be the expression. The novel, in short, cannot rise above its determinations, only renew them.

This is also evident in its failure to escape the conventions of the eighteenth- and nineteenth-century Victorian novel, which are ill-adapted to conveying its socialist vision. The naming of characters according to their moral qualities, for example Crass and Slyme, suggests an inability to change which is at odds with Owen's educational efforts and the frequently repeated belief that people can take charge of their circumstances. The resort to individual charity is one solution to the problem of poverty found in the Victorian novel and it recurs at the end of *The Ragged Trousered Philanthropists*. Barrington's Christmas presents to the children and his £10 gift to Owen suggest that conventional plot resolutions dominate the novel's socialist vision. Individual kindness succeeds where Owen's educational efforts fail. A novel devoted to the critique of capitalism very nearly ends by celebrating Christmas in the spirit of Dickens, with Barrington as Santa Claus (p. 575). Moreover, the disillusion with the possibility of collective action encourages us to read the final paragraph of the novel in a providential rather than a political way. The light that 'riv[es] asunder and dissolv[es] dark clouds which had so long concealed the face of heaven' (p. 587) conflates socialism with religion. In a truly Victorian manner, *The Ragged Trousered Philanthropists* concludes by counselling us to trust in a power greater than ourselves.

The novel also shows its debt to Victorian fiction by Owen's frequent attempts to describe society as a whole. This corresponds to the convention of the omniscient narrator in nineteenth-century fiction who is able to survey the totality of society from his or her privileged position. Similarly, plot devices, such as inheritance in *Great Expectations* or metaphors such as the web in *Middlemarch*, make visible the links between different parts of society. Owen differs from the omniscient narrator of Victorian fiction to the extent that he comprehends the totality of society in economic rather than legal, moral or metaphorical terms. Tressell's attempt to present a panoramic view of society does, however, fly in the face of late nineteenth-century developments in the form, when 'the attempt to write epically comprehensive novels of national analysis was abandoned for more specific concerns'.[7] To a certain extent, *The Ragged Trousered Philanthropists* dramatizes this tension between a general picture and local anxieties in the relationship between Owen and the philanthropists. Owen's unified view of the social formation is implicitly called into question by the miscellaneous 'narratives' of the philanthropists, who talk 'at the top of their voices, each one telling a different story' (p. 140). These different narratives never cohere and they anticipate, in a small way, the modernist emphasis on multiple and competing realities, on 'the progressive disintegration of those meticulously constructed "systems" '[8] which were so characteristic of the nineteenth century.

This raises the question of the relationship between Tressell's novel and modernism. The fact that *The Ragged Trousered Philanthropists* was finished in 1910, the year, according to Virginia Woolf, in which modernism began, does not of course make it a modernist novel. Nevertheless, the modernist reverence for 'high' culture and its repudiation of 'popular' culture[9] is clearly relevant to Tressell's treatment of this issue. If John Carey is right in his claim that 'the principle of modernist culture . . . was the exclusion of the masses . . . the denial of their humanity',[10] then Tressell's novel is modernist to the extent that it uses 'high' culture to divide the 'civilized' from the 'uncivilized', reducing the latter to the status of 'savages' and 'wild beasts' (pp. 431, 544). Tressell may believe that 'high' culture should be available to all, but his contempt for those who do not appreciate it allies him with modernist mandarins like T. S. Eliot, whose negative attitude towards the populist character of twentieth-century society Carey has so carefully documented.

The modernist stance towards culture, then, provides an additional context for understanding the problem of culture in *The Ragged Trousered Philanthropists*, which we have mainly considered in relation to nineteenth-century socialism. It also highlights certain modernist tendencies in the novel, which may otherwise remain hidden. There are, of course, many modernisms, and Dada is as different from Cubism as the aesthetics of Filippo Marinetti are from those of T. S. Eliot. Bearing that reservation in mind, we can say that Tressell's novel touches on such modernist preoccupations as formal experiment, the use of symbol and the nature of fiction.

Simplifying greatly, the formal experiments of modernist art were an attempt to organize the complexity of experience by creating works whose internal order respected that complexity but made little or no attempt to represent it.[11] The formal experiments of *The Ragged Trousered Philanthropists* do not, as in modernist art, constitute the subject of the work itself. Owens's diagrams, lectures, dialogues and his staging of 'the great money trick' (p. 211) are all possible solutions to the constant problem of 'his inability to put his thoughts into plain language' (p. 149). Tressell gears formal experiment, in other words, to a true knowledge of reality, whereas, by contrast, modernist art assumes that reality is elusive. For the one, art is a means to an end, for the other it is an end in itself. However, this difference is not absolute, for Tressell's socialist ambitions are reflected in the modernist aim of bringing 'past and present together [to win] release from a merely repetitive history and from a perpetual present lacking any hope of transformation'.[12] The difference lies in the fact that, for Tressell, this transformation is social, whereas for the modernists it is largely individual. Tressell wrote within a tradition that connected art and social transformation, a tradition which atrophied under modernism.[13]

The main image in *The Ragged Trousered Philanthropists* is that of a house. The philanthropists' renovation of a house called the 'Cave', a name which carries Platonic connotations, is used to show how the philanthropists participate in their own repression. Barrington, by contrast, uses the image of a house to illustrate the co-operative nature of socialism. 'The men who put the slates on', he remarks, 'are just as indispensable as the men who lay the foundation' (p. 497). This image does not function in the way that the symbol functions in modernist literature. One clear difference is that Tressell uses the image to illustrate an idea, whereas the symbol is deemed to have its own reality. However, Tressell's image is not totally divorced from the modernist symbol. For example, one characteristic of the symbol is to break down oppositions and present conflicting meanings simultaneously, and this is precisely how the house functions in Tressell: it at once signifies capitalism and socialism, thereby dissolving the opposition on which the novel depends. Momentarily, form dominates content, making *The Ragged Trousered Philanthropists* more a modernist than a realist novel.

One feature of the modernist novel is its exploration of the nature of fiction.[14] This does not occur in a self-conscious way in Tressell, but he is concerned, as we have seen, with how newspapers and popular fiction disguise, divert or otherwise deflect their readers from a true knowledge of 'reality'. This assumes that the distinction between fiction and reality is clear-cut, but in fact the novel shows that this is not the case. Tressell may claim that 'he has invented nothing' (p. 14), but this is evidently not so: the spontaneous combustion of Belcher on a railway platform is not an actual event but an allegorical comment on greed, as well as an eruption of the book's suppressed violence. It is an example of how Tressell has not only drawn on the diverse conventions of a rich novelistic tradition but has also deployed all the resources of fiction, plot, characterization, imagery and so forth to convey his vision. This vision is itself an interpretation of how things are which, as Owen's anxieties testify, seems to defy representation. Consequently, it is only ever a partial account of events, which means it is closer to the philanthropists' limited understanding than Tressell would care to admit. The hierarchical relation between 'truth' and 'fiction' begins to weaken, and so too does the one between 'high' and 'popular' culture, since that is ultimately dependent on the former: the 'popular', it will be remembered, is the realm of error and exaggeration. In short, the fictional nature of *The Ragged Trousered Philanthropists* means that we cannot place too much trust in Tressell's confident belief that 'fiction' can be disentangled from 'reality'. Indeed, Owen, who believes in the self-evident nature of 'reality', is also the character who wonders if he is mad:

> As he thought of this marvellous system [capitalism], it presented itself to him in such an aspect of almost comical absurdity that he was forced

to laugh and to wonder whether it really existed at all, or if it was only
an illusion of his own disordered mind. (p. 369)

Tressell's interrogation of fiction is perhaps seen most clearly in
chapter 29, 'The Pandorama'. The pandorama is a wooden box
with a roller on which to attach and rotate pictures illuminated by
candles (p. 301). It is decorated in the same Moorish style which
Owen had chosen when asked to design a room in the 'Cave',
which raises interesting questions about the importance of the
Eastern motif in a novel that uncritically accepts the tenets of
imperialism. The key feature of the pandorama is that its
mechanisms of representation are clearly on view. This, rather in
the manner of Brecht's epic theatre, prevents the audience from
identifying with what they see, as does the distancing commentary
of Bert, the young apprentice. The purpose of the pandorama is to
show how representations are constructed, so that the audience
realize that what they see is not a reflection of how things actually
are. Bert never allows the pictures in the pandorama to become an
absorbing narrative. He disrupts the sequence of events by
occasionally turning the handle backwards so that the audience are
jolted out of the 'story', and have to reconsider what they have
already seen (p. 302). Bert also exposes the ideology in expressions
such as 'An Englishman's Home' by dramatically juxtaposing its
connotations of property, privacy and liberty with an image of
poverty: 'a father and mother and four children sitting down to
dinner – bread and drippin' and tea' (p. 303). Other juxtapositions,
such as that between the rich and the poor, show that this is not the
ordering of providence, but a particular economic arrangement
maintained by state violence (p. 302).

It is with the pandorama that we at last get some *rapprochement*
between the idea of 'high' and 'popular' culture. Indeed, it would
not be too much to say that with the pandorama we move beyond
the novel's polarized conception of culture. The pandorama is used
to present the same critique of society as was offered by Owen,
the representative of 'high' culture in the novel, but since it
invites audience participation and creativity in the form of song
(pp. 302–3) it promises a more 'popular' and co-operative approach
to social transformation than the lectures of either Owen or
Barrington. The pandorama is the meeting-place of Tressell's
nineteenth-century socialism and his more muted twentieth-

century formalism. The relationship between these elements of *The Ragged Trousered Philanthropists* has gone unnoticed by criticism, which has, in any case, taken little account of his work. One reason for this neglect is that a novel which advocates the virtues of 'high' culture has not itself been classed as part of the canon. The exclusion makes Tressell's point almost as powerfully as he does, but not half so passionately.

Notes

[1] Robert Tressell, *The Ragged Trousered Philanthropists* (London, 1997 [1914]). Page references are to this edition and are inserted in the text.

[2] Gareth Stedman Jones, *The Language of Class: Studies in English Working-Class History* (Cambridge, 1983).

[3] Ross McKibbin, *The Ideologies of Class: Social Relations in Britain 1880–1950* (Oxford, 1990).

[4] Chris Waters, *British Socialists and the Politics of Popular Culture 1884–1914* (Manchester, 1990), 9. Waters gives a full account of the problems socialists had with the expansion and commercialization of leisure. A very good collection which also looks at working-class culture and class politics is John Clarke, Chas Critcher and Richard Johnson (eds.), *Working-Class Culture: Studies in Theory and History* (London, 1979). See also John Walton, 'Residential amenity, respectable morality and the rise of the entertainment industry: the case of Blackpool 1860–1914', in Bernard Waites, Tony Bennett and Graham Martin (eds.), *Popular Culture Past and Present* (London, 1982), 133–45.

[5] McKibbin, *Ideologies of Class*, 36.

[6] T. W. Adorno, *The Culture Industry* (London and New York, 1991), 100.

[7] Geoffrey Hemstedt, 'The novel', in Laurence Lerner (ed.), *The Victorians* (London, 1978), 19. For a full account of Tressell's relation to the novel tradition and to working-class fiction see Jack Mitchell, *Robert Tressell and The Ragged Trousered Philanthropists* (London, 1969) and, for a feminist perspective on the novel, see Pamela Fox, *Class Fictions: Shame and Resistance in the British Working Class Novel 1890–1945* (Durham, 1994).

[8] James McFarlane, 'The mind of modernism', in Malcolm Bradbury and James McFarlane (eds.), *Modernism: A Guide to European Literature 1890–1930* (Harmondsworth, 1991 [1976]), 80.

[9] Peter Nicholls, *Modernism: A Literary Guide* (Basingstoke, 1995), 12.

[10] See John Carey, *The Intellectuals and the Masses: Pride and Prejudice among the Literary Intelligentsia, 1880–1939* (London, 1992), 21.

[11] See Bradbury and McFarlane, 'The name and nature of modernism', in Bradbury and McFarlane, *Modernism*, 19–55; Nicholls, *Modernisms*, 36; and Peter Faulkner, *Modernism* (London, 1977), 16 and 18.

[12] Nicholls, *Modernisms*, 253.

[13] Ibid., 10.

[14] See John Fletcher and Malcolm Bradbury, 'The introverted novel', in Bradbury and McFarlane, *Modernism*, 394–415.

7

Fire and Horror: the Representation of Teesside in Fiction

ANDY CROFT

Most of Sheila Kaye-Smith's 1928 novel *Iron and Smoke* takes place in the Sussex landscape familiar to her readers. It begins, however, in 'Eden-in-Cleveland', on the edge of 'the Great Smoke itself – Middlesbrough and all the fuming travail of the Tees marshes, a land of everlasting fog', an opportunity for Kaye-Smith to rehearse some familiar oppositions between North and South, new and old, money and land, disruption and tradition, dirt and art, industry and nature. The effect is to transform the romantic conventions of the opening courtship scene into the abduction of Persephone, the expulsion from Eden:

> He leaned beside her on the balustrade, his elbow scarcely more than an inch from hers. The nymphs and fountains had come back into his imagination with the silence and the big white moon that had now entirely lifted herself above the arabesque of the hills. The silence seemed to be part of the moonlight . . . it seemed part of his dream of a temple-like house with shimmering white façade – fluted pillars supporting a huge three-cornered architrave, and on the lawn before it the freckled pool of a fountain where a naked nymph stood pouring water from a shell. He fearfully broke the silence and the dream of the white house.
> 'Jenny.'
> She turned her face towards him in relief. The last few moments had been unendurable to her in their embarrassment. He saw her eyes look out sweetly and wonderingly from under the pale frizz of hair on her forehead, while her bosom heaved the laces of her gown. He trampled on his dreams and kissed her.

'Oh . . . !'

The start, the quiver of her under his lips, told him, if he had wanted telling, that he was the first who had ever been so bold. But though startled she was not dismayed. Her recoil was no more than the natural recoil of surprised innocence. He kissed her again, and there was none, only a fresh and sweet delight. He was touched by her yielding. His heart woke – he seemed to clasp his nymph.

'Jenny – darling little Jenny. I love you.'

As he spoke the moonlight suddenly changed, going up on a sheet of flame. The night turned crimson, and for a moment Humphrey felt his heart bound with fear, but next he remembered the blast furnaces at Carlingrove. This was not the first time that he had seen them belch into the night, wiping out moon and stars, transforming the peaceful fields of Eden-in-Cleveland into some landscape of fire and horror, a frontier-stretch of hell.[1]

This is worth examining for a number of reasons. First, it is an extremely rare reference to Teesside in British fiction. Although it has a combined population of over half a million people, the area has rarely been written about, the experiences of its people rarely written up. There is no room, for example, for any entry on Teesside in Margaret Drabble's *Oxford Companion to English Literature*. Although the case of Teesside is an exceptional and an extreme one, the fact that Drabble does find room for entries on 'Wessex' and 'Barsetshire' is a reminder that it is part of a much wider omission from the central canon of English fiction, traditionally uncomfortable with writing about region, industry, class and work (the blurb on a recent Penguin edition of *Sons and Lovers* seems to think that the novel is set in the *Northamptonshire* coalfields).

Second, it is an example of the way that 'Teesside' – on the few occasions it appears in fiction – operates as a kind of topographically inexact, mythical landscape, 'Eden-in-Cleveland', a 'frontier-stretch of hell'. Even Pat Barker's *Union Street*, though recognizably set in Middlesbrough, carefully avoids identifying the town beyond the end of the street, while the geography of Barker's *A Century's Daughter* is extremely elastic. This no doubt reflects a widespread popular uncertainty about the identity, not to say the location, of the industrial conurbation at the mouth of the Tees, comprising Middlesbrough, Stockton, Hartlepool and Redcar.[2] At the end of Kingsley Amis's Booker Prize-winning novel, *The Old Devils*, Muriel Thomas finally leaves her husband and moves, much to everyone's disbelief, to Middlesbrough – or 'Yorkshire or Cleveland or whatever it is called these days' (as if to make the point, 'Middlesbrough' was not even spelled correctly in the first edition of *The Old Devils*).

Third, it exemplifies the fictive representation of Teesside as a shorthand for the uncivilized and barbaric, the desolate and the hopeless. At the end of *Steel Saraband*, a 1938 novel by 'Roger Dataller', an unemployed steel-worker leaves South Yorkshire in the futile hope of finding work on Teesside. In Margaret Drabble's 1969 novel *The Waterfall*, Jane finds a sad little letter from her estranged husband, written shortly before they separated, when he was working in Middlesbrough. One of the details by which Graham Greene established the loneliness of Fred Hale in *Brighton Rock* is the fact that his only relative is 'a second cousin in Middlesbrough' (who does not even turn up for the inquest). In *Keep the Aspidistra Flying,* George Orwell used the 'unemployed in Middlesbrough, seven in a room on twenty-five bob a week', three times in one chapter to haunt poor Philip Ravelston:

> in a way, of course, he knew . . . that life under a decaying capitalism is deathly and meaningless. But this knowledge was only theoretical. You can't really *feel* that kind of thing when your income is eight hundred a year. Most of the time, when he wasn't thinking of coal-miners, Chinese junk-coolies, and the unemployed in Middlesbrough, he felt that life was pretty good fun.[3]

Huddled in their 'frowzy beds, bread and marg and milkless tea in their bellies', a people and a place Orwell had never seen are reduced to a single, simple, timeless history, a negative phenomenon, unable to speak for themselves, the music-hall poor, as exotic as 'Chinese junk-coolies'. A few years earlier, J. B. Priestley described Middlesbrough in *English Journey* as 'more like a vast, dingy conjuring trick than a reasonable town', while Aldous Huxley compared the development of Middlesbrough to 'a fungus, like staphylococus in a test-tube of chicken-broth' (although he admired the ICI works at Billingham, which he thought was like 'a magnificent kind of poem'), and the film-maker John Grierson called Teesside 'a dangerous jungle'.[4]

Teesside, then, is rarely a real place in fiction, more commonly a 'frontier-stretch of hell', an underworld populated by Morlocks, a

City of Dreadful Night. At the heart of Margaret Drabble's *A Writer's Britain*, a coffee-table study of writing with a sense of place, is a study of the 'Industrial Scene'. There are vivid, ambivalent accounts by George Borrow of Merthyr and by John Dyer of Leeds, Charlotte Brontë on the West Riding, Ebenezer Elliott on Sheffield, Dickens and Mrs Gaskell on Manchester, Sillitoe and Lawrence on Nottingham, Bennett on the Five Towns, even Orwell on Wigan. But for the 'massive engineering feats . . . the building of railways . . . the explosions and blazing furnaces of the Industrial revolution' (which Teesside might be said to represent almost more than any other part of Britain), Drabble has to turn to Tolkien's *Lord of the Rings,* with its teeming orcs and goblins, 'spawning' in the dark and evil industrial landscape of Mordor.[5] Compare this description of nineteenth-century Middlesbrough from Storm Jameson's 1927 novel *The Lovely Ship*:

> The night was dark, with a moonless sky pressing down on the sinister flaming labyrinth of furnaces and shafts. Every few minutes a column of flame-driven smoke shot up into the sky, illuminating the iron-workers' quarter and the docks beyond. A blade edge of river flashed in the short-lived glow, and the sky was flushed with a tawny bloom like the bloom on dusk-red berries . . . The darkness throbbed with a steady beat as if some monster were alive and moving in the night near her.[6]

Or this 1914 poem by A. E. Tomlinson, born in Middlesbrough but by then a student at Cambridge:

> Tumult of furnaces;
> Red and ominous, splashing with flame the wash of the river;
> Red and seethed as a jungle dawning, transfused through the mist;
> Red as the ebb-swilled flats at sunfall, glazed and a-quiver
> Red, and primordially dour, as the hell of the Yiddish Christ
>
> Tumult of furnaces;
> Intoned, sacramental, the oaring that climbs from the blasts;
> Eery their asthmatic vomiting, baffling the sloth of the night;
> While the long geyser flames tongue and leer as the darkness lasts
> Staining the low-banked clouds with the bubbling crater's light.[7]

Or this 1930 sonnet by Wilfred Gibson:

> Across the Cleveland countryside the train
> Panted and jolted through the lurid night
> Of monstrous slag-heaps in the leaping light
> Of belching furnaces: the driving rain
> Lacing the glass with gold in that red glare
> That momentarily revealed the cinderous land,
> Of blasted fields, that stretched on either hand,
> With livid waters gleaming here and there.
>
> By hovels of men who labour till they die
> With iron and the fire that never sleeps,
> We plunged in pitchy night among huge heaps –
> Then once again that red glare lit the sky
> And high above the highest hill of slag
> I saw Prometheus hanging from his crag.[8]

This Teesside is a dangerous, exotic, fallen world, a part of England which writers do not have to know in order to know, a mythical, nightmare Teesside of the imagination. Muriel Thomas writes long letters to her friends in *The Old Devils*, reassuring them that there really is life so far north. They, however, are not fooled: 'the theatre, what's she talking about? In Middlesbrough? It can't be the theatre as *civilised folk* think of it . . . If you want my opinion, she's protesting too much. Life's not turning out to be much fun, how could it in a hole like that . . .'[9]

The fictional representation of Teesside is therefore a kind of imaginative hole, an extraordinary absence in the literary record. Middlesbrough Borough Council's Tourism Office recently designed a number of literary itineraries to bring coach-tour operators into the area: 'James Herriot Country' (Thirsk), 'A *Woman of Substance*/*To Hold That Dream* Country' (the TV serials were filmed in Richmond), the '*Nicholas Nickleby* Tour' (Dickens visited Barnard Castle while he was writing the novel), the '*Dracula* Trail' (Whitby), 'the Wonderland Tour' (Lewis Carroll lived in the village of Croft as a child) and '*Brideshead Revisited* Country' (the TV adaptation was filmed in Castle Howard). A remarkable achievement, to miss Teesside altogether, as though the cultural identity of the area can best be defined by omission. This essay is an attempt to describe the hole the size of Teesside in British fiction, to explain its shape, and to ask why there are so few familiar, recognizable, resonant images of Teesside in British fiction.

As the historian argues in Mark Adlard's *Interface*, a 1971 science-fiction novel set on twenty-second-century Teesside (now called T City), the roots of the 'De-Naissance' can be located in the nineteenth century :

> James Watt was hammering, chipping, and filing away at his primitive engines with all the passionate frenzy of Michelangelo hewing his Moses out of Carrara marble. But nobody knew and nobody cared. Nobody made an act of imaginative sympathy which would have brought the steam engine into the mainstream of thought and feeling. This divergence led to the exclusion of the engineer and all his works from the subjects considered worthy of treatment by an artist . . . The situation was made worse by the provincialism of the old capital and the south. As always, the people of London couldn't believe that anything important was happening outside their city boundaries. And to the superficially educated gentry of what used to be called the Home Counties, the development of railways in the north was no more than a threat to fox hunting and grouse coverts . . . The building of railways in England was the most gargantuan enterprise undertaken by mankind since the building of the pyramids. As if by divine ordinance England produced, at exactly the same time, its greatest crop of poets of genius. But what did the poets write about?[10]

Nevertheless, as other chapters in this collection demonstrate, most comparable industrial areas of Britain can boast stronger identities, constructed in large part by regional novelists who were committed to what the Halifax novelist Phyllis Bentley called 'locality, reality and democracy', and who successfully insinuated a sense of their part of Britain into a wider, popular, national identity. Why, then, has Teesside been so curiously absent in English fiction, even in those historical moments – say, the 1840s, the 1930s, the 1950s – when 'England' was discovered to lie outside the traditional centres of political and cultural authority, and when regional writing was understood to express something important about 'Englishness'? Why is the birthplace of the railways, the Victorian industrial experiment which for many years set the *world* price of iron and steel, almost entirely absent from the dream we have of ourselves which we call English literature?

Part of an explanation may be found in the relative lateness of industrial development on the Tees, particularly the gold-rush towns of Middlesbrough and (West) Hartlepool. At the beginning of the nineteenth century there were 900 people living in Hartlepool; by the end of the century there were 60,000; in 1820 there were just fifteen people living in Middlesbrough; by 1900 there were 96,000. These were unskilled, immigrant (and often polyglot) frontier towns, built, owned and politically dominated by a tiny and alien Quaker bourgeoisie living in rural north Yorkshire. This was an unskilled working class, lacking the autodidact culture of education and self-improvement which Nonconformity provided in other parts of the country, and whose trade unionism was dominated by small craft unions. Its formative political culture was Labourist, rather than Radical (as in Manchester) or Syndicalist (as in south Wales) or Marxist (as in Scotland). It was the WEA rather than the National Council of Labour Colleges that met the educational aspirations of working people on Teesside. To go to university was to leave home.

To become a novelist one had to leave Teesside. E. W. Hornung, for example, grew up in Stockton, a long way from the world of his best-selling gentleman burglar, 'Raffles'. Naomi Jacob, the most prolific and popular novelist to come out of Teesside, left her schoolteaching job in Middlesbrough and emigrated to Italy when the education authorities objected to her wearing trousers (only one of her seventy-five novels, *The Beloved Physician* – a medical romance based on the smallpox epidemic of 1898 – is set in the town). Although Harold Heslop started work in the ironstone mine in Boulby, his novels are set in South Shields (where, as a young miner, he won a Durham Miners' Association scholarship to study at the Central Labour College in London). That professional Scot, Compton Mackenzie, was actually born in Hartlepool, while the reputation of Teesside's most distinguished writer, Gertrude Bell (whose father was a Teesside ironmaster) is based on her travel books about Iraq.[11]

As these rapidly developing communities were emerging, an influential group of writers calling themselves the 'Bards of Cleveland' (John Wright, John Walker Ord, Henry Heavisides, Thomas Cleaver, Tom White, Elizabeth and George Tweddle, James Milligan and Angus MacPherson) sought to develop a popular sense of a regional identity in relation to Victorian England around Teesside's most famous son, Captain James Cook. It was an ambitious project, to say the least, inserting Teesside into the claims of a national imperial mission. 'Can Cleveland's vale produce no warrior's name?' asked George Tweddle; his answer was unequivocal:

> Upon your hills he bounded young and free,
> In all the pride of boyhood's joyancy,
> And when in foreign climes 't was his to roam,
> 'Mongst savage hordes where ev'ry face was strange,
> Oft would his soul across the ocean stray,
> When rest he sought at close of weary day,
> And in delightful reveries would range
> The verdant hills and valleys of his home.[12]

This was only a local variation on a major theme in late nineteenth-century verse, the homesickness of the builders of empire finding solace in images of pre-industrial, rural England. But Tweddle was also campaigning to restore the Cook monument, a campaign which was directed *against* industrial Teesside ('ye, vile, money-grubbing Cleveland slaves!').[13]

It was crucially an *anti-industrial* vision. At the moment when modern Teesside was making itself, the local literary intelligentsia took a strategic decision to define the place as a rural, anti-industrial landscape, whose tenuous historic claims were missionary and exotic rather than technological or economic, rooted in distant colonies of the mind rather than among their neighbours, turning their backs on the Tees and staring into the past, out to sea. Tweddle's long sonnet sequence (published in 1870) begins with a defiant personal definition of ideological geography:

> I've sat on Rosebury with many a bard
> Whose harp-strings, once so musical, are mute
> On earth for ever: we full well did suit
> Each other, in congenial regard
> For the loved landscape here unfurled to view.
> Yonder towers Guisboro's fine old ruined Arch,
> Memento of the Past – our onward march
> Mark'd by yon blast furnaces; churches not a few,
> Towns, farmsteads, rivers, fields of every hue –
> As grass and corn, and fallow – and o'er all
> The watchet ocean; prospects that ne'er shall pall
> Upon one's taste: the picture is ever new.
> We may roam far and wide before we see
> A finer sight than here from Rosebury.

Apart from the technical limitations of this kind of writing, what is most striking about it is the determined limitation of its vision. Behind the laziness of the language lies the careful construction of 'Cleveland' as a pre-industrial, rural idyll somewhere in northern Italy. The deliberate archaisms are part of Tweddle's attempt to present himself as the heir to a local, oral literary tradition, self-consciously derived from Caedmon (the poet as harpist, the archaic diction), and set in opposition to the industrial Tees and the 'vile necessities of trade'.[14] The religiosity of the diction sets the shepherd-poet and his Arcadian view apart from the world of the 'manufactures':

> Not among smoke of busy, crowded town,
> Where manufactures for the world are made,
> And man's best nature seems all trodden down,
> To suit vile necessities of trade,
> Has my life's Spring been past: but I have learnt
> To gaze upon each mountain, brook and plain,
> With poet's rapture; and my soul would fain
> Attempt a task for which it long has burnt
> With the unquenched fire of holy zeal, –
> To chaunt the beauties of my native vale,
> Preserve each legend, and record each tale.
> That aged grey-beards, e'en from sire to son,
> Have told, of love despised, or battle won,
> And add my mite unto the public weal.

Having thus been invited to see Teesside as an unnatural aberration, it is hardly surprising that so many visiting novelists were blinded by what they saw on Teesside. The consequences of this may still be seen in dialect poetry on Teesside, which is commonly rural, unlike, say, the traditionally urban dialect poetry of Lancashire or the West Riding. Even A. S. Umpleby, a schoolteacher from industrial Haverton Hill, and a major voice in local dialect writing, wrote mainly about the moors and the fishing villages on the Yorkshire coast. On an altogether different level, it may also be seen in those contemporary Teesside writers – Eleanor Fairbairn, Robert Holman, Tanya Jones – whose work is located in rural Cleveland, or those who – like Jane Gardam and Barry Unsworth – have written with such distinction about the sea.[15] In Mark Adlard's 1978 novel *The Greenlander*, the

Whitby whaling fleet passes the mouth of the Tees. The year is 1830:

> here, at the mouth of the Tees, all was peace and the beauty of undisturbed nature. This gentle estuary and its neighbouring coast were remote from any kind of business enterprise or economic endeavour. Here there wasn't anything that could testify to the reshaping hand of man. The river was asleep between its sandy banks in a dream of seals and sea birds . . . 'I've heard of an old crossing place where the monks from Whitby used to go over on their way up to Durham. It's got a name, I think.' He pondered for a moment. 'Middleburg or Middlesburg.'
> 'Pooh ! Middleburg or whatever you want to call it! Nothing but a handful of sheep and a few owld folk.'[16]

The Teesside economy – traditionally dominated by the heavy industries of mining, railways, iron and steel, shipbuilding, the docks (later petro-chemicals) – afforded few prospects of employment for women. The sociology of Teesside was dominated by a closed culture of aggressive, physical, masculinity (Gladstone once called Middlesbrough, admiringly, an 'Infant Hercules'). Women were, by definition therefore, excluded from the central experience of industrial Teesside – heavy, dangerous, collective, manual work in the traditional industries – as well as its labour movement and the culture of its working men's clubs.[17] And yet the overwhelming number of novelists who have tried to represent Teesside in fiction have been women. The horrified results were thus inevitably circumscribed by the reactions of writers who were outside the world about which they were writing. This is literally true of a writer like Lady Bell, whose 1907 documentary study of Middlesbrough, *At the Works,* was based on her investigations into the living conditions of her husband's employees, and which was in effect a form of Edwardian travel writing (significantly, none of her many plays and novels were set on Teesside). Mary Hervey, the heroine of Whitby novelist Storm Jameson's 1930 *The Voyage Home,* is also an outsider. She may be sympathetic to the conditions of the Middlesbrough poor, but her sympathy, like her vision of the town, has its limits, for she too is an ironmaster:

> The drive took an hour and a half, and though to the last half of it she was never out of sight of the town, she rarely saw it – squalid, conceived

overnight in the ugly haste of industrial opportunity, without a single gracious or redeeming line. Iron works and furnaces faced it across the bleak estuary of the Tees, grey slag tips, squat sheds, monstrous gas retorts, cylinders, tall black shafts . . . There were children in the grime-eroded houses she was passing, but they might have been dead for any sound they made. Even the two playing languidly in the gutter were silent, scarcely moving their limbs out of the way of the wheels. Mary had opened a soup kitchen, which her daughters attended faithfully: perhaps soup every other day is little comfort to small hungry stomachs – but she had done what she could . . .[18]

Jenny Bastow, the main character in Kaye-Smith's *Iron and Smoke,* has grown up on the edge of industrial Teesside, but she moves to Sussex at the start of the novel. When she returns, she is a stranger, sharing Kaye-Smith's narrative perspective; she is uprooted 'from the warm, pollen-scented May of the southern fields to the thin cold May of Cleveland, where the buttercups had scarcely begun to bloom':

> The long vault of Darlington station was cold and howling with winds, and as the train ran out towards Thornaby and Middlesbrough the grey sky was smeared with scuds of evil-scented smoke. She noticed the stunted trees that could not grow in the sulphur-laden atmosphere, the cottage windows that were grimy with smoke, the cottage gardens that were starved for the smoke-hidden sun.
>   'Lor!' shrieked her Brighton-born nurse in fear, as an emptying truck sent a stream of molten flame down the side of the great slag heap outside Dinsdale. The falling night seemed full of evil eyes, as flames winked from the mouths of ovens and kilns or flew from the tops of chimneys. The works of Dorman, Long and Co. just outside Middlesbrough were going full blast.[19]

Ellen Wilkinson was MP for Middlesbrough East when she wrote her 1929 novel *Clash*. But though it contains a highly sympathetic portrait of Middlesbrough, it is hardly any less of an outsider's view. During the General Strike the autobiographical heroine Joan Craig and her Marxist boyfriend Gerry Blain visit 'Shireport':

> The tall dark chimneys of the chemical works stood black against the red glow of the iron works across the river. These giant industries thrilled Blain. The struggle to control them seemed the biggest thing in

life to him. If only this strike could take them out of the hands of men like his father, the men to whom they represented only percentages and dividends – figures in a ledger – and put the workers in control . . . To Blain the working class, the men crowded into his meeting that night, had become the Hidden God.[20]

Significantly, the most sustained fictional representations of Teesside contain hardly any men at all. In the novels of Thornaby-born Pat Barker, men are either at work or looking for work; they have died or deserted their women who survive as best they can. Her children are fatherless and her women are husbandless (one of her novels is called *The Man Who Wasn't There*). Barker's 1982 novel *Union Street* is set in the 1970s, when Teesside was still hailed as 'the city of the future'. But the march of industry means little to Iris King, the formidable matriarch of the street:

She hadn't always lived in a nice house. She'd been born and brought up in Wharfe Street, near the river. As a young woman she'd battled her way out of it, but it was no use. She was no longer in Wharfe Street, but Wharfe Street was still in her. She remembered it. Knew it. Knew every brick of it. When she thought of Wharfe Street, she remembered Mrs Biggs. She'd lived in the end house, the one nearest the river, and the wall-paper had peeled away and hung in strips. She'd kept herself to herself. She was a clean-living, even religious woman, respected, if not much liked. Then her son, who was a bit not all there, had molested and strangled a little boy and left his body on a rubbish-tip. Then nothing that Mrs Biggs could say or do would save her. On the night before they hanged her son, somebody had gone and smeared dogshit all over her windows and all over her front door. And they'd gone on doing it too.

They never let up. She went loony in the end and had to be taken away.

And she remembered blonde Dinah, traipsing about the room in a night-dress with bloodstains on the back. There'd been men there, it hadn't been just women, but she hadn't cared.

Animals.

They were going to pull it down now, that was what they said, it was all coming down. Too late. Too late for her.

You could talk about it to people and they would say they understood. But they didn't, not really. Nobody who hadn't lived there could understand.[21]

Choosing to write about the experience of women on the economic margins has enabled Barker to write about the whole life of a declining industrial town. By the time *Union Street* was published, Teesside was in economic crisis, and Cannon Street, on which the novel was based, had long been demolished. This is, therefore, a kind of historical fiction. The sense of horror is still there in Barker's 1986 *A Century's Daughter*. But the horror is for what has been lost. The novel is an elegy for industrial Teesside. Eighty-year-old Liza Jarrett is taken to see the Transporter Bridge over the once-busy Tees:

> The river crawled away from them, streaked blue-purple, like cigarette smoke unfurling. The wind wrinkled its surface, a cold wind of the North Sea, and Stephen was afraid for Liza and tried to shield her body with his own.
>
> 'It's colder than I thought,' he said.
>
> 'Oh, it's always cold by the river.'
>
> A man in a peaked cap came to collect their fare.
>
> 'Can you still walk across?' Liza asked, craning her head back to see the walkway.
>
> 'No, love. Shut that off a few year back.' He winked at Stephen. 'Ovver many buggers topping 'emselves.'
>
> The platform clanged to a halt: the barricades swung open. Liza got back into the car and Stephen drove a few hundred yards up the road.
>
> High, barbed-wire fences enclosed work yards that would never work again. The wires throbbed and hummed as the wind blew through them. Bits of cloth and polythene clung to the barbs and snapped.
>
> 'Come on,' said Liza. 'I want to get out.'
>
> She walked a few steps, holding on to the side of the car. In her mind's eye she saw this place as it had been. Tall chimneys, kilns and furnaces loomed up through the brown smoke of a winter afternoon. Trams rattled, hammers banged, furnaces roared, and always, day and night, columns of flame rose up into the sky.
>
> 'There's nothing left,' she said, and, although she'd known that it must be so, her voice was raw with loss.[22]

This Teesside is no longer defined by the horrified reactions of outsiders. The fire and smoke have gone, and in their place is revealed a place where people live and work.

The old industrial Teesside of 'fire and horror' has been replaced by a different vision of hell – a working town without work. If Teesside has at last found its novelist in Pat Barker, her subject is not work and heavy industry, but the passing of that kind of history, as though industrial Teesside could only find its fictional place in industrial decline.

Notes

Earlier versions of this essay have appeared as ' "A hole like that": the literary representation of Cleveland', *Cleveland and Teesside Local History Society Bulletin*, 58 (1990), 31–42, and as 'A sense of place', broadcast on BBC Radio Four, 8 July 1991.

[1] Sheila Kaye-Smith, *Iron and Smoke* (London, 1928), 3.

[2] For the purposes of local government, the towns of Teesside, which were once part of County Durham and the North Riding, have in recent years been relocated first in Teesside and then in Cleveland; citizens of Teesside presently belong to no county.

[3] George Orwell, *Keep the Aspidistra Flying* (Harmondsworth, 1962 [1936]), 90; Orwell later visited Teesside, staying in 1944 on his cousin's farm outside Stockton, where he began writing *Nineteen Eighty Four*.

[4] For Aldous Huxley's visit to Teesside, see David Bradshaw (ed.), *The Hidden Huxley: Contempt and Compassion for the Masses* (London, 1994).

[5] Margaret Drabble, *A Writer's Britain* (London, 1979), 233.

[6] Storm Jameson, *The Lovely Ship* (London, 1927), 224; it has been suggested that the twenty-first-century Los Angeles depicted in *Blade Runner* is based on Ridley Scott's native Teesside.

[7] A. E. Tomlinson, *Candour* (London, 1922).

[8] See Mary Ashraf (ed.), *Political Verse and Song from Britain and Ireland* (London, 1975), 335; see also C. Day Lewis, 'Hail Teesside!', in *The Complete Poems of C. Day Lewis* (London, 1992), 720.

[9] Kingsley Amis, *The Old Devils* (Harmondsworth, 1987 [1986]), 379.

[10] Mark Adlard, *Interface* (London, 1971), 108. Coleridge and Wordsworth visited Stockton several times between 1804 and 1820, staying with Mary Wordsworth's family and with Thomas Hogg, Shelley's friend and first biographer; Byron's first wife was the daughter of a mayor of Hartlepool.

[11] The Scottish poet Kathleen Jamie was also born in Redcar; Philippa Gregory wrote the first of her best-selling Wideacre trilogy while living on Teesside in the 1980s; Nathaniel Hawthorne wrote *The Marble Faun* in Redcar; Sir Michael Tippett's first opera, *Robin Hood*, was written for and performed by unemployed ironstone miners in East Cleveland in 1934.

[12] George Tweddle, *Cleveland Sonnets* (Stokesley, 1870); Tweddle edited a weekly newspaper and a quarterly journal, and published many of the Bards of Cleveland as well as his *People's History of Cleveland* and *five* separate collections of his own *Cleveland Sonnets* between 1870 and 1890.

[13] The figure of James Cook is still central to the self-image of Middlesbrough (even though Cook left the area long before Middlesbrough was built and the house of his birth has been transported to Melbourne, Australia) – a scale model of the *Endeavour* swings, somewhat bizarrely, from the roof of the main shopping centre, a museum and a primary school are named after him, while the town's most famous work of public art, Claes Oldenburg's 30-foot metal sculpture, *Bottle of Notes*, consists of two layers of handwriting taken from Cook's journals. Until the abolition of Cleveland County Council, drivers approaching Teesside on the A19 were welcomed to 'Captain Cook Country'.

[14] According to local legend, Beowulf is buried on the Cleveland coast (a connection suggested on the Hartlepool coat of arms with a rebus which

reproduces an image from *Beowulf*); an important exception to the anti-industrialism of these poets was the poet John Wilkinson, an engineer from North Ormesby, in Middlesbrough.

[15] See also Jane Gardam, *The Iron Coast* (London, 1994).

[16] Mark Adlard, *The Greenlander* (Harmondsworth, 1980 [1978]), 4; several Teesside children's writers like Theresa Tomlinson and Julian Stretton have also set their novels in pre-industrial Cleveland.

[17] Consider the almost unanimous political silence which greeted the discovery – at the height of the Cleveland child abuse affair – of *Paris Sixty Eight*, a violent pornographic novel written by Middlesbrough Labour MP, Stuart Bell.

[18] Storm Jameson, *The Voyage Home* (London, 1930), 3.

[19] Kaye-Smith, *Iron and Smoke*, 159.

[20] Ellen Wilkinson, *Clash* (London, 1929), 83.

[21] Pat Barker, *Union Street* (London, 1982), 186; see also Barbara Gamble, *Out of Season* (London, 1985), a novel about a fatherless boy set in Redcar. When *Union Street* was filmed (as *Stanley and Iris*), Jane Fonda played the role of Iris.

[22] Pat Barker, *Century's Daughter* (London, 1986), 215.

8
Tone of Voice in Industrial Writing in the 1930s

SIMON DENTITH

Why industrial *fiction*? Why should the *novel* be considered such an appropriate form for those aspiring to give an account of working lives, and of the lives gathered together by industrial society? Why use this form, rather than, say, autobiography, or more academic modes of social history? This is not only my question; it preoccupied Raymond Williams, for example, especially as he was writing *Border Country* in the 1950s, at the same time he was writing his academic books – *Border Country* being a novel of working life that was in part autobiographical, but which sought to give an account of a 'whole way of life' in order to make sense of the individual lives lived within it. So what could the novel capture that social or demographic history could not? This preliminary and fundamental question can be put to many of the industrial novels of the 1930s, which, like Williams's fiction, seek to represent working lives usually excluded from the knowable communities of the novel. Why did so many working-class writers want to write fiction; what did the novel offer them that other forms of writing did not? I suggest one answer to this question: that the novel provided, as one of its characteristic modes, the use of irony, but that, in part because of this inheritance of irony, fiction was especially hospitable to a different kind of irony that was in fact a characteristic resource of the speech communities from which the novelists emerged. So I offer 'irony' as an answer to my question, but I seek to distinguish between different kinds of irony in the industrial writing of the 1930s, in the hope of specifying a particular working-class pattern of intonation and evaluation to be found there.

I am approaching, then, what I consider to be one of the characteristic notes of working-class writing in the 1930s – a particular tone of voice, which can be described provisionally as one of sardonic worldly wisdom, characterized often by ironic understatement or by the choice of telling anecdote. Given that they wished to write novels, what were the generic resources available to working-class novelists in the 1930s, as they sought to find appropriate ways of writing about the working lives – or non-working lives – of the people of their own class? 'Generic resources' here means rather more than the question of what kinds of writing they could draw upon as models – though this is an important question also, and Ken Worpole, in *Dockers and Detectives*, has shown, very suggestively, how 'realist' or 'expressionist' modes might speak with more or less appropriateness to the differing forms of life of diverse industrial communities.[1] This is certainly part of my topic; but I want to consider what can be described as the 'oral generic resources' available to these writers; that is, I wish to think about the way that working-class writing might draw upon the intonations, idioms and patterns of address that characterize the speech communities from which they come. To come at this aspect of my topic, I shall allude to some of the autobiographical writing of the period, presuming that novelistic modes are less prominent in this writing. My principal examples will be drawn from *Love on the Dole* (1933), but I shall allude to other writing as it seems appropriate.

In doing so, I shall be writing in the mode of 'sociological poetics', to use that phrase of Pavel Medvedev; that is, I seek to trace in the utterance (written utterances, in this case) the social relations that are realized in and through it.[2] This is partly a matter of genre, understood here as a learnt and shareable manner of speaking or writing in which certain attitudes and social relationships are implicit. But it is also a matter of particular intonations, of the ways in which specific speakers or writers realize those generic possibilities and negotiate the particular occasion of their speaking or writing.

I begin with a characteristic sample of Greenwood's prose, taken from near the beginning of *Love on the Dole* when the young Harry Hardcastle is still working in the pawnshop:

In the staring gas light, the women, throwing back their shawls from their dishevelled hair revealed faces which, though dissimilar in features, had a similarity of expression common, typical, of all the married women around and about; their badge of marriage, as it were. The vivacity of their virgin days was with their virgin days, gone; a married woman could be distinguished from a single by a glance at her facial expression. Marriage scored on their faces a kind of preoccupied, faded, lack-lustre air as though they were constantly being plagued by some problem. As they were. How to get a shilling, and, when obtained, how to make it do the work of two. Though it was not so much a problem as a whole-time occupation to which no salary was attached, not to mention the side-line of risking life to give children birth and being responsible for their upbringing afterwards. Simple natures all, prey to romantic notions whose potent toxin was become part of the fabric of their brains.[3]

Although much of the book is focalized through Harry Hardcastle, this is not; it provides a range of insights of which he is incapable, and which are part of the knowledgeable, demystifying tone in which the narrative of the book is largely conducted. Where does this tone come from? One answer would be to point to the novelistic tradition on which Greenwood is drawing, so that we could look back to Arnold Bennett and perhaps even to George Gissing as providing some of the generic resources which Greenwood is using here. Bennett is clearly one of the models for *Love on the Dole*; the very first paragraph of the book refers to Manchester and Salford as the 'Two Cities', echoing Bennett's 'Five Towns'; and perhaps some of the monumentalizing tone of the book derives from him – by which I mean the way the book at times looks down at Salford from a great height, and offers it for the reader's consideration as a kind of unchanging solid fact. I suggest Gissing because of the more sardonic tone which you can hear in the passage that I have just quoted: 'The vivacity of their virgin days was with their virgin days, gone; a married woman could be distinguished from a single by a glance at her facial expression.' This is certainly constructed in a rather elaborately literary way; the sentence moves into a tone of slightly weary knowledgeableness for which Gissing provides a model. However, the paragraph then modulates into a tone which I do not think can be found in either Bennett or Gissing, which seems to me to be a distinctively working-class tone, as in 'not to mention the side-line of risking life to give children birth'; here, the sardonic understatement emerges from a writing situation which presumes a shared knowledge, between writer and reader, of just how big a consideration is being alluded to in this lightly dismissed aside.

It would be possible to trace similar modulations of this ironic-to-sardonic tone throughout the course of the novel, tracing in it comparable combinations of more or less literary and oral sources. Indeed, the position of ironic knowledge occupied by the narrator with respect to his working-class characters is effectively a structural principle of the novel, which not only proceeds along a narrative of disillusion as it takes Harry Hardcastle from youthful optimism about the world of work to adult unemployment and despair, but pervasively subjects Harry to a sometimes laborious irony *en route*. For example, this is how he is described as he makes his way home, while still an apprentice, on a Saturday lunchtime:

> Harry, among the twelve thousand, dirty faced and jingling his money, swaggered home, walking with the rest of the street-corner boys. This Saturday feeling was intoxicating. He was happy, contented, oh, and the future! A delightful closed book full of promise whose very mystery enhanced its charm. It justified, fully, his choice of occupation. There was something indefinable about Marlowe's, something great and glorious, something imminent, but, as yet, just out of reach. Optimism told him to rest content, assured him that joys undreamt of were in store. And who can question optimism? It seduces. Anticipation filled him with unwonted buoyancy, with sensations of reckless abandon. (p. 54)

Greenwood strikes one of the characteristic notes of his novel here, allowing us to share some of Harry's excitement, but indicating, none too subtly perhaps, the disappointment that is in store for him. The very point of the book, one might say, was this act of demystification, by which the realities of industrial life will be revealed to Harry and to the readers. The note is struck again in the following passage, when Harry is about to be moved up from general dogsbody to be put in charge of an actual machine:

> The human nature in him, though, found errand running become stale and uninteresting: he fretted for promotion, never allowed an opportunity pass without pestering Joe Ridge, the foreman, who, as often as not, answered, snappily: 'Aw, f' God sake gie o'ever mitherin' me, son. Y'll be shoved on a bloody machine when it's y' turn. Tek things easy while y've chance. When y' workin' agen a stop-watch y'll

be bloody sick o' sight o machines. Blimey, some o'you kids don't know when y're cushy. Hop it now, Ah'm busy.' Sorry, though! Sorry to be entrusted with a lathe; a machine. Machines! MACHINES! Lovely, beautiful word! (p. 69)

Unlike in the previous quotation, however, the voice of an older, more experienced worker is present explicitly here. Indeed, it is worth enquiring from what perspective the novel's pervasive irony emerges. One such position is indicated here – it is that of the older worker who knows what is in store for those who are following on.

Elsewhere in the novel the position of superior knowledge, which generates the text's pervasive local ironies, is that of a higher educational level and more sophisticated political understanding – the position, indeed, of Larry Meath and the members of the Labour Club, in whose company Sally Hardcastle finds herself feeling inadequate:

> Their conversation, too, was incomprehensible. When the talk turned on music they referred to something called the 'Halley' where something happened by the name of 'Baytoven' and 'Bark' and other strange names. They spoke politics, arguing hotly about somebody named Marks. Yes, they were of a class apart, to whom the mention of a pawnshop, she supposed, would be incomprehensible. (p. 97)

The ironies here, I take it, are not difficult to decode, though they are relatively complex. There is a simple irony against Sally's ignorance, as in the misspellings of Beethoven, Bach and Marx. But there is a more generous irony too, I presume, in that Sally's supposition about the extent of the social ignorance of the other members of the Labour Club is itself an unfair projection, from her own limited experience, of just what educated members of the working class might know. At all events, the local ironies against the two Hardcastles, brother and sister, are part of a structural principle of irony which underlies the book, with varying presumed positions of knowledge sustaining it.

Insofar as there is one predominant situation sustaining this tone of ironic knowledge, however, it seems to me to be centred on the induction into work. One of the characteristic tropes of industrial fiction, unsurprisingly, is the transition into work, and accompanying that trope are the ironies that can be generated from the passage from innocence to experience. Often – as slightly in the case of *Love on the Dole* with the figures of Joe Ridge and Larry Meath – there is an older or more experienced worker on hand to articulate the fuller knowledge to which the whole book is tending. This is a trope which is by no means confined to the 1930s; it is an important aspect, for example, of Sid Chaplin's *The Day of the Sardine*, written in the late 1950s, where the boy's passage into adulthood and the world of work is guided by two important figures: his mother's lodger, and the First World War veteran with whom he works on a building site. What the young man learns is as much as anything a *style*: of reserved judgement, rueful acceptance, ironic judgement. The persona which Chaplin adopts, however, is more openly sardonic and knowing:

> Maybe you'll laugh at me but the first day was like shifting a mountain. It seemed it was never going to end. Didn't need a ball and chain: the shovel served. Yet it wasn't the shovel. It was that sun blazing down, that beautiful sun, and knowing that it was going to blaze all a long day of lost chances. Yet it had nothing to do with the sun. It was being tied and knowing that you were tied for life.[4]

I hope I have sufficiently suggested the place of irony in *Love on the Dole* as a structural principle of the novel. In this it resembles not only other contemporary industrial fictions, but also, of course, a predominant strand in the history of the novel, from *Don Quixote* onwards. While the particular social location of comparative knowledgeableness may alter (and this matter is obviously of crucial importance in the fiction that we are considering), an ironic gaze at the delusions of the protagonist is one of the principal generic possibilities that the novel provides. That, it may be said, is what novels do. But as I have suggested, this possible perspective on its own is evidently insufficient as an account of Greenwood's use of irony, because he is also drawing on a characteristic working-class tone, widely present in the writing contemporary with him, but also to be heard in working-class writing – not just novels – throughout the twentieth century. A canonical example, indeed, can be heard in the sardonic title *The Ragged Trousered Philanthropists*. But drawing on non-novelistic examples, and restricting myself to the writing of the 1930s, I think the tone that I am seeking to specify can also be found in the writing of Bert Coombes, of Jack Common and in other authors gathered together in the collection *Seven Shifts* which Common edited in 1938. I recognize that there are difficulties in making this case, if only because of the striking regional diversity of the writers that I have mentioned. How could such an elusive thing as a tone of voice carry across distances, and be heard in patterns of intonation as distinct as those of Lancashire, Tyneside and south Wales? Despite these regional differences, and the differing verbal styles that accompany them, working-class irony nevertheless remains a common way of negotiating shared experience, which is in part a class experience; in the particular ways that different writers draw on this tone of voice there can doubtless be traced individual temperamental differences as much as regional and social ones.

In an essay on Jack Common's autobiographical fictions *Kiddar's Luck* and *The Ampersand*, Michael Pickering and Kevin Robins write of ironic humour that it is in fact a distinctive tone of proletarian class- and self-consciousness, expressing moods that range from laconic resignation to buoyant self-confidence and pride. It is precisely this humour and irony that allow Common (like the working-class raconteur) to explore his own life at a distance and for its generality.[5] Common's irony in the autobiographical fiction can in fact be playful, even elaborate and literary, as in this passage where he is discussing the 'blunder' made by his unborn self in choosing to be born to working-class parents in Newcastle rather than to some more prosperous possibilities:

> I at once came under the minus-sign which society had placed upon my parents. They were of no account, not even overdrawn or marked 'R.D.', people who worked for a living and got just that, who had a home only so long as they paid the weekly rent, and who could provide for offspring by the simple method of doing without themselves . . . A sad mistake; though millions make it I think it still deserves a mourning wreath.[6]

Common in fact is a virtuoso of the ironic attitude, translating what Pickering and Robins rightly see as attributes of working-class speech into extended literary flights of fancy.

In the remainder of this chapter I want to explore some of the various moods to which these two critics point, and ask what happens to irony when it makes the transition from being used by a working-class raconteur to being present in the more formal protocols of publication – a transition which is more complex than they suggest, as Common's prose itself makes especially clear.

I think a version of this ironic humour can be found, for example, in the following passage by Will Oxley from his contribution to *Seven Shifts*; this passage should surely be placed at the 'buoyant self-confidence and pride' end of the spectrum suggested by Pickering and Robins:

> I was a hero for four years once, but the War stopped. They gave me a gratuity and sent me home. The gratuity I spent like a hero, then I turned round to look for the next thing. The next thing was the Labour Exchange where they allowed you benefit for War services rendered. But hero-worship quickly dwindled. There are plenty of heroes in the economic field; they get battered by big guns constantly and nobody says, 'Brave man'. I became a mere unit in the unemployment scheme and as the months went by the blessings of peace fell thick upon me. The mere inflation of being physically safe shrunk to nothing. I had no inner resources, no faith in God, and all my gratuity was spent, so I began to lose faith in myself. The job which seemed so easy to get when I came out of the army began to look as far away as first prize in the Irish sweep. I still haven't got it.[7]

You can hear the accents of speech quite near the surface of this writing, which gives me more confidence in advancing essentially a *speech* genre as one of the resources which feeds into Greenwood's writing.[8] At the risk of laboriousness, it is worth trying to explicate some of the implicit valuations that are being carried by the irony here. Principally, I take it, there is an irony here *against* the clichés of official discourse with respect to the War – that first sentence, 'I was a hero for four years once, but the War stopped', neatly skewers the way that official discourse can switch on and off the attribution of heroism as it suits. Similarly, the phrase 'and as the months went by the blessings of peace fell thick upon me' alludes feelingly to the realities of unemployment and the disproportion of the clichés that abounded in the period to those realities. In this passage, then, Oxley confidently manœuvres his way around a variety of conflicting discourses, and gets them into proportion via unstated valuations and presumed shared assumptions.

Writing of this kind seems to me to be characterized by just that buoyancy of which Pickering and Robins speak, though its actual topic is a *loss* of self-confidence caused by unemployment. It can be readily contrasted with the much quieter and more matter-of-fact manner of Bert Coombes in *These Poor Hands* in 1939 – generally intent, one might say, on giving as clear and straightforward an account of a miner's life as possible, with a presumed audience ignorant of the realities of such a life and for whom Coombes has to explain things carefully and unambiguously. But even in this prose there are moments of sardonic understatement or quiet irony which indicate a particular evaluative attitude on Coombes's part to the material which he recounts. One such moment, taken almost at random in the text, occurs after a description of a mining accident in which a young man, Jack Edwards, is killed:

> Because he was classed as single, Jack Edwards of the noble ideals and kind actions was counted to be worth eighteen pounds. On the night of his death I heard a fireman warn a haulier who was noted for his brutality to be careful how he handled a new horse. He did not ask him to stop beating this horse; he warned him to be careful not to let an accident happen to him, because he had cost the company forty pounds. I did not relish the idea that I was worth only half as much as a horse.[9]

This is a fairly characteristic sample of Coombes's writing. He is very careful to insist on exactly the necessary minimum information for his reader to gauge the force of the anecdote – the fireman's warning, for example, to the brutal haulier, is to be understood not as emerging from compassion for the horse, but out of concern for the company's investment. The force of the anecdote depends on the two incidents – the man's death, the fireman's warning to the haulier – being left to stand next to each other in the most directly unstated way; while the conclusion arrives in a tone of understated bitterness ('I did not relish . . .') which is strongly redolent of Coombes's attitude throughout the book, well described by John Lehmann, I think, as 'sensitive unhysterical truth with just perceptible undercurrents of stolid bitterness'.[10] Here, in marked contrast to the tone of Oxley's writing, the irony signals a moment of internalized bitterness rather than extrovert virtuosity.

Finally, in the prose of Jack Hilton, we can hear another and more accomplished writerly version of the tone of voice I am

trying to elucidate. In the following passage, about his first day at
work, there is an obvious comparison to be made with the irony
that governs Greenwood's prose in *Love on the Dole*:

> January 21, 1912, was the historic workday of my life. I'd long looked
> forward to it. By law every lad and lass became half man, or half
> woman. The half-time system allowed them to enter factories. *Laissez-
> faire* had been interfered with by those 'fools' in Parliament; often much
> to the disgust of our parents. They had known what it was to go into
> factories at nine, and they said that it had never done them any harm
> and thought we were being pampered. Those who were human and
> made the laws decreed that nine was too young and that twelve was old
> enough. Bless them for their humanity, and damn them for their
> conservatism, I think now. I was glad then of the privilege they con-
> ceded. I never liked school, and to be rid of it for half the time, and to
> take on real work, instead of blind alley work, seemed wonderful. I
> wanted to be like the other men-boys, to look down on errand, lather
> and news-boys. I wanted to be able to wear my cap on one side, to
> smoke a cigarette, and to use language that would become my
> manhood. I wanted to be a half-timer, and still more to be a full-timer.
> I'd have regular hours and the nights to myself. I'd be a little somebody
> at home, and mother would give me the deference due to a worker. I'd
> be able to open my mouth, and my younger brothers and sisters would
> not have to give me their lip. Soon I'd be full-time, and then would
> follow my first new suit. I dreamed it all rosily and wanted to grow to
> manhood sooner than time could fly. I'd looked forward to the
> confirmation of my faith, WORK.[11]

The irony here, while comparable to Greenwood's at the expense of
Harry Hardcastle, is clearly very different from it also. It springs
from fundamentally the same situation, that is, from the position
of adult knowledge about the world of work, by comparison with
youthful naïvety. It even shares the same typographical convention,
the resort to capitals, to emphasize that naïvety – in this case WORK,
in the case of Greenwood, MACHINES. But, perhaps surprisingly in
view of Hilton's politics, the ironies here are much less laboured,
gentler even, than those of *Love on the Dole*. Perhaps because this
is autobiographical writing, Hilton is looking back on his own
adolescence in a more indulgent spirit than that in which Greenwood presents the symptomatic case of Harry Hardcastle, so that
his foolish ambitions and petty vanities appear as evidence of the
absurdity of late childhood, in a light which is at once benign and

amused. Where there is irony at others' expense rather than at himself, Hilton assumes just that sardonic tone which I have been trying to explicate: '*Laissez-faire* had been interfered with by those "fools" in Parliament; often much to the disgust of our parents'; again we can see the way that judgements operate in unstated ways, where the commonplaces of conservative rhetoric appear, as it were, in inverted commas. Unusually, Hilton makes these judgements more explicit a couple of lines later, where he adds: 'Bless them for their humanity, and damn them for their conservatism, I think now.' It is a neatly turned phrase, and partly serves to remind us of the position of adult knowledge from which the whole passage is written. But this is a particularly confident adult knowledge, confident, that is, in its judgements, and without Greenwood's somewhat defeatist sense of foreboding.

Irony as a *spoken* form clearly depends upon the existence of shared, implicit values among those who use it – between the working-class raconteurs supposed by Pickering and Robin and those who listen to them. Often the force of it depends upon a shared knowledge of particular working conditions or hardships endured, or of the stupidities and tyrannies of authority or employers. Such irony allows the expression of shared values without their being explicitly stated. It depends closely upon the immediacies of the speech situation and the abilities of those around to understand it, and it often takes the form of ritual jokes or practised routines. If all this is true, then there must come a question about what happens to irony when it is translated into writing, where the face-to-face intimacies of the speech situation are absent. I have presumed that the particular tone of voice that I have been trying to explicate can be heard more readily in autobiographical writing, though even here it is a matter of writerly skill to find a manner, a pattern of phrasing, delicacy or bravura where necessary, to reproduce or translate that tone of voice without all the rich resources of intonation and expression provided by speech and its immediate context. Whether or not autobiography makes this tone of voice especially audible, the novel's own history as a form makes it especially hospitable to the ironic or sardonic tones of working-class speech, to the extent that it is often difficult to disentangle its generic endowment from the more socially specific speech resources of the communities from which the novelists spring.

Related to this is the question of the presumed address of the writing that I have been discussing, because the intimacies of the speech situation are clearly very different from the comparative anonymity of written publication. One large context for much of this writing in the 1930s is indicated by Andy Croft in *Red Letter Days*: the politics of the Popular Front, and the attempt to speak across class lines and to construct solidarities between people in doing so.[12] It may be that a consciousness of this larger context (of the knowledge, that is, of a sympathetic reading audience) made it easier for writers to translate attitudes grounded in the pragmatics of speech into the written forms at which I have glanced in this chapter – so that the writing, both autobiographical and novelistic, could be successful in making available, to a readership beyond the immediate 'audience', a set of attitudes towards, and evaluations of, the experience of a working life. As I have said, I think you can hear the accents of both individual and community – a particular tone of voice – more strongly in the autobiographical writing that I have quoted than in the fiction. But I also think that the speech genre which this writing draws upon can also be heard in some of the fiction of the 1930s (and from other moments in the twentieth century), and it is one of the most powerful, and characteristic, resources of industrial fiction.

Notes

[1] Ken Worpole, *Dockers and Detectives* (London, 1983).

[2] See M. M. Bakhtin/P. N. Medvedev, *The Formal Method in Literary Scholarship: A Critical Introduction to Sociological Poetics*, trans. Albert J. Wehrle (Cambridge, 1985).

[3] Walter Greenwood, *Love on the Dole* (Harmondsworth, 1969 [1933]), 30–1. Page references are inserted in the text.

[4] Sid Chaplin, *The Day of the Sardine* (Buckhurst Hill, 1989 [1961]), 72.

[5] Michael Pickering and Kevin Robins, 'A revolutionary materialist with a leg free', in Jeremy Hawthorn (ed.), *The British Working-Class Novel in the Twentieth Century* (London, 1984), 79.

[6] Jack Common, *Kiddar's Luck* (Glasgow, 1974 [1951]), 7.

[7] Will Oxley, 'Are you working?', in Jack Common (ed.), *Seven Shifts* (Wakefield, 1978 [1938]), 105.

[8] For the notion of 'speech genres', see Mikhail Bakhtin, *Speech Genres and Other Late Essays*, trans. Vern W. McGee, ed. Caryl Emerson and Michael Holquist (Austin, 1986).

[9] B. L. Coombes, *These Poor Hands: The Autobiography of a Miner Working in South Wales* (London, 1939), 60–1.

[10] John Lehmann, quoted in Andy Croft, *Red Letter Days: British Fiction in the 1930s* (London, 1990), 92.

[11] Jack Hilton, 'The plasterer's life', in Common (ed.), *Seven Shifts*, 9–10.

[12] Croft, *Red Letter Days*.

9

James Hanley's The Furys: *Modernism and the Working Class*

JOHN FORDHAM

This chapter identifies the Liverpool-based fiction of the working-class writer James Hanley as part of the historical trajectory of European modernism, which was first geographically located in Balzac's mid-nineteenth-century Paris and later developed in Dostoevsky's late-century St Petersburg. Balzac and Dostoevsky are here deployed not as earlier models for working-class realism, but as cultural signifiers of a developing aesthetic in which representations of reality are problematized by the textual presence of a set of overdetermined class relations.

The modified modernist paradigm here offered recognizes the 'differential' nature of modernity which is determined by a series of conjunctural and transitional moments. In terms of a novelistic response, these moments are represented within what Bakhtin calls the novelistic 'chronotope': the spatial concentration of various expressions of subjective temporality defined by conscious or unconscious class affiliations. The objective effect of a set of differential subject positions is to reveal not a single but a complex and overdetermined reality. What is taking place here is not only the rise of 'realism' as the literary branch of bourgeois ideology, but also the development of a parallel and contradictory modernism which, at the same time, subverts the triumphalism of bourgeois thought. By this is meant that, while it is often the case that the primary drive in the bourgeois novel is toward resolution and settlement, particularly in the English novel, the so-called European realist tradition is often much more toward isolation, disintegration and crisis. Such an assertion relies on an understanding of modernism as a gradual and emergent discourse within the 'realist text', the effect of which to the latter is to threaten its disruption and breakdown but ultimately not to eradicate it altogether.

Such a version of 'modernism' has implications for other kinds of writing, particularly that which has been conventionally represented as 'social' or 'socialist realism'. With the rise of British working-class writing and its coming to maturity in the 1930s, those struggles which have already been described become more urgent. Urban social conditions, to which only oblique reference has been made by bourgeois writers, are now being represented from within by the very class which suffers them; yet these texts are similarly defined by socio-cultural conflicts: this time new forms of working-class expression against a recently consolidated bourgeois aesthetic. James Hanley – originally a merchant seaman from the Liverpool working class – was first published in 1930. He is now known – if he is known at all – mainly through two surviving Penguin Modern Classics which drift in and out of print: *Boy*, his second novel (1931), and *The Furys*, his fifth novel and the first in a pentalogy (1935).[1] Hanley, along with other writers emerging from Britain's industrial provinces (F. C. Boden, J. C. Grant, Rhys Davies), was forging a radical modernism out of a new impulse for internal narration within the working class which, in its attention to the squalor and deprivation of that environment, moves beyond the parameters of 'the Real' to more expressive metaphors of a modernist class consciousness.

However, while Hanley's contemporaries – mostly worker-writers from the mining community – follow in the immediately recognizable 'tradition' of Lawrence and the exemplary model of Zola's *Germinal*, Hanley's own work – as Ken Worpole argues[2] – benefits from an itinerant's wider access to other European writers, notably Balzac and Dostoevsky, the greater of his acknowledged influences. Like theirs, Hanley's representations of the modern city are characterized by both the totality of social conjunctions and an intensity of subjective experience. Just like Paris and St Petersburg previously, Liverpool's position as the 'second city' of Britain in the transition from 'liberal' to 'monopoly' capitalism was typically contradictory: defined on the one hand by a rapid expansion of its modern infrastructure (transport and shipping), while on the other by a continuing simultaneous dependence on an older imperialist system of labour and distribution. Into the city continued to flow – particularly from Ireland – a dependent citizenry whose consciousness was collectively shaped by the experience of an antiquated agrarian economy. For them, the experience of the city was that it was both familiar in its hierarchical social relations and unfamiliar in its bewildering monolithic modernity. Hanley's family came to Liverpool as migrant workers in 1908 from a settled existence in Dublin, sustained by its pride and confidence in an Irish maritime inheritance. That encounter of a migrant sensibility with the modern city is primarily what informs Hanley's early works and particularly the long project of novels, *The Furys* chronicle. In the first two of the sequence – *The Furys* and *The Secret Journey* (1938)[3] – Balzacian and Dostoevskian ideological conflicts are reproduced in early twentieth-century Liverpool: pre-industrial Ireland with dockland modernity; family and Catholic values against youthful dissent; individual ambition against collectivity; maritime romanticism versus urban expressionism; bourgeois versus working-class aesthetics.

Hanley's modernism in *The Furys* chronicle is defined by the textual imbrication of these socio-cultural conflicts, the primary signifier of which is its punning title, invoking both the modern figure of the Irish migrant and the legendary name of the daughters of night and darkness. While there are no exact parallels with Aeschylus, the novel consistently evokes the Oresteian original: the Fury family suggests both an Atrean dynastic order and their erstwhile pursuers. The Furys, like the house of Atreus, are accursed, symbolic of a once proud family or nation, fallen from the natural state of Irish grace, divided by enmity and ambition in the 'maelstrom' of the modern imperial city, and 'scattered over the earth' (*F* 37). Peter, the modern Orestes, youngest son and failed priest, is both destroyer of his mother's aspirations – in that he is sent home in disgrace from the seminary – and avenger: the slayer of the moneylender, Anna Ragner, who holds the family in the iron grip of debt. Peter's initial action brings down upon his own head the anger of his race because he was the hope of maintaining its spiritual purity, now threatened by modernity's corrupting influence. The second action provokes the greater anger of modernity itself in the guise of the mob and the judiciary. The Furys are thus pursued and haunted by the material consequences of their own rage which reinvokes their dual aspect:

the city environment has transformed them into what their name implies, 'the angry ones', the modern dwellers of the abyss. Yet they still retain, primarily in the mother's purity of aspiration and allegiance to Catholic Ireland, their alter-identity of 'the kindly ones', implicit in which is the Furys' dynastic or noble role as cultural guardians.

While the mythic dimension can be said to suggest a dominant literary orientation in *The Furys* chronicle, its modernism is both supported and undermined by the interplay of other components or voices which constantly contend for a privileged reading. Such a narrative strategy recalls Jameson's concept of a 'decentering' in Balzac. Just as Balzac's 'fantasm' of the restoration of the *ancien régime* paradoxically reveals 'the Real' – that is, 'the fallen world of capitalism' – as the bedrock of resistance to such wish-fulfilment,[4] so Hanley's *The Furys* projects the unfallen world of pre-capitalist Ireland as a 'fantasm' whose limitations are defined by the 'Real' of working-class Gelton (Hanley's fictional Liverpool). Moreover, as also in Balzac, such textual conflicts are primarily revealed in Hanley's representations of familial relations, which are not only psychoanalytic but social: in Jameson's terms, 'socially coded or symbolic positions'.[5] Most exemplary of that symbolic level are Hanley's women, particularly the mother Fanny and her sister Brigid. They represent the 'purer' line of descent, the Mangans, tracing their ancestry back to the profession of sea-captains and, through the only surviving male, the stroke-smitten grandfather, Anthony, to the days of the Great Famine.

Initially, the two sisters are represented as essentially antithetical. The spinster Brigid, descending on Gelton from Cork ostensibly to bring home the disgraced Peter, provokes the old antagonism when Fanny had made, in Anthony's words, the 'tragic mistake' (*F* 37) of marrying into the disreputable Fury family. The sudden symbolic appearance of old Ireland in the midst of a family of Irish migrants reveals not only the sharp distinctions between the degraded slums of 'Hatfields' and the relative tranquillity of provincial Cork, but also the latter's 'spiritual isolation' (*F* 105) compared with the divided yet more vibrant world of the metropolis. That complex way of seeing does not privilege any essentialist view of Irish Catholic society, yet Ireland does remain a value, the dream of a restored lineage and stability, and from that perspective the two sisters represent a point of resistance to the brutalizing and racist environment with which the Furys daily contend. Brigid Mangan might be scheming and self-obsessed but she is also representative of that older Irish insouciance which resists metropolitan adapt-ability. It is her sister Fanny who has yielded to its necessity in order to survive: 'for she and not Brigid had tasted fully of the fruits of that malignant, if not bestial curiosity, that strange wilful, bat-like groping into all the sacred recesses of life, that seemed the horror not only of Hatfields but all Gelton' (*SJ* 25).

Brigid is invulnerable to Gelton's anti-Irish abusiveness; sailing proudly through the city in her provocative emerald green, she survives through her ability to distance herself from the surrounding turmoil, imagining herself back in her own house in Ireland, where she was 'immune from the storm and stress of the world [. . .] the very spirit of the house in the Mall seem[ing] to have floated down on her in tranquillity and peace' (*SJ* 341). Fanny, however, has to struggle daily with the oppressive cares of poverty and debt. Her 'heroism' is of the quality of Dostoevsky's Mrs Marmaladov, worn down by the sheer drudgery of keeping the household from the workhouse, yet dreaming still of the 'beautiful life'. Peter's failure at the seminary signals the end of her dream to reproduce some familial dignity, yet her father, disabled as he is, remains the silent though eloquent witness to that vanished world:

> This imprisoned and ageing flesh was but the magic mirror through which she could see like many bright suns the happy days of her childhood in Ireland. Through him she could resurrect those times past and gone. She could put out her hand and touch them, those magic and lovely days. [. . .] In such moments her whole soul surrendered to a feeling, delicious, joyous, and yet melancholy, to which she could give no utterance. (*SJ* 180)

While Fanny and Brigid are closely associated with an Irish age of innocence, the other Fury women are surely representative of the family's metropolitan fall from grace. Maureen, the only daughter, is perceived by Brigid to have been 'coarsened' and 'ruined' by the jute factory and an ill-matched early marriage to the pious yet dull Joseph (*F* 155–60). Yet Sheila, Desmond's wife – whom Fanny calls 'his beautiful prostitute' (*F* 140) – is a more ambivalent figure. Paradoxically, she, too, cherishes the memory of another life:

Imagine a valley, a valley so green that there is no other green like it in the world, and in this valley and on the bank of an old river a large white house. [. . .] In the winter I used to love the rain, and all the smells that come into the air, wet leaves, wet grass, glistening moss on the banks, the dull leaden sky, the running water, the flights of birds over the house, just as it was getting dusk. [. . .] I had all this to myself, and nobody to say nay to even my smallest wish. Everything was mine, everything. I was free as the birds in the air. (*SJ* 349)

What Sheila brings to Gelton – and what so fascinates Desmond and her lover, Peter – is not only a scent of rural Ireland but a mystique about her origins, which are rooted in an extant yet declining Anglo-Irish aristocracy. Again, what is very reminiscent of Balzac here is the instinctual recognition in Hanley of familial relations as fundamentally social as well as psychic. If anything, Sheila's class position is a more entrenched and imperially complicit one than Brigid's. Yet she has 'escaped' to the *déclassé* house of a trade-union activist. No precise reason is given, except that, similar to the way that Brigid is 'beckoned' by 'an almost magnetic power' from Gelton's pubs (*F* 194), Sheila finds something compelling and transforming about her immersion in city life: 'Here was a meaning to life after all. People doing things, men working, women working, night and day, eating, sleeping, seeing. Everything became orderly, chaos vanished. Existence had a purpose. One was beginning to grow' (*SJ* 353). Thus the dream of rural or provincial stability is eclipsed by the delimiting power of the city's reality. While nation and religion constitute the bedrock of colonial resistance for the Irish working class, they are also perceived, ironically, from a different class perspective, as archaic and conservative. Sheila, at the symbolic level, represents the dual aspect of modern Ireland: in her associations with rurality, the pure idea of motherland (a child of nature habituated to lonely walks along the shore), and as metropolitan prostitute, the 'fallen' or immigrant culture of the mainland. However, the desire for 'growth' is a strong suggestion that, for all its faults, it is with the latter that any hope of social transformation lies. Emblematically, the political activism of her husband, Desmond, and the intellectual rebellion of her lover, Peter, are the radical alternatives to the 'heroic' quietism of the Furys.

Indeed, the essential opposition of the two sons, Desmond and Peter, rehearses the familial and ideological struggle in Balzac's *The*

Black Sheep between two brothers: the Napoleonic 'man of action', Philippe, and the artistic and sensitive, Joseph. The first novel, *The Furys*, invokes those responses through the emblematic watershed of a significant public event, which in Bakhtin's terms, assumes a formative role as the novelistic 'chronotope'. Here Hanley discloses his debt to the Russians in that, for his central spatio-temporal device, he invokes Pushkin's 'public square', the place of 'licence' in which the variety of temporal representations and consciousnesses of the social totality is assembled. Pushkin rejected aristocratic habits in the Russian theatre, proclaiming that 'national tragedy' was born in the public square.[6] Thus, in *The Furys* the social event of the strike brings together the various conceptions of historical time within an epochal and crucial present, yet in their various ways these conceptions struggle both backwards into 'historical inversion' – a consciousness which prefers the past – and forwards 'along the historically productive horizontal'.[7] On such a principle, that which has already been shown to be classically inspired can be considered to be 'mythic time'; the pre-colonial experience of the Mangans might be termed 'Irish time'; while the third temporal component which confronts both of these – the prospect of social change in a new epochal phase of modernity – can be designated 'future time'.

The date of the novel's setting, 1911, is itself chronotopically significant. The year was a crisis point in the history of Liverpool's working-class struggle. *The Furys* has two strike scenes which ostensibly read as a meticulously researched realist account of the infamous Bloody Sunday of 13 August 1911, the crucial event in the Great Liverpool Transport Strike. The narrative perspective follows a number of protagonists caught up in the brutality of police action: notably Desmond Fury, the railway union official and his neighbour the Orangeman, Andrew Postlethwaite. The two men are habitually antagonists, the mere presence of so many 'Billies' in Desmond's Catholic community provoking a perpetual hostility. Such a tendency to provocation is, moreover, underpinned by Andrew's determination to be singular in a crowd in which few are distinguishable. Emerging red-faced from a pub, he confronts Desmond while dressed in a check suit, white cut-away collar, red and white spotted tie and light-brown boots, looking 'more like a bookmaker's clerk than a loco man' (*F* 259). Yet Postlethwaite's determination to be 'out of place' among the 'drab crowd', a homogeneous 'forest of heads' (F 261, 263) is precisely where Hanley's character, as well as being socially representative, assumes the form of the grotesque, a gross parody of Orange Order insensibility and a textual counter to Brigid Mangan's vivid green.

However, this image of a particular kind of 'Irish' resistance assumes a quite different significance when juxtaposed with another individual figure who stands outside the crowd. Observed on the balcony of a hotel is an apparently 'bibulous gentleman' in 'full morning dress' (F 269, 270) adjusting his pink buttonhole, again an egregious grotesque, an incongruous sight of colourful prosperity amidst the various tones of grey. It takes only the briefest parade of conspicuous wealth to provoke the inevitable hurling of a brick and the consequent mounted charges of the police. The *agent provocateur* disappears but sets in train the desired effect. Andrew Postlethwaite himself receives a baton to the head while protesting the indiscriminate beatings and terrorization. As he falls, Desmond Fury literally leaps into retaliatory action and, with prodigious strength, brings down the rider from his horse. The public square has now become a 'battlefield' (F 276), yet the chronotope of the strike produces new forms of consciousness out of the clash of old antagonisms and polarities: symbolically both Orangeman and Catholic, against the repressive and conspiratorial modern state, now forge a new union and class solidarity. However, Hanley also has at his disposal another symbolic vocabulary which is at once consciously modern and traditional:

> A baton was something more than a piece of weighted wood. It was the symbol of authority, it had no respect for neutrality. The very hand that wielded it succumbed to its power. Its sickening hum, as it swung to and fro in the air, had taken the place of the indistinct hum. Its song had assumed control. It had taken the place of hooter and whistle, of all the concourse of sounds that usually came from the industrial ant-heap. Trains, trams, ships, docks, cars, machines were silent. On this Sunday afternoon there was only the yelling mob, the red-faced and sweating police, and the stiff wooden interrogator that sang ceaselessly through the air. (F 276)

In other words the causes of the violence lie not with any class or individual but in a contemporary version of an ancient malevolence now risen out of the ground of industrial societies. In this sense, Hanley's protagonists again assume the guise of grotesques, absurdly drawn figures in a modernist 'Inferno' struggling to free themselves but ultimately trapped and powerless. Such is the modernist aesthetic which increasingly dominates *The Furys* chronicle as it develops in the first three volumes: the representation of a pervasive urban threat, whether it takes the form of the casual curiosity of neighbours, the jeering of a music-hall audience or the full-blooded fury of the hue and cry.[8] As in the demonstration, these collective images are not those of a working class united in pursuit of a common goal, but the manifestations of an undifferentiated menace, or the uncontrollable chaos of nightmare.[9] In a sense, this is why Hanley's grotesques remain so conspicuously colourful against the darker tones of the city. As the mob threatens to overwhelm, to annihilate, the individual human subject, so the individual acts become yet more absurdly idiosyncratic, as though some essential humanity were determined to remain observably vital and indissoluble.

Seen in this way, the expressionist figuration is not totally dissimilar to the putatively more political discourse of a realistically described industrial action, since both are, in a modernist sense, concerned with the processes of social transformation and an insistence on human vitality in the face of a moribund social domain. As Hanley's Bloody Sunday is carried over into the night and the authorities attempt to clear the streets of a growing spontaneous assembly, Peter Fury is struck by 'something nightmarish about the sudden change' (*F* 326). It is at this moment that he has a chance encounter with the curiously named Professor Titmouse, another grotesque, absurdly dressed in a tailcoat, grey trousers, elastic-sided boots and a deerstalker hat. As Peter's self-appointed guide through the maelstrom, he is both the medieval Mephistopheles and the predatory street 'brownie' (homosexual), an old evil and a new emanation from the unconscious. Yet the spell he holds over Peter also evokes Strindberg's *The Ghost Sonata* in which The Old Man guides and manipulates The Student in order to experience vicariously the pleasures he can no longer enjoy:[10] as the professor's vitality wanes, so Peter's increases in intensity. Sensing the young man's fascination with the sights and sounds of the riots, the professor lures him to the central square where, mounted on the back of an elevated stone lion, they are able to witness the second and most violent confrontation of the strike.

The image immediately recalls Yevgeny, in Pushkin's 'The Bronze Horseman', who takes refuge on just such a statue as the flood waters of the Neva swirl around his feet.[11] As in the Russian original, the city's streets are transformed by the immanence of cataclysm, but instead of the water, it is Gelton's disaffected crowds who 'like some vast silent river' threaten to swallow them up (F 342). Trapped by the proximity of the 'maelstrom', Peter is forced to watch as the violent scenes end in a conflagration of buildings, transfiguring the people as 'Goblins from the Inferno' (F 344). At the violent climax, the professor embraces Peter in a fit of sexual excitement, an act which repulses the young man, causing him to jump from the lion and take his chance with the crowd.[12]

Peter might be disturbed, but the whole experience is curiously stimulating, as is revealed later when Peter becomes embroiled in a street clash with armed troops. This time, it is Sheila who guides the young man through the streets and the atmosphere is charged equally with the *frisson* of sexuality and physical danger. As the two figures are caught up in the crossfire of guns and rudimentary weapons, Sheila falls to the ground, spattered with the blood of a young man, whose chest oozes 'a veritable fountain'. Although unharmed, her 'expressionless' face surrounded by its 'welter of blood' (F 499) resembles the pallor of a corpse, making Peter's labyrinthine escape with her to the house 'through dark passages, through entries' evocative of both the Orphic myth and some heroic rescue from a front-line offensive (F 500–1). In the succeeding pages of the chapter, the dark figure of the professor appears again, hovering in the form of a disembodied voice, goading Peter toward the sexual act, which takes the form of a kind of blood rite, mingling feelings of revulsion and elation: both contamination – 'Oh! the blood!' – and purification – 'When had he knelt like this before? Ah yes! When he had received his first Communion' (F 501–3). It is significant that those complex motivations are prompted within the social parameter or chronotope of public space, in which '*crisis,* radical change, an unexpected turn of fate takes place, where decisions are made, where the forbidden line is overstepped, where one is renewed or perishes'.[13] The voice of the professor constantly projects the contradictory imperatives of desire and duty out of the anathema of violent extremes. The batons and flames of the riot and the horrific sight of the dead man provoke the emotional crisis point – 'that fountain of blood keeps bursting up, taking fire, that burning sword' (*F 507*) – around which contradictory meanings are generated, questions raised. Sexuality in Hanley is finely balanced on the borderline between the prison house of guilt and the free space of liberation: the act which either propels Peter into the 'social rottenness', where 'ideals are stinking in the heap', or guides him toward 'that flashing light [which] clouds out everything' (*F 507*).

Again, what singles out these figures from the industrial landscape is that quality of the grotesque which transforms the everyday into the exceptional, provokes the moment of crisis in contemporary working-class experience which holds out the possibility of personal, social or political change. Yet that also signals a crisis of representation comparable with other self-reflexive modernisms. Hanley's representations of reality do not in any sense reaffirm the primacy of 'realism', but constitute a point at which, in the struggle to articulate a working-class conscious-ness, 'the Real' itself is both problematized and redefined. As part of the resistance to the reality of urban societies, working-class narratives often rely on a collective memory of premodern social relations and modes of living, or on the settled and entrenched values of industrial communities; yet at the same time the modern-ized urban environment offers, as it did in former transitional moments, the possibility which premodern or more traditional societies could not: that of social transformation. In such conflicts lies the essence of working-class modernism: not a reaffirmation of 'realism' but the textual representation of a socio-cultural complexity and irresolution. It is such an aesthetic – a modernism of the working class – which refuses the temptations of any bourgeois closure and asserts a new priority of struggle and process.

Notes

[1] London, 1935. Page references to this edition (identified as *F*) are inserted in the text.

[2] Ken Worpole, *Dockers and Detectives: Popular Reading: Popular Writing* (London, 1983), 77–93.

[3] London, 1938. Page references to this edition (identified as *SJ*) are inserted in the text.

[4] Fredric Jameson, *The Political Unconscious* (London, 1989), 180–4.

5 Ibid., 180.

6 See Mikhail Bakhtin, *The Dialogic Imagination: Four Essays* (Austin, 1990), 132.

7 Ibid., 148–57.

8 See also Peter Fury's flight from the crime scene in *The Secret Journey*, 566–9, and the public pillorying inflicted on Joseph Killkey in *Our Time is Gone* (London, 1949), 406–10.

9 I am indebted to Ken Worpole for pointing this out.

10 August Strindberg, *The Ghost Sonata*, in *Plays: One*, trans. Michael Meyer (London, 1989), 166.

11 Alexander Pushkin, 'The bronze horseman', in *Pushkin: Selected Poems* (Harmondsworth, 1964), 243–5.

12 Cf. Professor Warschauer (Warremme) in Jacob Wasserman's *The Maurizius Case* (London, 1930); he is a predatory homosexual who, to the seventeen-year-old Etzel von Andergast, is both dubious mentor and initiator into the city's iniquities:

Warschauer had a passion for all sorts of human assemblies, whether processions, public exhibitions, demonstrations of strikers or mere street gatherings; the crowd had for him an irresistible attraction. He was happiest in confined spaces, when he was wedged in amongst thousands of his fellows, and skilful speakers were exciting the mob to fanatical demonstrations; and he explained to Etzel that what he enjoyed was the intoxication of the bliss of depersonalization and anonymity. (p. 233)

13 Mikhail Bakhtin, *Problems of Dostoevsky's Poetics* (London, 1984), 169.

10

Lewis Jones's Cwmardy *and* We Live: *Two Welsh Proletarian Novels in Transatlantic Perspective*

ROLF MEYN

In the United States the decade of the Great Depression fostered not only a theoretical discussion of what was to be called proletarian fiction, but also the production of some seventy novels in this field. One has to keep in mind, however, that very few of these novels were actually written by working men or women. Michael Gold, the 'Dean of American Left Letters', was thrilled when he found out that Jack Conroy, author of *The Disinherited* (1933), was a genuine member of the working class and glorified him as 'a proletarian shocktrooper whose weapon is literature'.[1]

But whatever the class of the authors, a proletarian commitment existed. Harvey Swados, himself a young radical in the 1930s, sees a dominant trend at work in the literature of that decade: 'To answer the question of who we are, the novelist of the thirties often tried to find out where we had come from, to retrace the footsteps of the preceding generation and determine the direction in which they pointed.'[2] Sometimes in single novels, sometimes in trilogies, the years from the turn of the century to the Great Depression came under close scrutiny. John Dos Passos's merciless dissection of American history, culture, politics and politicians of this period in his trilogy *USA* (*The 42nd Parallel*, 1930; *1919*, 1932; *The Big Money*, 1936) was the most famous example of a search into the past in order to explain present and future trends. That he 'looked forward to ruins, back to hope',[3] that he came up with a radical critique of capitalist society, based on Karl Marx and Thorstein Veblen, made him a revered master of literature for writers on the left on both sides of the Atlantic. His formal experiments, a collage of historical biographies, newsreels, stream-of-consciousness auto-biography entitled 'camera eye' and traditional fictional characters whose fates highlighted social and economic tendencies, con-tributed to his fame. Communists and fellow-travellers forgave him the unfavourable portraits of fanatic party members in *1919* and his growing cultural conservatism, which became evident in *The Big Money* with its plea for a return to Whitman's 'story-book democracy'. More importantly, here was a writer who, with the help of brilliant stylistic innovations, interpreted life in America in terms of class antagonism, though without the telos of revolution and a future classless society.

The probing of past and present in order to point the way into the future appeared in a variety of forms during the 1930s. Michael Gold's *Jews Without Money* (1930), a fictional autobiography, reviewed the struggle of his immigrant parents in the Lower East Side Ghetto of New York to secure a decent life for themselves and their children. Gold's version of Jewish American history led straight to world revolution, as the last pages of the book testify. Jack Conroy's *The Disinherited* (1933) portrayed the narrator's driftings through the United States from the First World War to the first years of the Great Depression. Like Lewis Jones's Len Roberts, the narrator Larry Donovan was a miner's son whose episodic adventures were intensified by the inexorable course of history that ended in economic depression and misery, but also in Larry's conversion to a class-conscious proletarian. Other writers pre-ferred, like Dos Passos, to use the trilogy to bring their messages home. In her three novels *Pity Is Not Enough* (1933), *The Executioner Waits* (1934) and *Rope of Gold* (1939), Josephine Herbst utilized the form of a family saga to juxtapose a disintegrating middle class and a rising proletariat in a developing class war. James T. Farrell, in his three novels *Young Lonigan: A Boyhood in Chicago Streets* (1932), *The Young Manhood of Studs Lonigan* (1934) and *Judgment Day* (1935), minutely described the disintegration of a weak and sensuous protagonist, a member of the lower middle class, whose skidding downhill was accelerated because parents, teachers and priests had lost all moral authority. At the end of the last novel Paddy Lonigan, knowing his son would die soon of double pneumonia, watches a group of young Communist anti-war demonstrators marching into a better future.

It is interesting that two Welsh writers of the 1930s, Kate Roberts and Lewis Jones, looked at the same historical period. Roberts's *Feet in Chains*, published in Welsh as *Traed Mewn Cyffion* in 1936, covers almost forty years of a family's history in 133 pages. The story begins in about 1880 and ends in the years of the Great War which, as in many novels of the 1930s, is seen as the outcome of industrialization and capitalism, symbolized by the quarries. The war is also the final point in the family's falling apart. *Feet in Chains* is not a proletarian novel, but the anti-war and anti-capitalist bias links it to that genre. The protagonist's son muses, after he learns of his brother's death in France:

> They [the Welsh people] came to realise that, in every country, there were people who regarded war as a good thing, and were taking advantage of their sons to promote their interests. These were 'the Ruling Class', the same who oppressed them in the quarry, who sucked their blood and turned it into gold for themselves. Deep down, they believed by this time that some people were making money out of the war just as they had made money out of the bodies of the men in the quarries.[4]

In Jones's *Cwmardy* the protagonist Len Roberts comes to a similar conclusion, although the experience of the Great War on the 'home front' is not the last station on his journey to ideological certainty.

Carole Snee sees *Cwmardy* and *We Live* firmly rooted in the realist tradition, 'the most readily available mode of expression for writers not schooled within a literary tradition'.[5] The traditional realist novel emphasized individual consciousness and thus was part of bourgeois philosophy and the forms shaped by it. Yet, by adding a 'conscious ideological or class perspective', it was able to 'undercut the ideological parameter of the genre, without necessarily transforming its structural boundary'.[6] Although Snee does not specify the 'ideological perspective', her definition comes close to what in the 1930s was understood as 'socialist realism'. It never became a doctrine which working-class literature was to follow in Britain and the United States, but Communist writers like Lewis Jones shared the conviction that it was their task to show the essential – not just accidental or illusory – traits of reality, by revealing the historical tendencies inherent in that reality and by making clear the inevitability of the victory of the new over the old social forces.[7]

Such historical tendencies were the inhumanity of capitalism and the cyclic economic crises it ran into, the sharpening class struggle and the proletariat's growing determination to fight oppression and exploitation. The writer who explored these tendencies was necessarily tendentious; literature was seen as a weapon in the class struggle. This was the tenor of the debates at the American Writers' Congress in 1935, which was initiated and influenced by the Communist Party of the USA. Michael Gold ended a long discussion about the bourgeois origins of many authors of proletarian novels with the blunt verdict: 'The man with the revolutionary mind can write a revolutionary book.'[8]

How familiar Lewis Jones was specifically with the concept of socialist realism, as it was proclaimed at the Soviet Writers' Conference in 1934, and the general debate about proletarian literature, is not clear, but these ideas were well known and widely debated in Wales in the period. In fact Jones's novels contain all the criteria considered essential by left theoreticians of the 1930s as well as by recent scholars. Walter B. Rideout's taxonomy based on themes (strike novel, stories of conversion to Communism, tales of decay of the petty bourgeoisie, novels about 'bottom dogs' – the lowest social stratum[9]) and Barbara Foley's paradigm of genre and politics of form (proletarian fictional autobiography, proletarian *Bildungsroman*, proletarian social novel and collective novel[10]) can all to some extent be applied to *Cwmardy* and *We Live*. The strike of 1910, the General Strike of 1926 and a stay-down strike in the mid-1930s are pivotal events in the novels, without turning them into fully fledged strike novels. The theme of the decay of the petty bourgeoisie is touched upon in the suicide of the shopowner and his wife and their son's awareness that, despite his intellectual abilities, his poverty will never allow him to win a place in middle-class society. Len's biography in *Cwmardy* is largely a conversion story, as it is told in so many proletarian novels of the 1930s. The bottom-dog theme is also relevant in Jones's two novels, though in a different way. In Edward Dahlberg's name-giving novel *Bottom Dogs* (1930), in Nelson Algren's *Somebody in Boots* (1935) and in Tom Kromer's *Waiting for Nothing* (1935) the protagonists either do not have the energy to rise from the lowest layer of society or are so taken up by their struggle for survival that they seem to be doomed; all the more, because they have lost their sense of human solidarity. In *Cwmardy* and *We Live* the miners and their families are reduced to bottom-dog status in times of hunger wages, drawn-out lock-outs or unemployment, but they violently refuse to accept this fate. A growing sense of solidarity but also defiance, instilled into them by tireless leaders, keep them from resigning themselves to this degradation.

In *Cwmardy* the forms of proletarian fictional autobiography and proletarian *Bildungsroman* overlap. Unlike Jack Conroy in *The Disinherited*, Jones does not resort to the mode of first-person narrative. That he rejects the role of the witness telling the story of his life is due to his intention to create a 'collective work in the sense that my fellow workers had to fight the battles I tried to picture, and also in the sense that I have shamefully exploited many comrades for incidents, anecdotes, typing, correcting and multifarious details connected with writing'.[11] Len Roberts's career bears such a close resemblance to that of his author that both novels are partly fictional autobiographies. In a sense, Len's death in Spain is almost prophetic: Jones died while he was working for Spanish Aid. John Pikoulis even hints at some psychological connection between Jones's illegitimacy and the familial structures in the novel: Big Jim and Shane are not married, the strength of feeling Len has for his sister Jane is the result of Jones's own revulsion towards his absent father, and Len also suffers, like Jones, 'from a deficient or withdrawn mother'.[12]

Cwmardy, as has been suggested, is also a proletarian *Bildungsroman*. Usually the development of the protagonist's class consciousness is its main theme. This is mostly completed towards the end of the novel, after the protagonist has renounced the bourgeois myth of upward social mobility open to everyone and embraces the notion of rising with the proletariat instead. The change of mind is a long process in an exemplary character's mind, as the following passage from Jack Conroy illustrates:

> I no longer felt shame at being seen at such work as I would have once; and I knew that the only way for me to rise to something approximating the grandiose ambitions of my youth would be to rise with my class, with the disinherited: the bricksetters, the flivver tramps, boomers and outcasts pounding their ears in flophouses. Every gibe at any of the paving gang, every covert or open sneer by prosperous bystanders

infuriated me but did not abash me. . . . I felt like a man whose feet have
been splashing about in ooze and at last have come to rest on a solid
rock, even though it lay far below his former level.[13]

Len Roberts's conversion, however, is not a problem of class
consciousness. When his mother encourages him to study hard so
that one day he can win a scholarship and go to college, his mind is
already made up: 'No, mam, . . . I don't want to go to any schools
after I finish this one. What I want is to go to work with dad in the
pit as soon as I be old enough.'[14] In this respect the pastoral scene
at the beginning of the novel is symbolic. Len and his father look
down from the mountain crest into the smoke-filled valley of
Cwmardy, where even the grass ceases to grow. Len has little
interest in the beauty of the landscape around him – his eyes are
fixed on the pit. When Big Jim tells his son to descend with him, he
follows willingly, 'being always eager to get near the pit that stood
at the top end of the valley'.[15] From the very beginning of the novel
Len is portrayed as a character who is deeply attached to the place
and the people to which he belongs.

The proletarian *Bildungsroman* differs from its bourgeois
counterpart in a number of ways. Both share protagonists who are
set apart from their peers by some traits – sensitivity, intelligence,
the determination to gain deeper insights and, though not always,
physical appearance. Both forms contain a story of apprenticeship,
a transformation from ignorance (of self) to knowledge (of self),
and at the same time a transformation from passivity to action. In
a proletarian *Bildungsroman*, however, the protagonist's knowledge (of self) is never an end in itself, but part of a totalizing
'truth' in the form of political values, an ideology or doctrine; in
other words, the proletarian form is far more deeply embedded in
the structure of a *roman à thèse* or ideological novel.[16] The latter
presents models of confrontation: Capitalism versus Socialism,
Fascism versus Democracy, Liberalism/Labour/Social Democracy
versus Communism. All these ideological conflicts are 'resolved by
a narrative supersystem that in itself is ideological and that
evaluates competing ideologies: only one of them is "right", while
the others are discredited'.[17]

In *Cwmardy* and *We Live* all three phases of the proletarian
Bildungsroman are at work: hero's separation; hero's development;
hero's absorption in a larger entity. Len's ideological apprenticeship

progresses through several stages. After his initiation as a collier and the confrontation with the miners' brutal exploitation in the pit, he soon qualifies as an agitator capable of leadership in a forthcoming strike. Len's rise is so rapid that it somewhat mars the credibility of the story, although it is in fact part of the fictional autobiography: the author himself became an organizer at a very early age. In Len's case, the author emphasizes, the rise is not surprising, since he reads a lot and 'has a capacity for deep thinking': separation enables development. All he needs is someone 'who could inspire him, a person whose words and actions would serve as a focus for his thoughts, a man he could look up to as an example'.[18] This man is Ezra Jones, the miners' leader. He becomes Len's 'donor' or mentor, a figure of great importance for the protagonist's transformation from passivity to action.[19] This tellingly happens in chapter 10 of *Cwmardy*, entitled 'Cwmardy goes into Action'. Len becomes Ezra's devoted disciple in the ensuing strike, but soon 'goes into action' himself. For it is Len who encourages his fellow workers to continue when his donor is in danger of compromising after ten months of strike and massive employment of policemen and soldiers. After the victorious strike, it is due to Len's speech that the miners decide to join the Federation: the absorption of the hero and his actions into the larger entity is at work.

The wider development has theoretical as well as actual status. Len's groping for an ideology he can endorse goes on. He and Ezra's daughter Mary organize a 'circle' in order to uplift the community's education. The subjects Len and his friends discuss take an 'increasingly Socialist bias', and well-known 'Liberals and theoretical Socialists' are invited to lecture. Marx and Socialism become chief topics in the discussions which soon spill over to the pit.[20] That is a national issue: the hero's energy has wider, international directions.

Len's apprenticeship ends in the Great War, which even Ezra justifies. Unlike his father Big Jim, Len volunteers only reluctantly, but is rejected as medically unfit for service. Yet the war also holds Cwmardy in its tight grip. Enforced increase of productivity in the pit and scanty food rations make life almost unbearable for the miners and their families. Len soon learns to see through the patriotic platitudes of pit-owners and trade-union officials, but the final destination of his ideological journey is signalled by the emergence of another donor in the person of a speaker. The reader never learns his name; he is just introduced as a 'young man' who 'called himself a revolutionary'.[21] Similar figures appear in quite a few proletarian novels – their only function is to promulgate the essentials of Marxist ideology. Len is shocked by the speaker's assertion that only an armed uprising of the workers can overcome the resistance of the capitalist class, but he and many of his fellow workers agree with the young man that the war they suffer from is a conflict between capitalists which leaves the workers as helpless pawns in the game.

Cwmardy ends, as it began, with a mountain scene. Ezra, Mary and Len look down into the valley which again is covered by a filthy blanket of smoke. More important than the scenery, however, is the conversation they have. Ezra's fatalistic opinion is that there will always be conflicts between capitalists and workers as long as the world is inhabited by masters and servants. Len's contrary assertion that man's (and hence the worker's) fate is in his own hands marks the end of his apprenticeship and his awareness of his role as the focus of a proletarian *Bildungsroman*.

We Live differs from *Cwmardy* in that it lacks all elements of the proletarian *Bildungsroman*. Instead it is closer to a *roman à thèse*. Ezra turns into an opponent when Len receives ideological guidance from the Communist Party. The conflict between the two men takes on tragic dimensions, not only because Ezra is Len's father-in-law but also because both are deeply devoted to the workers' cause. But for Len – and the author – Ezra is a Parliamentary Socialist, an adherent of 'the old trade union industrialist philosophy of determinism and fate',[22] and his ways of dealing with the class struggle in the pits are outdated now. To do justice to him, the author allows the blameless proletarian Big Jim to defend Ezra when he sells out to the company by taking a job in Lord Cwmardy's office: 'Us can't blame a man for that, mun. It is human nature. A man have got to live whatever he is, and you can't throw blame on Ezra when rotters like you do leave the Federashon and let him starve in the gutter.'[23] Most of the older men agree with Big Jim, while the younger ones condemn Ezra. The split in the working class has become a generational conflict. Luckily, the community of Cwmardy is spared the consequences of an Oedipal battle because of Ezra's timely death – another example of the 'jumpiness' in the structure of the text of which the author was himself aware.[24] Ezra is denounced as a 'Social Fascist', a term the Communists used in their attacks on Labour in Britain, Social Democracy in Germany and Socialists in the United States in pre-Popular Front days, but Ezra is nevertheless utilized by the Communist Party after his death. At the request of Mary, herself a party member, her father is given a 'red funeral with the Party in charge'.[25] In the light of how he was treated by the Communists when still alive, this is certainly macabre, even if one takes into consideration that the Popular Front ideology has taken hold by now, symbolized by the scene in which Ezra's coffin is carried to its grave by six party members and six members of the Federation committee. Harry Morgan, a party official, leaves no doubt that only the party is entitled to enter into Ezra's heritage: 'We grieve for him to-day, but we also glory in the knowledge that the foundations he laid are safe in the hands of the Party and the people.'[26]

A *roman à thèse* excludes romance and most of the elements of a family saga. Len's and Mary's lives are completely consumed by their work for the party, which becomes the surrogate for family life and children. Mary's delicate health does not allow childbearing anyway. Mary even rises to the rank of a county councillor, whereas Len, out of work, is made an organizer for the unemployed. The party line is proclaimed by Harry Morgan, who in some scenes resembles a cold apparatchik. Len is different because his sense of solidarity with his fellow workmen is sometimes stronger than his obedience to the party line. On his initative, the miners decide on a stay-down strike against the advice of the party. Len is neither the stalwart but somehow flat character who as organizer or strike leader plays a dominant role in many proletarian novels, nor is he, like his wife, a proselyte operating from the basis of a newly acquired *Weltanschauung*. Instead he is a protagonist who focuses conflicting loyalties and issues with regard to the miners of Cwmardy and the party's long-term strategies. The description of the stay-down strike, a crucial feature of the mid-1930s conflict on the south Welsh coalfield, highlights both the reality and the impact of working-class solidarity. In the dark-ness of the pit the miners lean on each other when the fight for a union of their own and a minimum wage threatens to tire them out. Above, their wives and friends desperately fight the police to send food down to the half-starved working men. That they come up as winners in a conflict they began against the party's advice demonstrates where Len's deepest loyalty belongs.

The struggle is not only Len's: the individualistic element of the *Bildungsroman* in *Cwmardy* is surpassed by a more generalized consciousness in *We Live*. Mary is made of sterner stuff than Len. She is 'her husband's superior intellectually, having the capacity to think more coherently and feel less acutely'.[27] She also gains a fuller understanding of revolutionary politics. This does not turn her into a 'Boudica of the barricades, cool, ruthless, efficient',[28] however; Jones still relates to contemporary reality. The Communist Parties in Europe and the United States were largely masculine preserves. Women organizers as party members were active in industries with a predominantly female workforce, as in the textile mills and the garment industry in the United States. Women writers – to name only Mary Heaton Vorse, Agnes Smedley, Josephine Herbst, Grace Lumpkin, Fielding Burke and Clara Weatherwax – were authors of proletarian novels in which female protagonists and their actions are presented as important contributions to the fight for a classless society. This is to some degree the case in Jones's *Cwmardy*, but more strongly so in *We Live*. Women's oppression is linked with the exploitation of the working class, as symbolized in the seduction of Len's sister Jane by Evan the Overman's son and her subsequent death in childbirth in *Cwmardy*. Wives are depicted as suffering as much from economic exploitation as their husbands. The American women writers, as well as Lewis Jones, emphasize that working-class solidarity is not only achieved through unity among the workers, but also by their wives joining picket lines, protest marches and demonstrations. Mary is one of them. Although childless, Len and Mary, supported by the enduring loyalty of Big Jim and Shane, form an exemplary proletarian nuclear family in which the traditional bourgeois hierarchy has been replaced by husband and wife working hand in hand for a better world.

Internationally conscious as the 1930s leftist *roman à thèse* must be, *We Live* concludes with the Spanish Civil War and its impact on Cwmardy. Anti-Fascism is referred to earlier in the novel when Dimitrov and his stand at the trial of Leipzig are glorified as a lone Anti-Fascist action,[29] but the sudden switch towards the end from domestic to international affairs is another example of Jones's 'jumpiness', though it is true that the war in Spain was the *cause*

célèbre of the Popular Front years. Welsh miners indeed volunt-
eered in relatively large numbers to fight in the International
Brigades. Len Roberts, rejected in the Great War, is now sent by the
party to fight in Spain, because only the most trusted, that is the
politically reliable, men are thought to be worthy enough to go.
After all, as Harry Morgan argues, 'the front-line trenches of
democracy' have been shifted from Cwmardy to Spain.[30] Len's
heroic death on a Spanish battlefield, surrounded by slain enemies,
is prophetic. With the benefit of hindsight, the moment fore-
shadows the end of the doomed Spanish Republic, but the *roman à
thèse* is more positive: *We Live* ends in an act of defiance. Despite
Len's death Mary, Big Jim and Shane join the welcome demonstration for the returned brigaders. Marches and demonstrations
against capitalism and fascism were considered proper endings for
proletarian novels by quite a few authors.

   In spite of their differences, both *Cwmardy* and *We Live* fit into
the category which Barbara Foley calls 'proletarian social novel'.
This form 'denotes a multi-protagonist work of fiction using
traditionally realistic techniques of representation'.[31] As a proletarian *Bildungsroman, Cwmardy* focuses on Len Roberts and his
donors, his father included. As an ideological novel, *We Live*
centres on Len, Mary and Ezra and their political involvement. But
in both novels Jones introduces other characters in order to
investigate relations among the working class of Cwmardy and to a
lesser degree between classes. Big Jim, the hard-working, outgoing
proletarian who never loses his joy of living and his fighting spirit,
whether directed against Boers, Germans or capitalist exploiters
and their mercenaries, seems to be created in direct contrast to his
brooding, sensitive son. In addition, many other figures and their
interactions with the main characters Len, Big Jim, Shane, Mary
and Ezra are part of the social fabric: Jane herself is offered in the
opening chapters as a physical realization of the once beautiful but
now ravaged valley. Jones's vivid descriptions of working conditions in the pit and life in the grimy valley of Cwmardy add an
authentic touch to the story of a tightly knit Welsh mining town in
an era of social and political turmoil. Class struggle is part of the
people's life and is interpreted from a Manichean perspective as a
battle between 'the forces of goodness and the forces of evil'.[32]
Jones's message is that the workers can only win this battle if they
develop an almost Whitmanesque sense of class solidarity. Len and

Big Jim Roberts are embodiments of the author's belief in the proletariat's ability to achieve that victory.

Notes

[1] Michael Gold, 'A letter to the author of first book', *New Masses*, 10 (1934), 26.

[2] Harvey Swados (ed.), *The American Writer and the Great Depression* (Indianapolis, 1966), xxix.

[3] John P. Diggins, *Up from Communism: Conservative Odysseys in American Intellectual History* (New York, 1975), 265.

[4] Kate Roberts, *Feet in Chains*, trans. J. I. Jones (Ruthin, 1996), 120.

[5] Carole Snee, 'Working-class literature or proletarian writing?', in Jon Clark, Margot Heinemann, David Margolies and Carole Snee (eds.), *Culture and Crisis in Britain in the Thirties* (London, 1979), 167.

[6] Ibid., 169.

[7] Barbara Foley, *Radical Representations: Politics and Form in U.S. Proletarian Fiction, 1929–1941* (Durham, 1993), 83. Foley quotes from Mossaye Olgin's review of Granville Hicks's anthology *Proletarian Literature in the United States*.

[8] Michael Gold, 'Discussions and proceedings', in Henry Hart (ed.), *American Writers' Congress* (New York, 1935), 166.

[9] Walter B. Rideout, *The Radical Novel in the United States 1900–1954: Some Interrelations of Literature and Society* (New York, 1992), 171.

[10] Foley, *Radical Representations*, 263–4.

[11] Lewis Jones, foreword to *Cwmardy: The Story of a Welsh Mining Valley* (London, 1978 [1939]), unpaginated.

[12] John Pikoulis, 'The wounded bard: the Welsh novel in English: Lewis Jones, Glyn Jones, Emyr Humphreys', *New Welsh Review*, 26 (1996), 23–4.

[13] Jack Conroy, *The Disinherited* (Westport, 1982 [1933]), 286.

[14] Jones, *Cwmardy*, 26.

[15] Ibid., 4.

[16] Susan Suleiman, *Authoritarian Fictions: The Ideological Novel as a Literary Genre* (New York, 1983), 65, 71. Although Suleiman only analyses French novels, the basic structure she discovers can be found in many ideological and proletarian novels of the 1930s. See also Rolf Meyn and Oliver Scheiding, 'Treason, treachery and betrayal: politics, ideology and the process of disillusionment in the literature of the Spanish Civil War', *Zeitschrift für Anglistik und Amerikanistik*, 42 (1994), 27–37.

[17] Suleiman, *Authoritarian Fictions*, 71.

[18] Jones, *Cwmardy*, 152.

[19] Suleiman, *Authoritarian Fictions*, 65.

[20] Jones, *Cwmardy*, 246.

[21] Ibid., 270.

[22] David Bell, *Ardent Propaganda: Miners' Novels and Class Conflict 1929–1939* (Umeå, Sweden, 1995), 91.

[23] Lewis Jones, *We Live: The Story of a Welsh Mining Valley* (London, 1983 [1939]), 191.

[24] Jones, foreword to *Cwmardy*, unpaginated.

[25] Jones, *We Live*, 200.

[26] Ibid., 201.

[27] Ibid., 83.

[28] Pikoulis, 'The wounded bard', 25.

[29] Jones, *We Live*, 25.

[30] Ibid., 307.

[31] Foley, *Radical Representations*, 362.

[32] Julian Symons, *The Thirties: A Dream Revolved* (London, 1975), 107.

11

'Two Strikes and You're Out': 1926 and 1984 in Welsh Industrial Fiction

JAMES A. DAVIES

Welsh industrial fiction is heir to the nineteenth-century novel. The latter contains so many seminal scenes: Stephen Blackpool, in *Hard Times* (1854), discovering he can speak, movingly, to a strike meeting, 'wi'out bein moydert and muddled',[1] only to find himself embarked on a tragic sequence; Margaret Hale, in *North and South* (1854–5), rushing to help the millowner, Thornton, as he confronts angry strikers, her action triggering mutual sexual attraction that ultimately leads to marriage; Maheu, the sensible, hard-working miner in *Germinal* (1885), finding his voice, for the first time, when part of a deputation to the manager, so that 'things stored up in his heart, that he did not even know were there, now came tumbling forth in a great outpouring of emotion'.[2] His wife becomes the most determined of the strikers; their lodger, Étienne, emerges as the miners' 'undisputed leader', and Zola comments: 'In reality he was climbing a rung of the social ladder into the ranks of the detested bourgeoisie.'[3]

These scenes, these novels, are important points of reference for any discussion of strikes in fiction. They not only point to the obvious dramatic potential of confrontations between masters and men and within the ranks of masters and men, but also to the transforming power of the industrial stoppage, the way in which strikes change lives. In these scenes workers discover unsuspected oratorical resources, women reject stereotypical roles and, as Zola's comment reminds us, the changes can have social as well as personal implications.

Such ideas can be found in three Welsh novels dealing, at least in part, with the 1926 General Strike (nine days in May) and the continuing Miners' Strike that lasted until November: Gwyn Jones, *Times like These* (1936), Lewis Jones, *We Live* (1939) and Raymond Williams, *Border Country* (1960).[4] In *Times Like These*, Edgar Evans, not noticeably articulate or successful in private matters, comes fully to life as a union leader: 'his powerful, passionate speech was reserved for miners' meetings' (p. 106). Though rural taciturnity characterizes most of the railwaymen in *Border Country*, Jack Meredith, a signalman, previously only a name in the text, by refusing to strike emerges as a man of strong principles expressed through tersely cogent utterances; by refusing to work overtime after the strike he ensures that all three signalmen are re-employed. Further, strikers not only emerge as fine orators and/or men of principle but also as skilled organizers. Gwyn Jones's Edgar Evans becomes local organizing secretary and instructs his committee:

'If we take our little district as a whole, and that is what we have decided, we have a number of things to consider. Here they are: food and clothing; information and propaganda; sports and entertainments; transport and permits; finance. I don't say as we won't find anything else, but those are the chief items.' He was enjoying himself. (p. 152)

Oliver Biesty, all his life a miner, is put in charge of permits and also 'enjoyed an increasing importance and satisfaction' (p. 153) as he gives or refuses permission for strikers to do small jobs. In *We Live* are strike committees, organized soup kitchens, Federation hand-outs, leafleting, with Lewis Jones's main characters, Mary Jones and Len Roberts, well to the fore. Even in *Border Country*, though the local railway workers are too few and too self-sufficient to require a complex infrastructure and are, in any case, only out for the short-lived General Strike itself, Morgan Rosser has to organize the withdrawal of labour and keep his colleagues informed by means of meetings and notices.

Mary Jones, the heroine of *We Live*, is pushed on to a platform, 'where, for the first time in her life, she made a speech' (p. 177), thus neatly combining the realization of personal potential – she speaks very well – with a new role for women. Dai Smith has noted 'the full, sympathetic treatment of women' in both Lewis Jones's novels;[5] a central theme of *We Live* is the rise of Mary Jones during 1926 to a position of influence as public speaker, Communist Party member and demonstrator. *Border Country*, on the other hand, is a very male book: there are no women strikers, and the wives, though anxious, hardly change their routine during the short stoppage. For Mary Biesty in *Times Like These*, however, the long strike is catalytic in that, though she is not directly involved, it impels her towards important decisions. The strike makes the thought of living in the Valleys more and more intolerable. She braves her father's anger to break with her miner-fiancé and move to London to continue her secretarial career. The narrator is supportive: 'Her manners, her speech, and her clothes were all improving' (p. 24), he writes, using that last word without apparent irony.

Lewis Jones's is the darkest account of 1926. In *We Live*, in possible defiance of meteorological accuracy, even the weather is dreadful, with drizzling rain and a 'wind [that] moaned along the telephone wires, lashing the people's faces and bending their heads to the muddy earth' (p. 153), a Zolaesque scene if ever there was one. Enforced leisure is given over (almost totally) to political discussion and agitation. Despair, hopelessness and poverty are strongly emphasized. But even in this novel, limited as it is by Lewis Jones's Marxist agenda, strikes increase awareness of possibilities beyond the routine, even though Lewis Jones does not allow career development outside the workers' movement: Mary Jones becomes a dedicated party leader, and, seemingly as a consequence, even her health improves.

Both Gwyn Jones and Raymond Williams are more realistic, less fettered by political dogma. In *Times Like These*, a new life develops during the long hot summer of 1926. The mines are silent, smoky air disperses, the river runs clean. Despite the obvious problems there are, for many, temporary satisfactions and glimpses of better things. Gwyn Jones makes much of that marvellous summer in the description of strikers bathing in a river pool called the Horse Washings:

> To this new Horse Washings, as to Arden, many men did flock every day, and fleet the time carelessly, as they did in the golden world . . .
>   These were the Arcadian characteristics of the strike – the soft swirling of bodies in water, the soft pad of feet on turf, the crumble of brown soil, sappy chew of grass, the fly and leaf stippling the smooth river pools . . . [and] Tempe and its shepherds piping in the shade. (p. 205)

Shakespeare and classical pastoral: here is a highly educated narrator offering up this group of leisured miners to readers who resemble him. The passage treads a fine line between mockery and the sense of this idyll being too good to last; but even the latter does not subvert these periods of sheer enjoyment at being freed from work underground.

Strikes hint at possibilities beyond strike-led tasks. Some remain hints: Edgar, flushed with organizational success, 'wouldn't mind' (p. 158) being in Parliament, though nothing comes of that. In Raymond Williams's Glynmawr most have small second incomes from rural pursuits. As the General Strike begins, Harry Price is typical in calculating he can replace some lost income through his beehives, flower-garden and vegetables. What intensifies, even when the strike is over, is the sense, new to some, of a more meaningful alternative to work on the railways: 'Like Harry with his gardens, Morgan [Rosser] found, as the summer months passed, that the journeys with the van were his real work, his actual centre, while the work at the box was just done in the margin, for a wage' (p. 154). His life is transformed: the 'journeys with the van', selling produce in the Valleys, begin Morgan's new career. He enjoys 'the business feeling of it' (p. 155), leaves the railway and becomes, of course, a successful businessman.

When Dickens observed the Preston strike prior to writing *Hard Times* he praised the workers' discipline and solidarity.[6] In the novel itself he criticized strikes because, in them, 'private feeling must yield to the common cause'.[7] This is, of course, usually the case, but what both Dickens and Mrs Gaskell failed to see – and Zola saw all too clearly – was that strikes also fostered individualism, bourgeois instincts, as with Étienne, Edgar, Len and Mary, Morgan Rosser. To put this another way: strikes can be understood as a qualified version of the carnivalesque, expressing, here, unrestrained individualism as well as communal eruption. To adapt Lynne Pearce: strikes are 'sites upon which all manner of voices . . . break free from hierarchical . . . control',[8] upon which the roles of masters and men are, at least temporarily, reversed, and new, individual voices are heard. Even the family can, in this special sense, be carnivalized, as economic power passes from father to child – for example, within the Biesty family of *Times Like These*, increasingly sustained by daughter Mary's remittances – and conventions break down. Gwyn Jones's realism exposes the treatment of the Roberts family in *We Live* as essentially sentimental.

Given their iconic status in Welsh working-class culture, the treatment of the General Strike and subsequent Miners' Strike in these three famous Welsh novels is strangely indirect, at times almost marginal. Gwyn Jones's account of 1926 concentrates on Luke's and Olive's honeymoon and early married life, on Mary Biesty's account of her visit to London, on the ending of her relationship with Edgar, on family rows over her future and on a fight between two friends over a girl, this last being one of the novel's finest set-pieces. Like his namesake, Lewis, Gwyn Jones is not blind to the organizing, the appeals, the problems of the poor, the harshness of means-testing, the increase in debt, the loss of pride, the fear of winter and the ever-darkening political context. But his deepest imaginative engagement is with familial and personal relationships, and with what we now call leisure activities, such as walks, open-air activities, games, chat. As one character exclaims: 'Why – to a lot of us this ain't a strike at all. It's a holiday' (p. 189).

In *We Live*, from the start of the General Strike to the miners' return to work, Len is mainly absent, at first working for the Communist Party in the city (preparation for leadership, says Mary, in a bourgeois moment), then in prison following a fracas with the police. This, of course, allows Mary to play a more central role. But in this novel the events of 1926 are dominated by two incidents. The first is the horrific sequence during which the shopkeeper, his business in ruins, kills his wife and then hangs himself; the second is a demonstration against the local Council – the members of which are solidly working-class, miners' leaders elected by those who are now striking – for failing to provide relief. The first is individualism taken to chilling extremes, the second is focalized through the characters of Len and Mary so that the mass demonstration becomes a struggle between new and old leaders. In *Border Country*, during the fine May weather, Glynmawr's 'adjustment to the strike was quite quickly made' (p. 125). Here, indirectness is all: the railwaymen spend more time in their gardens and read the notices and telegrams from bosses and union that arrive at the quiet country station. The only real dispute, in which Morgan Rosser has an influential role, is over the terms on which they return to work.

In all three novels, the communal events of 1926 in a sense take second place to assertive individualism. This last is part of a

paradox, for all three novels also stress the helplessness of striking
workers in the grip of larger forces, sensed, for example, by Luke in
Times Like These: 'All these forces working above and about him –
still they baffled him' (p. 125). Gwyn Jones, uniquely, also insists
that the owners and managers, like their workers, 'felt that the
strike was something over which they had no control' (p. 84). The
paradox is, of course, that the general helplessness and strike-
induced calls for solidarity generate individualism (the bourgeois
impulse) through glimpses of better alternatives and the desire –
sometimes satisfied – to seize the day. We can note the (almost
certainly unintended) symbolism of the ending of *We Live*: the
workers march, their leader, Mary, is provided with a car.

Fifty-eight years after 1926 was the Miners' Strike of 1984–5. It
lasted a year, from March to March. I study these events in three
novels: Raymond Williams, *Loyalties* (1985); Tom Davies, *Black
Sunlight* (1986); Roger Granelli, *Dark Edge* (1997).[9]

Loyalties is a wide-ranging novel which, for much of the book,
uses the valley mining community of Danycapel as a positive point
of reference in a complex, uneasy, dishonest, at times traitorous
world dominated by a powerful upper middle class with fashionable socialist inclinations. During the Miners' Strike Danycapel is
described from afar as an idyll: 'the upper slopes of the mountain
were suddenly bright with the red gold of bracken and the pale
gold of larch . . . The sun was catching the smoke and making a
strange lattice of beams and arcs: insubstantial and luminous
above the solid grey bed' (p. 329). Closer inspection certainly finds
economic deprivation and hardship, but more prominent are the
popular sustaining clichés of valley life and 1984–5. We discover
terraced houses like little palaces, memories of a heroic past, and
the discovery and application of entrepreneurial skills: raising
money, the bulk buying of food, assessing need, distributing.
'They're very close in Danycapel', we are told, 'They look after
each other' (p. 312). The familiar Williams ideas are centred on this
valley town: the knowable community, the importance of the
structure of feeling, and basic, working-class wisdom that is well
able to expose the limitations of Gwyn Lewis's Cambridge
education.

But, whereas in *Border Country* such values and exposing are
supported by the whole text, in *Loyalties* they are, almost
immediately, undermined. For the section entitled 'Danycapel,

October 1984' is followed by the climactic confrontation between Gwyn and his natural father, Sir Norman Braose. The latter dismisses the Miners' Strike as 'a morass of illusion and rhetoric' (p. 360), socialism as a dead end, and Gwyn as clinging, sentiment-ally, to a world – that of the socialist Valleys – which he left and to which, because of subsequent education, experience and position, he can never return. Sir Norman has been one of the novel's villains, showing little loyalty to Gwyn's mother, socialism or his country, but there is little doubt that he has the best of the argument with Gwyn. His ultimate intellectual superiority is buttressed by his 'green' credentials, his concern with nature con-servation to which he has devoted his later years.

Black Sunlight is a popular and iconoclastic novel. It questions received ideas, such as the glamorizing of 1926 as an 'epic fight' (p. 207), forgetting it was a wholesale defeat. It injects realism into accounts of the later struggle. A 'grim, sepia' print of 1926, with its ragged children, on the wall of the 1984 soup kitchen, points up the latter as 'a palace of wonder and surprise', pop music, mounds of donated food – Coca Cola, turkeys, sausages – and an 'avalanche' (p. 370) of donated chocolate. We are a long way from Williams's Danycapel. Through the long, hot summer of 1984 Tom Davies describes a holiday atmosphere: sport, leisure, day trips to the seaside. A cascade of donated wine and turkeys makes Christmas 1984 for many the best ever. All this, plus the excitement of flying pickets and fighting with the police.

Individuals emerge, men and women, to organize rosters, to raise funds and form support groups: 'the surprise discovery of the summer was the endlessly inventive eloquence of Dai Scaggs' (p. 372), thus extending the long line of those whom strikes made orators. In an echo of Morgan Rosser in *Border Country*, Gnasher, one of the valley characters, organizes the scavenging of tips for coal, mechanizes in part, whilst maintaining productivity by keeping the diggers high on amphetamines, and makes a fortune by selling high-priced coal to desperate businesses.

The mood darkens as the strike moves to its inevitable defeat and associated nihilism. The wives are more determined than the men to resist capitulation – a reflection of women's heightened profile during 1984–5, evident in all three novels, as well as a further reminder of *Germinal* – and so prevent safety cover at the local pit. This is near total collapse as the miners take it over in a final futile gesture. The least convincing part of the book is the injection of mystical symbolism: the Christ-like Huw crucified, literally, on barbed wire during fighting with the police, and bleeding to death in hospital, the village clock stopping, significantly, at three o'clock. Tom Davies's valley community is one of unbridled individualism, combining the rumbustiousness of Jack Jones with explicit sex, which might seem at odds with the saintly Huw's symbolic purpose: his death marks the destruction of the valley's soul and the loss of its life-blood in a generally bleak ending.

Roger Granelli's *Dark Edge* (1997) casts a decidedly drooping eye on the strike and valley life generally. Certainly its treatment of the family – that unit which, as Raymond Williams has shown, can be the industrial situation in microcosm – is bleakly pessimistic. The book is structured on the hostility between two brothers, one, Edwin, a miners' union leader, the other, Elliot, a sadistic police-man, which ends tragically. The novel suggests similar strike-induced tensions in other homes. As one of the main female characters reflects: 'the family was a "bunch". Full of secrets, repression, unrequited hopes and terminal disappointment' (p. 184).

Though there are the usual plus points, such as cleaner rivers, healthier pit-free lives, and women developing organizing skills through support groups, Granelli is even more iconoclastic than Tom Davies. Even the emergence of women is treated sceptically: the outside observer, a woman journalist from London, sees 'a crumbling man's world, with women as addendums . . . a world that was archaic and restrictive to her own sex' (p. 114). The benefits of nationalization are seen as, at best, dubious; community spirit fragments into terrace life and that on more affluent estates, and even the committed, such as Edwin, the book's hero, 'loved and hated [their] community' (p. 14). Doubts are cast on socialist solidarity, the coolly objective, Cambridge-educated union official Ceri Griffiths representing 'a new breed of socialism' (p. 63) alien to his worker-colleagues; the strike itself, and Arthur Scargill's role, are regarded with much cynicism. Even 'Welshness' comes under fire, described as 'a complex sense of inferiority balanced with aggressive pride' (p. 14), and as a 'strange blend of unreliable romance and the ability to plunge into dark despair as if it were a refuge, "Welshing" on their strengths and responsibilities' (p. 105). 'Nationhood' is dismissed as almost meaningless, the Welsh language as divisive. Further home truths are offered about mining: 'the work itself was disgusting' (p. 135) is a typical comment.

The novel's ending, alas, is an unconvincing mixture of poetic justice and politically correct incoherence. Elliot, the sadistic policeman, becomes a paraplegic after falling from a bridge during a fight with Edwin; it emerges that they are only half-brothers. Edwin substitutes a new Welsh patriotism for his socialism, but, oddly or opportunistically, decides both to learn Welsh and to leave for London, the attractive visiting woman journalist having offered to fix him up with a London college. Here is a further reminder of Zola, whose Étienne leaves the mining village for political work with Pluchart that will 'broaden his programme' (p. 495). Zola notes that this is a bourgeois tendency, and we might say the same of Edwin. Certainly, in Granelli's novel, strike and strikers are swept aside as the individual breaks ranks.

In *Seasonal Tribal Feasts* (1987) Stuart Evans, Swansea born and Swansea Valley bred, offered a view from Oxford of the miners' strike. It enters academic discussions about general social unrest, but the most revealing comment, hardly academic, is by the central character, Ben Oldfield: 'The summer of '84 I shall remember, I think, for an evening in a stuffy crowded lounge of what used to be called London Airport, drinking wine with a woman of gentle wit and surpassing charms on a hot night.'[10] We are, once again, a long way from Danycapel. In *Glass Shot* (1991), Duncan Bush's working-class hero, a tyre-fitter in Cardiff, passes miners' pickets as he drives through the Valleys. He calls them 'woollybacks' existing in 'only one more dirty-looking, Welsh, played-out little village . . . This isn't South Wales. It's Nineteen Fifty-Five',[11] gives them money to save them having to play cards for matchsticks, and responds positively to the power of the scab convoys ferrying coal to the steelworks. In both novels the message is that, outside the mining communities, few cared much or at all.

I began in the nineteenth century and to the novels of that period I now return. In his famous chapter on 'The industrial novels' in *Culture and Society* Raymond Williams concluded that fear of collective action was shared by all who wrote them. Perhaps because of that their works make much of individuals in action, and thus – unconsciously or consciously – of strikes as engines of bourgeois advancement. The same can be said of the three novels on 1926, even of *We Live*, where, in that novel, what is left out – the attractions of dispersal, and of advancement beyond the party or the valley community – is as potent as what we have, advancement through communism's hierarchy. My three novels on 1984–5 also insist on the individual gesture – the enterprising leave or are about to leave, or consider leaving, usually for England – but suggest the end of socialism, of working-class solidarity, even, perhaps, of tenable Welsh valley communities. The vulnerability of these last is emphasized further by those brief references in *Seasonal Tribal Feasts* and *Glass Shot*.

It would be comforting to say, simply, that these novels demonstrate that the world has moved on to become an arena for individual achievement. But this is to ignore the eager violence, particularly in *Black Sunlight*, *Dark Edge* and *Glass Shot*. Dickens (the creator of Steerforth and Bradley Headstone), Mrs Gaskell (Boucher) and Zola (Souverine) would recognize, particularly in that violence, the anarchic element, the nihilistic edge, in modern Welsh writing on industrial themes. Certainly in the cited novels by Davies, Granelli and Bush – and to some extent in Meredith's *Shifts*, that fine novel of deindustrialization[12] – there are, on the one hand, gestures towards middle-classness and, on the other, the desire to 'Let order die!'[13]

In my title, 'Two Strikes and You're Out', 'out' not only refers to disastrous personal or wider social consequences, but also means getting 'out', moving elsewhere to a better life that in these Welsh novels is essentially a bourgeois conception, an attractive middle-class existence invariably outside Wales. The Marxist optimism of *We Live*, the spiritual possibilities of *Black Sunlight*, and the gestures at Welsh and Welshness of *Dark Edge* – together a mixture of wishful thinking and confusion – reveal the writers' reluctance to accept the logical consequences of community collapse. The honesty of Gwyn Jones and Raymond Williams (to say nothing of Duncan Bush) is far more persuasive: they accept the decline of those communities, and know there is no going back. But, explicitly or implicitly, all these novelists recognize – even at times seem to celebrate – individual initiative in a manner that would have pleased their nineteenth-century predecessors who were afraid of the mob. All recognize the individual's pressing need to get out. It might also be said that not one of my novelists has much more of consequence to say to those who have to remain than Luke's despairing comment at the end of *Times Like These*: 'Everything do seem so useless, somehow' (p. 319).

Notes

[1] Charles Dickens, *Hard Times*, ed. George Ford and Sylvère Monod, Norton Critical Edition (New York, 1966 [1854]), 108.

[2] Émile Zola, *Germinal*, trans. Leonard Tancock, Penguin Classics (Harmondsworth, 1982 [1954]), 213.

[3] Ibid., 221–2.

[4] Gwyn Jones, *Times Like These* (London, 1979 [1936]); Lewis Jones, *We Live* (London, 1978 [1939]); Raymond Williams, *Border Country* (London, 1988 [1960]). Page numbers refer to these editions and are inserted in the text.

[5] David Smith, *Lewis Jones*, Writers of Wales (Cardiff, 1982), 59.

[6] 'On strike', *Selected Journalism 1850–1870*, ed. David Pascoe (Harmondsworth, 1997), 463–4.

[7] *Hard Times*, 110.

[8] Lynne Pearce, *Reading Dialogics* (London, 1994), 59.

[9] Raymond Williams, *Loyalties* (London, 1989 [1985]); Tom Davies, *Black Sunlight* (London, 1986); Roger Granelli, *Dark Edge* (Bridgend, 1997). Page numbers refer to these editions, and are inserted in the text.

[10] Stuart Evans, *Seasonal Tribal Feasts* (London, 1987), 212–13.

[11] Duncan Bush, *Glass Shot* (London, 1991), 56–9.

[12] Christopher Meredith, *Shifts* (Bridgend, 1988).

[13] Shakespeare, *Henry IV, Part Two*, 1.1, 154.

12

Arthur Seaton and the Machine: a New Reading of Alan Sillitoe's Saturday Night and Sunday Morning

KATHLEEN BELL

Alan Sillitoe's relation to the label 'working-class' has never been a simple one. Writing to *The Nottinghamshire Guardian* (where he had published some early short stories) to promote the forth-coming publication of *Saturday Night and Sunday Morning*, he advised potential readers: 'The novel is set in Nottingham and deals with working-class life there.'[1] However, by January 1959, in an article in *Books and Bookmen*, while relating his work as a writer to the jobs (and pay) of his brothers, Sillitoe was showing a little uneasiness with the slightly different label 'proletarian novelist', declaring, 'I have merely written a novel about working-class people, and my other novels will not always be of this theme.'[2] This comment suggests a limited view of the term, as though to be 'working-class' or 'proletarian' indicated subject rather than, for instance, form, theme or perspective.[3] More recently, while still asserting the importance of his roots, Sillitoe has opposed the label of 'working-class writer'.[4]

It is not hard to understand the reasons for the difficulties Sillitoe and other writers have had with this label. To be identified as 'working-class' is a useful way of gaining access to an audience. The label provides publishers with a means of categorizing and marketing a book and is popular with a wide spectrum of readers. While middle- and upper-class readers look for insights into a different way of life, it is possible for the working-class writer to use that label to address readers whose origins are similar to his own. Sillitoe's early eagerness for such an audience can be seen from his statement that 'Factory workers enjoy reading about their own environment, and few books allow them to do this.'[5] The 'working-class' label becomes a means of declaring kinship with family, friends and people of similar backgrounds, as well as resisting the idea that writing is an exclusively bourgeois occupation. It also affirms that to be a writer is to play a productive role in society and, perhaps, to be self-supporting. In his 1979 introduction to *Saturday Night and Sunday Morning*, Sillitoe recalls his ambition to earn £200 from the book, so that he could live on the proceeds while writing another, equally remunerative novel.[6] Similarly in *Books and Bookmen* he wrote of the importance of being a 'wage-earner' like his brothers Brian and Michael.[7] Such comments provide a helpful blurring of the customary distinction between 'job' and 'profession'.

However, for all the strengths of this approach, the coupling of the terms 'working-class' and 'writer' can nonetheless lead to marginalization, with the modifier 'working-class' limiting rather than enlarging the scope of the term 'writer'. It can be used to imply writing from knowledge rather than from imagination. Moreover, such labelling, acting as an insistent reminder of class hierarchies which are still strong, also tends to deny the writer the kind of teaching, influential and judgmental role which is so easily assumed by writers with a more securely respected place in the social hierarchy. This is reinforced by the way in which the term 'working-class' links its members to a place in the production process rather than to a social and hierarchical position. What working-class writers produce, the term might seem to imply, is not literature but mere product and to reject the term is thus to assert the autonomy of the author as opposed to the agency of the tool.

The advantages and disadvantages of this categorization are comparable to the effect of relating Arthur Seaton to his workplace role as capstan lathe operator – a role in which he is, for most of the book, distinguished by his strength, speed and efficiency, but in which the control over his environment he asserts elsewhere is contained and limited by the regular demands of the workplace. He is marked by a contradiction that is common in working-class protagonists in novels, in that the power with which he is endowed and which confirms his heroic status is in direct contradiction to his role in the workplace. Arthur may be a worker of exceptional ability, earning the remarkable sum of £14 a week, at the piece-work rate of 4s. 6d. per 100, but in earning this his body, and at

least some part of his attention, is subordinated to the manufacturing process.

This subordination is not immediately apparent. Arthur's speed
and strength are such that the workplace can initially appear a site
of liberation in which he is free to think for himself and imagine
acts of anarchic destruction against the institutions that would
control his life. It is here that he imagines dynamiting the factory
where he works, taking a pleasure (which we as readers are per-
mitted to share) in the prospect of 'the wonderful sight of gaffers
and machines and shining bikes going sky high' (p. 45). Here, as in
the pubs and streets of Nottingham, Arthur seems at first to
function as hero of folktale or myth, with the conventional skills of
trickster coupled with superhuman strength and endurance. It is
these powers which Arthur demonstrates in the first chapter of the
novel when, after consuming seven gins and eleven pints in a
drinking contest, falling downstairs, taking another two pints to
aid his recovery and vomiting the last over a man's best suit, he still
finds his way to the bed of another man's wife, able to contemplate
an hour of love-making before sleep. Arthur's creative lying, his
personal vengeance on those he takes to represent 'the forces of
righteousness' (p. 115) and his constant struggles for self-
preservation are familiar from tales as well-known and varied as
the *Odyssey* and 'Jack and the Beanstalk'. But while the character-
istics of the trickster hero are often, as Marina Warner points out,
diametrically opposed to those of the gigantic strong man,[8] Arthur
Seaton combines the identities of prankster and warrior hero. This
might seem to relate to the historical shift in conventions of
masculinity which is Warner's subject, but it may also be that a
hero who works on a production line, and is therefore
subordinated to a process controlled by others, requires more than
mere cunning or mere strength, but something of both.

While cunning and strength may seem to mark out Arthur as
hero, there are also structural elements which give him this role.
While he does not fulfil all aspects of the function of a folktale
hero as defined by Propp,[9] it is possible to recognize folktale
sequences within the narrative which briefly give Arthur the
function of hero. For instance, there are the three women (Brenda,
Winnie and Doreen) who represent a threat to his freedom and the
three pursuits by the swaddies (trailing him after his affair with
Winnie has begun, encountering him with Brenda and Winnie at

the Goose Fair and finally beating him up near the White Horse so that he seeks help from Doreen). Either set of events would parallel the formula of three battles with the villain and, although the outcome is Arthur's defeat, it could nonetheless be argued that he moves from these events into the folktale conclusion of marriage, survival and wisdom.[10]

In addition, external political and economic factors seem at first to give Arthur more freedom in his workplace than was available to the central figures of many previous novels dealing with the work environment. For example, Frank Owen in *The Ragged Trousered Philanthropists* and Larry Meath in *Love on the Dole* are more evidently subordinate to the workplace because the economic pressures of competition are felt more acutely in periods of recession. The nakedness of economic forces takes from Owen and Meath the degree of agency we expect in the heroes of novels; one can be saved only by a middle-class sympathizer with money to spare, while the other dies leaving his fiancée to show her understanding of economic pressures by embarking on a life of prostitution. Arthur Seaton, by contrast, is put to work at his capstan lathe in the 1950s, a period of economic boom and full employment, when his skill is a commodity in demand (although demand for labour is such that almost any pair of hands would do). Moreover, Arthur could not easily be punished for dissident political views or rebellious actions while he remains a useful commodity who could respond to discipline or sacking by quickly finding a similar job elsewhere. As Arthur reflects early on in the novel:

No more short-time like before the war, or getting the sack if you stood ten minutes in the lavatory reading your *Football Post* – if the gaffer got on to you now you could always tell him where to put the job and go somewhere else. (p. 30)

However, while the freedom from immediate economic pressure which Arthur Seaton experiences may liberate him from some constraints experienced by previous working-class characters, it has the additional effect of distancing Arthur from precise knowledge of the degree to which he is imprisoned within a specific social and economic role. Arthur's rebellion may lead him to the avoidance of some orthodoxies, but, for all the character's exuberant lies and linguistic flourishes, at times the narrator seems to be ironic at the expense of Arthur's lack of understanding. On occasion the narrative tone shifts from echoing Arthur to implying a critical distance between author and character:

> The difference between before the war and after the war didn't bear thinking about. War was a marvellous thing in many ways, when you thought about how happy it had made so many people in England. There are no flies on me, Arthur thought. (p. 29)

The final sentence, reminding the reader of Arthur's admiring relation to his own thought processes, effectively distances the reader from Arthur's point of view. His insistence on his own rightness is just sufficiently excessive to provoke the reader into questioning or even disagreement. There is plainly a contradiction between Arthur's mellow and uncritical views here (expressed as he is on the point of leaving for work with his father) and the anarchic anger he expresses elsewhere at government, taxation, Council House[11] and mass communication. However, the simplistic view Arthur takes of the causes of economic change seems to indicate that a life in which relative comfort can be bought by repetitive manual labour may also distance the worker from the harsher awareness of exploitation which had been experienced by his predecessors.

Arthur's class enmities are the product of inheritance rather than experience and thought; while he sees Robboe as the 'enemy's scout' and worker and boss as members of 'different species' (p. 71), he still believes, for most of the novel, that 'It was a good, comfortable life if you didn't weaken, safe from the freezing world in a warm snug kitchen . . .' (p. 54), voting Communist out of pity (p. 40) and feeling at home in an 'anarchistic Labour' (p. 146) environment more because of its familiarity than because of its political convictions. It is only after the personal disaster of being beaten up that Arthur reaches a new point of uncertainty, deciding that:

> No place existed in all the world that could be called safe, and he knew for the first time in his life that there had never been any such thing as safety, and never would be, the difference being that now he knew it as a fact, whereas before it was a natural unconscious state. (p. 213)

The phrasing of this passage calls into question all that the reader has been told of Arthur and his self-confidence in the first section of the novel. Moreover, it is at this point that Arthur's previous views about war as a source of happiness and economic security are undercut by the use of an image from the Second World War to stand for life as Arthur is now experiencing it:

> Life was like that, he thought, you floated down on a parachute, like the blokes in that Arnhem picture, pulling strings this way and that so that you could put out your hand to reach something you wanted, until one day you hit the bottom without knowing it, like a bubble bursting when it touched something solid, and you were dead, out like a light in a Derbyshire gale. (pp. 213–14)

Confronting his own lack of control over his circumstances, Arthur is compelled to draw on images from history and nature. The first image of parachuting into Arnhem sees Arthur as subject to orders at the moment when obedience to command has sucked the individual into an inevitable process which he can do nothing to halt. (Sillitoe's questioning of military hierarchies is common in his writing of this period and may derive both from his personal experience of army life and from a post-war awareness of the danger in unquestioning obedience to orders.) The second and third images – of bubble and (presumably) candlelight – place Arthur at the mercy of the mindless and cyclical processes of nature. Both images imply the loss of autonomy and power, as any sense of self is reduced to the agency of the tool. Critically, the image of the soldiers on parachutes is dissolved not into the moment of landing, when some degree of autonomy, however limited by circumstance, might seem to be restored, but into the bubble and light whose extinction is inevitable by the laws of nature.

The effect of the change on Arthur Seaton is echoed in the opening of the following chapter when he is suddenly injured by the drill:

> His finger jumped back from the drill and a mound of blood grew from his sud-white crinkled skin, broke, and ran down his hand. He wiped it away with a bundle of cotton-waste: a small cut, but the blood poured out, over his palm and down to his wrist. He drew a dry finger across

and diverted it to the floor, away from his bare sinewy forearm. He cursed the lost time, and set out for the first-aid department, to have his finger hockled and bandaged. (p. 219)

We understand from the text that a moment's imprecision in the tightly ordered sequence 'Turn to chamfer, then to drill, then blade-chamfer' (p. 42) has caused the drill to injure Arthur's finger, but the injury is expressed without any suggestion that Arthur is either responsible for it or has any control over the natural forces of his own body. It is Arthur's finger that jumps, not Arthur who withdraws it, while the blood pours out in such a way that it cannot be stopped but only diverted like a river.

This moment, although minor in terms of workplace injuries, is highly significant in terms of how both Arthur and the reader regard his work. Previously, despite forceful hints from the novel's imagery, it has been possible to perceive the machine and the factory as the source of such autonomy as Arthur possesses. It gives him space to pursue his thoughts and money to conduct his leisure activities. It is even the producer of bicycles like the one that Arthur rides on his outings to the southern Peak District. Moreover, Arthur is presented as supremely good at his job – the fastest in the factory – so that he appears to be in control of the industrial environment rather than controlled by it, able to regulate his own production to maintain his wages at the optimum level. From time to time he may find that his 'guts are rotten' (p. 52) but brandy and tea will improve his stomach to such an extent that he asks himself 'Did I really feel badly this morning?' (p. 55), being reassured by the knowledge that his wages will not suffer, while his work-rate is such that no one else's work will be hindered by his absence.

It is not until the end of the book that 'rotten guts' (p. 253) are acknowledged as a by-product of the work that Arthur Seaton finds he has little choice but to undertake. Only in the short second section is the illusion of Arthur's autonomy entirely dispelled as his need to write himself into the public arena becomes acute: 'you know that the big wide world hasn't heard from you yet, no, not by a long way, though it won't be long now' (p. 255). However, at this point in the novel Arthur has begun to define himself in relation to the world of animal existence and to display the passive vulnerability foreshadowed in the images of bubble and light caught in a gale. He is at the mercy of a political, social and economic structure which mimics the forces of nature in its impersonality and disregard for the humans it uses and consumes.

From the very beginning of the novel there are hints that Arthur is bound up in and part of a mechanized world; the drink that propels him downs the stairs at the White Horse, in triumphant anticipation of his later descent of the helter-skelter as the swaddies close in on him, is described as a 'high-octane fuel' which 'set him into motion like a machine' (p. 10). Similarly, Saturday nights are not merely 'the best and bingiest glad-time of the week' but subject to the 'slow-turning Big Wheel of the year' (p. 9), offering an early reminder that even the celebratory October Goose Fair is a mechanized pastime, a licensed period of carnival. The image of the Goose Fair's Big Wheel as the mechanized turning of the year emphasizes the passivity of characters and readers alike, even at their 'bingiest glad-time'; turning briefly to second-person narrative, the novel continues:

> Piled-up passions were exploded on Saturday night, and the effect of a week's monotonous graft in the factory was swilled out of your system in a burst of good-will. You followed the motto of 'be drunk and be happy', kept your crafty arms around female waists, and felt the beer going beneficially down into the elastic capacity of your guts. (p. 9)

Already the alcoholic rejoicing in the pub at weekends is seen as part of the bigger mechanical system of which the best workers, like Arthur, are part. The 'you' in this passage does not consist of conscious agents but of separated parts of people (arms, guts, etc.) whose systems are 'swilled out' and who 'follow' mottoes and 'feel' beer rather than drinking and enjoying it. The only activity allowed to 'you' is that which identifies masculinity, keeping 'arms around female waists', conventionally defining labour as male while again anticipating the threat to independent action which is found in women as symbols of domesticity.

The role of women is crucial in defining the relation between nature and machine. Despite his occasional Lawrentian readings of sexual relationships in terms of essential conflict, it seems evident that Sillitoe as a writer is capable of affection for women, rendering the three different characters of Brenda, Winnie and Doreen, for example, in a manner which suggests that there is more to them than

Arthur sees. Similarly, Ada, Em'ler and Margaret are endowed with character and individuality, despite their circumscribed roles in late-1950s society. However, the women in the novel are also given conventional functions, representing both naturalness as allure and the artificiality of social control. For instance, Mrs Robin engineers the apparently natural action of fainting to control her husband when he might be involved in a fight. Women are seen, through the novel's brief account of Doreen's view of Arthur, as seeking men with 'attributes of kindness and generosity, affection and industry' (p. 180). Thus, while men's concern is for sexual pleasure, the interests of women are aligned with those of the gaffers, requiring that the production line work smoothly and a man play his part in it for the support of wife and family. The allure that women represent may be natural as experienced by men but the novel suggests that it is only the adulterous passions of married women that fail to reinforce the economic interests of the factory owners. Thus the role of Doreen suggests an alignment between mechanization and nature.

Nature and the work of production are both contrasted and aligned in *Saturday Night and Sunday Morning*. Obviously there is a sharp visual contrast between the factory which pollutes the air of the surrounding streets and the fields and woods of Wollaton, Strelley, the Erewash valley and beyond. The natural setting at least offers freedom of movement, since Arthur's life here is not regimented as it is by the demands of the workplace. But at the same time, both nature and workplace are taken for granted by those who experience them; as Arthur realizes for a moment 'the funniest thing was that . . . you [did not] think about work when you were standing at your machine' (p. 43). Like nature, it provides an experience of rhythm and repetition and is a backdrop for an assortment of fantastic visions:

> Time flew while you wore out the oil-soaked floor and worked furiously without knowing it: you lived in a compatible world of pictures that passed through your mind like a magic-lantern, often in vivid and glorious loonycolour, a world where memory and imagination ran free and did acrobatic tricks with your past and with what might be your future, an amok that produced all sorts of agreeable visions. (p. 44)

This passage suggests the delusions presented by the machine's apparent liberation of the mind; the visions that play games with past and future as time flies may be 'agreeable' but they do not even, like the magic lantern show, belong to a world of shared fantasy. Instead, they are individual 'pipe-dreams' which, while they exist in solitariness, cannot be realized. Of course, by drawing attention to the vividness of Arthur Seaton's imagination, Sillitoe is sharing with us both its richness and Arthur's great potential; he also offers us, as readers, the opportunity to turn fantasy into fact. But in this passage, as in many others, there is no description of the content of the 'agreeable visions'; the language that draws attention to them, including the coinage 'loonycolour' gives sufficient impression of wonder and movement to convince us of Arthur's imaginative power but remains on the plane of abstraction rather than of concrete reality. Meanwhile Arthur's actions for the most part mesh with the rhythms of machine and nature alike. He may mitigate its worst effects on himself, whether by advising Brenda on her abortion or getting drunk in Ambergate during his military service fortnight. He may oppose its most extreme regimentation, as represented by Robboe, Mrs Bull and Rat Face. However, for all his fantasies of guns and explosions he is securely held by both nature and machine, accepting Doreen as the bait which will tie him forever to both.

To understand the relation of nature and the machine in *Saturday Night and Sunday Morning*, it may be helpful to think of nature not just as a series of places and experiences that can be enjoyed in freedom but as an area in which human agency is largely irrelevant. This aspect of nature is apparent in the sexual encounter between Arthur and Doreen immediately following their engagement, when both language and communication are lost: 'He spoke to her softly, and she nodded her head to his words without knowing what they meant. Neither did Arthur know what he was saying: both transmission and reception were drowned, and they broke through to the opened furrows of the earth' (p. 188). This passage leads directly to Arthur's famous canal-side soliloquy, too easily read as his continued defiance against the world. However the passage might also seem to refer to the role of the Fisher King in T. S. Eliot's *The Waste Land*, where fishing in a canal can be read as a symbol of sterility and death.[12] As Arthur fishes, he acknowledges his position within the production processes of capitalism, trapped by marriage as a fish is by bait, since domesticity will render him financially dependent on the system which uses his labour: 'you were roped by a factory, had a machine slung around your neck, and then you were hooked up by the arse with a wife' (p. 252).

This canal-side realization leads Arthur to a relative acceptance of his role within society. Again, his insights are not to be trusted. While taking the bait 'meant death for a fish', Arthur speculates that 'for a man it might not be so bad' (p. 252). At the same time he thinks himself out of the area of public concern in favour of the individual advancement which is offered by the consumer-driven capitalist society of which he has become part:

> So it looked as though they'd be all right together, he thought, as long as a war didn't start, or a trade slump and bring back the dole. As long as there wasn't a famine, a plague to sweep over England, an earthquake to crack it in two and collapse the city around them, or a bomb to drop and end the world with a big bang. But you couldn't concern yourself with these things if you had plans and wanted to get something out of life that you had never had before. And that was a fact, he thought, chewing a piece of grass. (p. 253)

While some of the dangers which Arthur raises are plainly absurd, the threat of the bomb was considerable at the time Sillitoe was writing. (His awareness of this threat and sense of the need for action can be judged by his presence on an early CND march.) Arthur, caught like the fish, ignores the threat but we as readers should be aware of the contrast between the nihilism that recalls Beckett ('Born drunk and married blind, misbegotten into a strange and crazy world . . .' p. 254[13]) and the apparent content with which he asserts, immediately after, that 'it's a good life and a good world' (p. 255), involving himself in the world of exploitation by smiling as he reels in a fish.

Obviously, fishing in a canal does not need to stand for something else but is a common enough activity. However, the parallels and differences that Arthur finds between workers and fish suggest some crucial difficulties in the role of Arthur as hero of the novel, difficulties which can be further explored by a comparison of *Saturday Night and Sunday Morning* with Sillitoe's slightly later novel about the Seaton family, *Key to the Door*. According to Sillitoe's 1977 preface, *Key to the Door* was 'in progress' during the same years as *Saturday Night and Sunday Morning* and was begun earlier although shaped into its final version rather later.[14] *Key to the Door* tells the story of Brian Seaton, Arthur's oldest brother, and culminates in a single, politically understood action, the deliberate refusal to kill a bandit who may or may not be a communist rebel.[15] Brian is unlike Arthur in many ways. He has experienced the economic depression of the 1930s more acutely. He is also more widely read, having a small library of stolen books and particularly treasuring his copies of *The Count of Monte Cristo* and *Les Misérables*. None the less, he is just as credible as Arthur as an inhabitant of Radford.

However, in the numerous rewrites of the novel, some no doubt in response to rejections from publishers and some in response to Sillitoe's own sense of what was necessary to explain Brian's action (which began, in early drafts, as the killing of the communist/bandit), Brian was given the kind of background which his brother in *Saturday Night and Sunday Morning* signally lacks. While Arthur Seaton plainly has a family and at times reflects on their past, he seems to live in a continuous present, seeing the future in terms of personal plans rather than political action. For Arthur the future exists only in terms of seasonal repetition ('the coming of summer (good); military training at the end of August (purgat'ry); Goose Fair in October (smashin'); Bonfire Night (good if you didn't get blown to bits); and Christmas at Christmas' (p. 149). Lacking any consciousness of the future other than repetition, he similarly lacks a sense of the past – a lack which may be related to his complete freedom from guilt about his actions. By contrast Brian, after his action, becomes aware of his own position between past and present:[16]

> it was the first time he realized that he had a past, and had not evolved out of a dream. He could say: 'I remember that time walking across the Cherry Orchard ten years ago and meeting Alma Arlington,' ten years being no longer a meaningless massive chunk of time, but something that could be dissected and sorted out, and called a past. In a week he would be on the boat, going back in a way to join himself up with this past, and the idea of it was one alternately of fear and distaste, as well as one similar to the feeling that came over him when reading the poems. Nevertheless little of the past was yet visible; and neither had he much vision of the future, but at least he knew that both existed. (pp. 385–6)

This sense of history – imprecise and nascent as it is – has to be understood politically. It derives from his actions and enables him to relate his politics to those of others, allowing Knotman to identify him as 'a socialist-anarchist' (p. 388). It is also derived from Brian's sense of a shared cultural awareness which enables him to see himself in relation to others. Significantly, his interest in literature has been prompted by the shared experience of listening to wireless serials of *The Count of Monte Cristo* and *Les Misérables* and it is these texts, rather than Knotman's copy of *The Ragged Trousered Philanthropists,* which influence his interpretation of the world. His imagination is something that can be shared with others, as when he identifies himself as Jean Valjean or signals 'Kubla Khan' in Morse code, in contrast to Arthur's individualist imagination which is limited to his ready lies and his solitary if fantastic musings at the capstan lathe. Arthur's sense of distance from such realities as Brenda's abortion, when he acknowledges 'He was only real inside himself' (p. 101), is symptomatic of his cultural aloneness.

Arthur's work, therefore, gives him the illusion of self-determined agency and personal space but he is caught by its structures just as much as he is at the mercy of the urges for food, sex and alcohol, which he experiences as necessity. Condemning the mass culture represented by television, his substitutes for its appeal – fantastic imaginings and ready lies – lead nowhere because they are pleasures he does not share with others. Being 'lost . . . among the people' (p. 192) may offer temporary relief from the threat that the swaddies increasingly represent but, as the moment of their attack looms, Arthur finds himself 'in solitude' and is planning an early night after watching television (p. 201). While Arthur's imagination suggests that he has the same potential for agency and independent thought that his creator has (and with which Arthur's brother Brian was endowed), he remains a character without the critical self-awareness which leads to political action. For all his strength, his illusions of agency fail to move him into the arena of political action but leave him, at the end of the novel, as little more than the tool of the machine.

Notes

[1] *The Nottingham Guardian* (6 September 1958), 4.
[2] Alan Sillitoe, 'The pen was my enemy', *Books and Bookmen*, January 1959, p. 11.

[3] Raymond Williams's comments on the 'lack of fit' between working-class experience and the inherited subject of the novel (in his essay 'The ragged-arsed philanthropists', *Writing in Society* (London, 1991), 239–68) should at least raise the possibility that working-class writing is capable of generating a new aesthetic, which would involve remoulding the inherited form and content of the novel.

[4] In informal conversation with the present author, Alan Sillitoe indicated that he found the category 'working class' a limiting one for a writer. Given the views of certain critics, this is hardly surprising. A useful account of some derogatory remarks (with a helpful response to them) can be found in Michael Wilding, 'Alan Sillitoe's political novels', in *Social Visions* (Sydney, 1993), 95, 139.

[5] Alan Sillitoe, 'Proletarian novelists', *Books and Bookmen* (August 1959), 13.

[6] Alan Sillitoe, *Saturday Night and Sunday Morning* (London, 1985 [1958]); page references to the 1985 edition are inserted in the text.

[7] Sillitoe, 'The pen was my enemy', 11.

[8] In Marina Warner, *Managing Monsters: Six Myths of our Time – The 1994 Reith Lectures* (London, 1994), 25, where she highlights, as an example, the contrast between Charlie Chaplin and Arnold Schwarzenegger.

[9] In Vladimir Propp, trans. Laurence Scott, revised and ed. Louis A Wagner, *Morphology of the Folktale* (Austin, TX, and London, 1973).

[10] Here I am drawing on Jack Zipes's use of Propp and helpful summary of Proppian functions in his essay 'The changing function of the fairy tale', *The Lion and the Unicorn: A Critical Journal of Children's Literature*, 12, 2 (December 1988), 7–31, see 10. It would be possible to find further parallels, for instance reading Brenda's pregnancy as the peripety which is only a temporary setback or taking Ada as the mysterious individual who helps Arthur as hero by the magical gift of advice on how to procure an abortion. However, while such instances do briefly help us recognize Arthur as hero through his function in the plot, a reading which depended too heavily on these aspects would oversimplify Arthur's role.

[11] To avoid confusion it may be helpful to note that the Council House is the name given in Nottingham to the very grand building in which the City Council has its headquarters.

[12] While I have no evidence that Alan Sillitoe had read *The Waste Land* or was directly influenced by it while writing *Saturday Night and Sunday Morning*, it would be remarkable, given his assiduous reading, his association with Robert Graves, his marriage to the poet Ruth Fainlight and his own poetry, if he did not know the work well enough to be influenced by it, whether at a conscious or subconscious level. There is certainly a conscious reference to *The Waste Land* in Sillitoe's 1960 poem, 'The rats', although its use there would not confirm my interpretation of the final chapter of *Saturday Night and Sunday Morning*.

[13] Samuel Beckett's *En Attendant Godot* was first published in Paris in 1952 and received its first performance there the following January. The English version, *Waiting for Godot*, was first published and performed in 1955, when the controversy it created was widely reported.

[14] Author's preface to Alan Sillitoe, *Key to the Door* (London, 1978 [1961]), 1–6; page references to the 1978 edition are inserted in the text.

[15] Sillitoe's 1977 'Preface' identifies the bandit as a communist (p. 2), but in the novel Brian alternates between identifying him as bandit and communist (pp. 368–9).

[16] The phrase is borrowed from the title of Hannah Arendt's 1961 collection of essays; the influence of Arendt's thinking may be evident in this chapter. I find her ideas helpful in the clarification she offers, although I do not always share her conclusions.

13

'The Uncertainties and Hesitations that were the Truth': Welsh Industrial Fictions by Women

STEPHEN KNIGHT

I

Like industrial work, industrial fiction is usually seen as a male sphere. Yet in early coal-mining, both on the bank and down the pit, in heavy industry, especially in wartime, and all the time in mills and light industry, women have often laboured as hard and with as many difficulties as men. In writing about the industrial world there has also been a recurrent presence of women, from both inside the working class, like Ellen Wilkinson and Ethel Carnie, and outside it, like Elizabeth Gaskell and Margaret Harkness.

Wales has been notable both for the extent to which its history has been changed by industrialism and also for the vigour with which its literature has responded to those changes. As Jane Aaron has noted,[1] the circumstances of women who were involved in industrial life, as well as the different interests of women writers, meant that few of them dealt with industrial topics: of the twenty stories in her recent anthology only three even mention industrial work, and it has only a marginal or negative role in their stories.[2] But part of the wealth of industrial fiction in Wales is that women have in fact made a contribution which, if not large in quantity, is nevertheless striking in both its quality and its different reading of the industrial world. Allen Raine, as Katie Gramich records,[3] included some industrial material in her novel *A Welsh Witch* as early as 1902 and, as this chapter will discuss, Kate Roberts, Menna Gallie and Margot Heinemann make widely differing and important statements on the industrial context. But the range and quality of that material is only one part of the story; in Welsh industrial women's writing, as elsewhere in the world, what is most marked is that, while women's voices are to a considerable extent consistent with the social politics of male industrial writing, and have clearly recognized the patterns developed by male writers, they also redevelop those formations: there are quite striking differences of formations, evaluation, tone and – most notable of all – genre to be found when women create industrial fictions.

Each of the women writers of the Welsh industrial novel discussed here has a specific relation with industrial society and its politics, but each grew up in a quite different context which influenced her development as a thinker and writer. Most strikingly, each operates in fiction in a way different from but comparable to male writers writing in her period and, to large degree, dealing with the same materials: if the women, as the title of this chapter suggests, write with less certainty and more hesitation than the men, that unsimplistic thoughtfulness is in fact a significant critique of and contribution to the genre.

II

Kate Roberts (1891–1985) is widely regarded as the major Welsh-language fiction writer of this century, and noted more for her brief but powerfully suggestive short stories than her few, and themselves rather short, novels. She was equally widely known as an activist on behalf of Welsh Nationalism in both political and cultural forms. Her best-known novel is entitled *Traed Mewn Cyffion*, which literally means 'feet in shackles' and is usually translated as *Feet in Chains*;[4] the title uses the exact words found in the Welsh Bible, where the English Authorized Version has 'Thou puttest my feet also in the stocks.'[5]

Roberts sets herself to write her own people's constricted story; though the novel is not at all religious in spirit, the title reference derives directly from the *gwerin* culture from which she came, the culture of a world that was communal, Protestant, Welsh-speaking and, at the same time, both rural and industrial. She was born in Rhosgadfan, Caernarfonshire, an area where most families lived on smallholdings but most of the men also worked in slate quarries spread between Snowdonia and the coast. This world was far from idyllic. A tremendous battle was fought between the slate miners and the brutal quarry owners at the end of the nineteenth century, and the climax was a two-year lock-out in the quarries run by Lord Penrhyn, who refused pay rises and banned any kind of union. The story of the strike is told powerfully in T. Rowland Hughes's novel *Chwalfa* (literally 'Upheaval', but translated as *Out of their Night*[6]) a northern variant on the honoured succession of male left-wing heroics for which the Welsh novel is well known.

However, Roberts does not describe the great strike, though her novel traces the story of a quarrying family from about 1890 to the Great War. In genre, position, interest and politics, this is a different narrative. As Noragh Jones has said, writing about Roberts's relation to traditional male-focused fiction, 'we have to rewrite the plot to make room for women's experiences'.[7] Jane Gruffydd, the focal figure of *Feet in Chains,* is married to Ifan, a slate miner, and one of her sons follows his father's work, like most of the men in the village. As Ned Thomas sums it up, the novel is clearly aware of the political situation in the quarries:

> Through Ifan we learn about the system of contract employment at the quarry, the scope it gave for bribing officials, and victimizing particular workmen. We learn, from the experience of one family, how illness meant the descent from simple poverty into poverty racked with worry and debts. Death strikes suddenly at the quarry face. The quarry-owners are far away, and English, and automatically hated. The union is just beginning to gather membership.[8]

Just as the men work on small farms as well as in the quarry, so the novel indicates the range and extent of women's work, character-ized by Noragh Jones: 'A housewife like . . . Jane Gruffydd who worked on the small-holding and made money from her poultry and her dairying still lived the old craft-based domesticity which demanded a vast range of skills.'[9]

This decisive move from the world of men's work to that of women was central to Roberts's well-known short story 'Y Condemnedig' ('The Condemned'),[10] in which a dying miner comes to appreciate his wife's presence and also her intense activity. On a much wider basis, *Feet in Chains* not only realizes women's work, but also charts a range of political issues as they impact on the domestic domain. Under the pressures of the modern world Jane sees her daughter

Sioned become a mean-minded urban bourgeoise, anglicizing her name in the process to Janet; Owen follows a structurally similar path away from the *gwerin* world through education, to become a teacher; Wiliam, who fully recognizes the economic pressures in the quarry, responds by travelling to the coal-mines of south Wales. But the starkest disruptive power of all is that of international politics: Twm, as bright as Owen but less steady, becomes a Welsh teacher (a sign of changing professional possibilities within the period of the novel), but is oppressed by a bad headmaster and joins the army. The most potent moment of the whole novel comes when the telegram from the War Office to Jane announces Twm's death only in English; the tragedy must be translated.

These powerful and defining experiences are mostly seen from Jane's own viewpoint, and the action all starts from and returns to the home she runs for her family. The genre is the family saga, and it is no accident that one of Kate Roberts's models was Chekhov, another specialist in the understated perception of historical change, seen from within the family. This is a deliberate and positive choice on Roberts's part. It may even be a conscious rejection of the male industrial novel: Jack Jones's *Rhondda Roundabout* and *Black Parade*, the heralds of the form, appeared in 1934 and 1935, and Roberts herself was living in the south at the time: trained as a Welsh teacher at the University of Wales in Bangor (like Twm), she travelled south (like Wiliam) and taught first in Ystalyfera and then Aberdare, both places steeped in the radical, populist traditions of south Wales.

Whether Roberts consciously set aside that tradition, or simply followed her own path – or both – *Feet in Chains* shows the capacity of a powerful and skilled woman writer to handle the industrial context as a formative element of the modern experience, but also as only one of them: the ultimate thrust of the novel is an implicit resistance to those forces. Derec Llwyd Morgan comments that Roberts has produced 'some of the most powerful social criticism made in Welsh Literature in the twentieth century'.[11] Jane at the end physically attacks the pensions officer who, she feels, insults the memory of her 'dear son' Twm; and Owen himself, thoughtful and recessive as he is, finally asks 'Why did they not rise up against such things?' (pp. 129, 133).

These moments have been taken as 'reflecting Kate Roberts' own decision to enter polemical journalism and politics on behalf of the Nationalists'.[12] In the same year that *Traed Mewn Cyffion* appeared she married Tom Roberts, editor of the influential Welsh nationalist weekly paper *Baner ac Amserau Cymru* (*The Banner and Times of Wales*); they edited it together from Denbigh, in north-east Wales, until his death in 1946, and for ten more years until she retired Kate Roberts herself ran this important organ of resistance to the forces that are recorded in her major novel as having negative impact on the structure of Welsh society. Through this and other writing, including her fiction, she was a major force in the Welsh nationalist movement and the associated campaign for the preservation and development of the Welsh language, as well as providing through her fiction a crucial role model for other women writers in Wales. In the power of her fiction, through the wide influence she had in Wales, in her combination of empathy with the oppressed and a stubborn sense of both the value and the possibility of principled resistance, Kate Roberts provided a model of fiction which includes the concerns of both women and men, which embraces the problems of industrialization, but is in no way limited to them or by them.

III

Menna Gallie (1920–90) was born in Ystradgynlais, just up the Swansea Valley from Ystalyfera, which Kate Roberts had recently left. Gallie's family was also Welsh-speaking, and she followed a version of Roberts's path, doing well at school and going on to the Swansea college of the University of Wales, where she studied English with Economics. But there the similarity ended; where Roberts moved around Wales in her career and marriage, Gallie married an academic philosopher turned political scientist and moved between Keele, Ulster and Cambridge before returning to south Wales when her husband retired.[13] She wrote in English, and for London publishers, and she wrote quite consciously, it would seem, against the existing models of the southern Welsh industrial novel.

Strike for a Kingdom[14] was published in 1959 but set in 1926, and both that date and the novel's title link it firmly to the English-language novels that dealt with the south Wales industrial dramas of the 1920s and 1930s, such as Gwyn Jones's *Times Like These*

(1936), set during the 1926 strike, and Lewis Jones's *Cwmardy* (1937) and *We Live* (1939) which relate a young man's growth into Marxism through the first three decades of the century.

Gallie grew up during the 1930s in Wales, and was also familiar in the post-war period with the heroic representation of coal-miners by the Polish artist Joszef Herman, herself acting as model for some of his paintings. But much in *Strike for a Kingdom* strains against the masculinist politics of traditional mining fictions. For one thing there is her characteristically humorous tone: she has an 'exuberant prose style and an inventive comic flair',[15] the jacket of the original publication compares her work explicitly with Gollancz stable-mate Gwyn Thomas, the ironic comedian of the Rhondda, and the similarity can be seen in her description of the village carnival:

> In a wave of catcalls and comments the Strike Committee men tried to form the procession up in twos: tutting and fussing and shouting orders to which nobody listened. At last they managed to get the smallest ones, two fairies in white and tinsel, to the front and the rowdy Red Indian jazz band at the back. The smallest fairy was already tired and sticky and trailed her curtain-rod wand in the dust. The mothers of the fairies hurried up to take their hands and give them courage. Next to the fairies were Joe Everynight's twelve children, all dressed in flour sacks, Spiller's Fine Ground. The smallest child's sack trailed to the ground and the sack of the eldest one scarcely covered her bottom. This one wore a card on her back, 'The Bread Line'. Their mother twitched them tidy. (p. 22)

But the blurb goes beyond Welsh comedy, indicating Gallie's major generic move by saying: 'This is a detective story that is as "different" as you could imagine.'

While the whole story is set in 'Cilhendre' – much like Ystradgynlais – during the summer of the six-month strike, its action opens with and focuses on a murder: the mine manager is found dead beside the river, and both a police inspector and a local figure are involved in solving the crime. At a stroke Gallie re-structured industrial conflict through the apparatus of a genre that was noted for being led by women writers like Christie, Sayers and Allingham.

But that generic shift is itself more firmly feminized when another body is found on the bank: a stillborn baby has been buried there very recently, and this inquiry leads even further away from industrial matters into the traumatic household of a dying woman and her neurotic brother. The discovery that he was both the distracted killer of the manager and, it seems, the incestuous father of the child directs the thematic thrust of the novel towards domestic crisis rather than political tensions.

But not all is so sombre or restricted. The viewpoints of women and children are used from chapter 1 on to give breadth to the normal narrow male focus of the Valleys novel, and Gallie uses her lighter tones, from irony to farce, in a way that Raymond Stephens sees as thematic: he feels her comedy 'is designed as a medium for the life-affirming qualities of the miners and their way of life'.[16] The presence of positive comedy is certainly marked. After a brief political comment on the strike, chapter 2 develops an amusing and highly coloured account of the village people, miners, women and children, all engaged in carnival play, but all aware of the dire political context:

> It was officially opened with a speech given by the oldest member of the Strike Committee. He was sixty-nine and still a collier, his face and hands very scarred and one eye was pulled badly out of shape. Old Eye was no Lloyd George, no orator, but miners have a touching faith in the Seniority Rule.
>
> 'Comrades,' he began, 'Comrades bach, we have gathered here to have a carnival. It is a good idea to have a bit of a spree, like, to cheer us up in these unhappy times. But, comrades, they are good times too, because they are showing that we *are* comrades, that we are one behind the other against those up by there who have brought us to this pass . . .'
> (p. 21)

The sequence supports Stephens's other comment that Gallie 'was haunted by the desire for the good community'.[17]

While this can be read as the result of a female intelligence re-handling the Valleys novel, the novel's focus of value is still male. D. J. Williams is a miner, graduate of Ruskin College, Oxford, Justice of the Peace, well-known poet and acknowledged village authority. It is he, acting as a father confessor, who works out what has been going wrong in the house next door, the source of both the dead baby and the manager's murderer. Gallie's English readers might well have seen him as a sort of genial witch-doctor operating among the intriguing tribes to be found in the then popular 'regional' novel. Welsh readers might well have seen more in his name. The writer D. J. Williams was the archetypal interpreter of the *gwerin*, and his *Hen Dŷ Ffarm* (*The Old Farmhouse*)[18] is a classic and very widely read statement of the values of place, people, poetry and Protestant religion. For Gallie to make such a figure the focal authority of a village much like her own in 1926 is to turn away from the leftist heroics of Lewis Jones and the early Gwyn Thomas and look back to a different focus of value, one much closer to Kate Roberts than the male writers that Gallie is eluding: Williams was one of the famous three who set fire to the RAF bombing school in the Llŷn peninsula in 1936, and so lit the torch of self-conscious Welsh nationalism: another was Saunders Lewis, who was a major supporter and colleague in Roberts's nationalist work over the next decades.

At the end of *Strike for a Kingdom*, D.J. reflects:

> That evening D.J. sat alone in the quiet kitchen. He, too, was feeling released and relaxed. Glad to be quiet, to be alone, to be able to think to himself. He sat in his chair, his face expressionless, his fingers tapping on the arm of the chair. When his mother came in after watering her flowers, she thought he was worrying too much and missing his friend, but she didn't speak. Her presence was for him part of the silence. Though his face looked remote and calm, he was excited and bubbling within; his poem was working out. His stomach was tensed, his fingers pulsating,the music was ordered and the words were coming right. He got up suddenly from his chair and reached for his pen and writing pad.The poem was coming. It would be all right.
> 'Earthbound and slothful, barely venturing forth . . .' (p. 200)

Gallie finally presents, in terms of the Welsh bardic tradition, the sombre male overview characteristic of the mining novel, a last generic element in this strikingly remoulded novel of south Welsh industry. *Strike for a Kingdom* expresses, through its apparent hesitations on genre and its apparent uncertainties of tone, Gallie's effort to give an account less simplistic than the male version of the industrial experience of villages like Ystradgynlais. That she was aware of both the difficulty and the importance of this project is clear when she makes her character D. J. Williams reflect how his native Welsh language is not adequate to deal with the complex industrial-ethical situation he is in; he needs another language to present 'the uncertainties and hesitations that were the truth' (p. 108).

Gallie's second industrial novel, *The Small Mine* (1962),[19] continues her rewriting of the industrial novel through recounting further events in Cilhendre. More than twenty years forward in time, the main village pit is nationalized. Joe Jenkins, a young upwardly mobile miner, gains his fireman's certificate and decides to move to a still private small mine, where he can earn more and so marry Cynthia, a smart young colliery clerk. The man he replaces, seeking vengeance on the mine-owner, wrecks the workings one Sunday. But Joe, conscientious in his work at least, is down the mine, and is killed.

So murder mystery emerges again as a generic variation, and once more inquiries follow, at some length, before the culprit is identified. Raymond Stephens is content to read the book as a version of the male industrial dramas and so thinks 'The novel never really recovers after Joe's death. Its emotional power is drained off.'[20] But it is clear enough from the start that the 'emotional power' of the novel is not simply masculinist, and a number of the patterns of *Strike for a Kingdom* are found again here, rather better developed and organized.

The opening shows Joe Jenkins underground in traditional male mode, but a woman's voice is plain in the narration, both relishing and mocking male heroics:

> In the other beams his face was black, beautified, dramatised by the coal, white eye-balls bright, a flash of teeth in the coal-rimed lips, the licked inner bottom lip wetly red, sensual, male. The others fell in behind him; the animals came in one by one, hurrah, hurrah. (p. 5)

As we meet Joe's family, the traditional pattern of big, dominant, if slightly stupid, father and patient, trusting, hard-working mother is abandoned: Joe's mother Flossie 'was a dark, darting, little woman, still trim and tight in the figure, bouncing with energy and long since out of patience and passion for her slow, kindly, insensitive husband' (pp. 7–8).

The first chapter deals with conventional enough themes: pit politics (with up-to-date issues like the problems of nationalization and even immigrant German workers), Joe's elaborate preparations for going out, his aspirations towards Cynthia. The genial encounter he has with the village children is also familiar enough, as the hero is usually kind to the young. But in this novel, these children will play an increasing role; like the women, they can have narrative authority: it is they who in fact will reveal the killer and they offer a form of wisdom and judgement, even (in chapter 14) a mock-trial, outside the adult male world of the usual pattern.

But if the first chapter is largely conventional, with some initial reorientation of viewpoint away from the masculine, the second clearly states Gallie's innovative purpose. Joe goes to the pub, talks to his mates, has sex with one of the pub women. Nothing strange about that in a manly text. But here most of the action, and all the evaluation, is presented through the resigned eyes of the woman brutally known to the men as 'Sall Ever-Open-Door':

> But she'd come to realise that there was something about her that communicated itself to men. There were men who knew by looking, catching on, that she was 'that sort', 'one of them'. She had to make no gesture, no indication; there was about her, around her, an acceptance, a servitude. She came to think of herself as belonging to a certain type of woman – she couldn't have been more explicit – a type whom men recognised; recognised as prey, as pleasure, as ease, as easy. She accepted the recognition, accepted its code. (p. 25)

Joe simply feels she is 'part of the night, the luck of the night, the pool for the leaping salmon' (p. 33). She, though, knows her minimal role, and the reader must respect that knowledge: 'She knew she had to give passivity; she concentrated on passivity as other women, the loved women, concentrated on fulfilment; this was one of the disciplines of loneliness' (p. 355).

Increasingly, the focus of narration and centre of interest is with the women. When the novel deals with work, it does so briefly: chapter 7, set in the pit, is just five pages long; the previous one, given over to the village women conversing in Cynthia's mother's shop and to Joe's subsequent encounter with Cynthia, occupies twenty-one pages, a long sequence in this short novel. The tone is vigorous as well as extended:

> Lil Cream Slices was buying navy blue school knickers from Mrs Griffiths the Stockings.
>   'Awful hard on her knickers, our Gert is. It's that old gym.'
>   'Jim? Jim who, in the Man's name?'

'Gym, girl, gymnastics, in school; wears the seat out in a couple of weeks, indeed to God. I'm buying and buying for that girl – well you know yourself, I'm forever in here for something. Education's a great thing, no doubt, but I wish it wasn't so hard on the knickers.' (p. 66)

Rich with casual comedy – and equally casual devotion to the church and the school – the passage, like the chapter, celebrates the industrial female as few texts have done. By contrast, brief to the point of reticence is the male drama of of Joe's transfer to the small mine; Stephens, pursuing his grail of the male novel, feels there is a symbolic theme here about the betrayal of the nationalized communal pit for the advancements of petty bourgeois capitalism,[21] but if that does exist in the novel it is only as a minor strand. Radical politics is also represented very briefly through Joe Kremlin, the 'old bolshevik' figure who often appears in the male fictions – but here his main role is to prompt the investigation into Joe Jenkins's death, not to construct any coherent political critique or hope for the future.

That future, in fact, is exclusively female. A classic ending to the male industrial novel is the hero moving on to another life, another set of intense experiences. Gallie turns this round. At the end of *The Small Mine* Cynthia moves on; she is saddened by Joe's death, but with her own resources, both emotional and financial, intact, she has arranged a job in Birmingham. The final pages show how she has survived both the handsome hero and the threatening attentions of the man who killed him – a sequence that in itself seems symbolic of Gallie's grappling with a dominating and single-minded masculinist genre.

IV

Different though Roberts and Gallie were in their contexts and concerns, they at least shared a background. Margot Heinemann (1913–92) was a London-based left-wing intellectual with only a political observer's knowledge of Wales, but her contribution to the reworking of the male industrial Welsh novel was as significant as that of the other two writers, and in some ways was both more complete and assured.

After graduating from Cambridge (where she studied English), Heinemann worked through the war years and after as a researcher and writer in the Labour Research Department, producing major papers and books on wages, health and economic policy, including a book advocating pit nationalization.[22] She joined the Communist Party in 1934 and, as Andy Croft shows, she remained one of its leading intellectual and cultural figures.[23] She stayed in the party when many left after the exposés of Stalinism and the invasion of Hungary in 1956, but the 'uncertainties' and 'hesitations' of those years seem to have sophisticated her position from one of a fairly hard-line leftist to that of a thoughtful analyst of people, politics and indeed the patterns of the industrial novel who in 1960 published *The Adventurers*.[24] It was successful, selling out quickly, and was reprinted in the 1962 Contemporary Fiction series by the widely read book club Readers' Union: people responded strongly to what Alan Sinfield has called 'the most positive and astute representation of working people that I have seen in the period'.[25]

Heinemann was an experienced writer and editor, albeit of non-fiction, and the book has a confident set of movements, rather different from the subtle statements about power in Roberts and the exploratory complications of tone and genre in Gallie. *The Adventurers* opens in what seems a familiar way. It is the Second World War, in Abergoch, a fictional mining area in mid-Wales. That relocation enables Heinemann to generalize about the Welsh mining industry, and also frees her fiction from the cultural imperatives of the south Welsh novel, from choirs to rugby and mountain walks; but not from politics – it seems likely that she knew that 'goch' in Abergoch means 'red'. Curiously the move also locates the novel in a area roughly similar to the setting of Raymond Williams's *Border Country* which also appeared in 1960 and which has some similarities to *The Adventurers* as a story about a young man's move away from Wales to a burgeoning career – and to the resulting relationships and evaluative comparisons with those who remained at home. Sinfield refers to both as examples of 'the revisiting fable'.[26]

While Williams's story has a modernist retrospectivity, Heinemann's begins simply enough. In the early years of the war, Dan, or Danny, Owen is an intelligent young man who refuses to be conscripted into the pits where his father and friends work. He wants to join the air force and, in any case, feels a person should 'bring to flower the talent you had in you' (p. 24). The local miners, led by his friend Tommy Rhys Evans, support him, in part on the grounds that the conscription is anti-democratic, in part because Danny, as Tommy says, 'could be something different altogether' (p. 22). The wildcat strike in the Abergoch pits is resolved by Lewis Connor, the area union agent, using Danny's alleged claustrophobia as the grounds for making him a special case. He is freed from jail, goes off to the air force, has a good war and goes on to a working man's college – not the Ruskin of reality, but Heinemann's invented Keir Hardie College at Cambridge.

Danny goes to Hardie, works hard and turns into a journalist in political economics. Heinemann's book still seems remarkably contemporary as the young Welshman, a Candide of the 1940s, enters journalism with high hopes and good intentions to serve his class faithfully after visiting a mine he writes up the men's work with admiration and respect and feels 'Although it was only talk, you were in some way joined to the work, like artist and model, both part of the same patient labour that ended in coal' (p. 135). This piece is admired by a radio journalist whom he knew as a tutor at Hardie, who represents a further stage in a possible career for an intellectual worker: Lena is from working-class Liverpool, another adventurer, but she is further along the career track and has an edgily defensive polish that Dan so far lacks: 'Lena came in, a dark purple coat over her arm. In black, with a heavy silver chain, like a slave chain, round her neck, and thick silver earrings, she looked older and smarter. Excluded, Danny rose' (p. 156).

So far Danny seems central among the 'adventurers' of the title and Heinemann seems to have set up a traditional Welsh *Bildungsroman* of a sensitive dissenting hero off on his adventures. But she takes a different turning: like Lena, he becomes enmeshed by chains of silver and is no longer excluded from the power élite. The story develops away from the cosy and easily outraged values of the usual Welsh industrial novel into an ironic and highly political narrative, showing Danny's steady corruption by the interrelated forces of the media, right-wing unions and capitalism. At the same time, and also moving away from the male protagonist beloved of traditional left fiction, he is decreasingly the focal figure as the novel goes on, and is ultimately just one of the characters who signify different political positions.

Heinemann shows how easy is the path towards career success and away from political purity. Danny does try to be loyal – his first feature is on mining issues and he does a radio talk for Lena on his experiences in the pit. Yet, subtly, his position is shifting: he arranges a radio programme but radical unionists take it over as a demonstration – they had not told him, they say, because they knew he would have to stop them. As Danny rises as a writer, he comes to the notice of powerful people: one of them is Murdoch, a prophetic name that here, Croft suggests, may be identified with Woodrow Wyatt, the Labour right-winger and godfather of many an alliance with business.[27] Danny begins to provide information for Murdoch's doubtful purposes and the crisis of betrayal comes when he shapes a television programme dedicated to destroying the campaign for union leadership by Lewis Connor, the miners' agent who saved Danny from the pits and, for all his own compromises, has remained too left-wing for the new powers in right-wing Labour and the unions.

While this media rake's progress has been going on, the novel has had little to do with Abergoch. Danny's career has been central, and other interest has focused on two parallel characters. One is Lena; the other is Richard Adams, a Cambridge leftist, well-born, an officer with a splendid war record, handsome, dynamic, ideologically committed to the Communist Party. Croft here sees the figure of the left historian E. P. Thompson,[28] and Richard's role in the novel is to play Danny's opposite. Socially descending, but never wavering from their political commitment, he and his wife end up in the Abergoch district: he is a social worker – the kind of job Danny rejected after leaving Cambridge because the money was so poor. Richard has other roles in the novel as well, representing the possibility of a cross-class coalition on the far left, and also being the focus for Heinemann's thoughts on the Communist Party trouble of the mid-1950s. He is perturbed by Khrushchev's revelations:

> It was one thing to see how injustice and cruelty could have happened and another to defend it as right. You expected the other side, the colonial lords of Kenya and Malaya, to use crude and brutal methods as the only means to prop up their own crude and brutal system. You didn't expect it of your own. (p. 304)

A hard-line rank-and-file member takes a different view:

> You middle-class comrades always do wobble when anything like this happens. You've no experience of the struggle, then. Of course it's

tough and hard – always been tough and hard – and you've got to be hard yourself. Workers realise that, they know what a fight is. The whole of life's a fight, for us. We're not wasting any tears on this bloody gang. (p. 304)

Heinemann does not resolve the issue – it was still a raw nerve on the left in 1960; but in the action a little later Richard's little son is lost, and then rescued with some affection by one of the workmen who took an anti-Communist stance. The idea of populism is not foreign to Heinemann, but the moment of sentiment, even sentimentality, is unusual in this rigorous-minded novel.

Closer to Danny in both class and trajectory, and indeed to become his wife, is Lena. The other women he likes either reject him (the upper-class Judy) or are effectively betrayed by him for career (his old Abergoch sweetheart Eva). Lena is strong rather than glamorous, moving with ease among the chattering classes of the day, and she presumably represents some of Heinemann's own experiences in the world of the media and politics; but the figure also suggests that women can have the same opportunities and temptations as men. It remains only a suggestion: unlike Roberts and Gallie, Heinemann does not explore this area further.

Lena is in fact a curiously recessive figure; only once does the novel explore her feelings in any depth and then it is because Danny himself is thinking about her, in a somewhat sexist way: 'He realised vaguely that Lena was insecure, and not only because she still had a good deal of her way to make . . . Lena, though, wanted more than this; or rather she wanted all this and the certainty of being altogether desirable as well' (p. 156).

Seeing the limits of Lena as a character makes it clear that, unlike Roberts and Gallie, Heinemann does not choose to use gender as a basis for destabilizing the traditional industrial novel. Intellectual as she was, her generic innovation lies along those lines. The title of Croft's article identifies the genre as 'socialist realism' and Heinemann evidently understands and can operate the basis of Lukács's account of historical politics in a text: though Lukács's *The Historical Novel* was not published in translation in England until 1962, its tenets were well known in left intellectual circles such as that of Heinemann and her partner J. D. Bernal. Danny is classically the 'mediocre hero' whom Lukács identified as the core of Scott's success in representing history not through a 'monumental historical figure' but, like Waverley, an ordinary weak person across whom the forces of the period would march.[29]

Such negative characterization is not all that occupies the historical politics of the realist novel, however, and nor does it in *The Adventurers*. Along the way there is a good deal of acute, if sometimes digressive, contemporary political analysis – such as the pressure on Hardie College to provide technical training rather than intellectual breadth; the way government planning is organized, or rather fixed; the struggle for power within the unions; the question of German rearmament. The plot is directly involved at this general political level when the last third of the novel brings its focus largely back on to Abergoch. Book 3 is entitled 'The Uneconomic Valley', and the issue is whether the Abergoch pits should be closed. The radical miners make too much trouble, the pits are not all that profitable, and international capital, mediated by Murdoch, would like to shut them down. The story moves out of Danny's ambit as the miners, now under the formal leadership of Tommy Rhys Evans, Danny's erstwhile wildcat supporter, backed by the local party led by Richard and by the high-level machinations of Lewis Connor, fight a battle for preservation that eventually is successful: it is they who now seem to be the adventurers of the title.

In the final sequences, Tommy returns to the centre of the action, and is now seen as the figure of value, greater even than the loyal Communists, Richard and Kate. Tommy has never left home. With a happy family, busy in his work, keeping things running, winning as many small battles as he can, he is the model of a leftist leader and acknowledged as something of a hero – including in one odd scene when Kate, Richard's politically committed and well-bred wife, suddenly realizes she loves Tommy, but in the same moment recognizes that it cannot be, and chooses to soldier on with Richard and the political struggle. Apart from this brief romantic distraction the novel is to its end politically strong, though not naïvely rosy; Tommy reluctantly accepts a move up into Connor's job and the final sense is that the struggle must continue:

> He turned back to the house. The valley lay quiet under the stars: only a distant sound of a car changing gear on the hill, and far off, in the bottom of the long cleft, the throbbing of the pumps at the pit, never ceasing, like the heart of the place. (p. 319)

For Tommy, like Richard and Kate, true adventure is true commitment, not the escape that Danny and Lena have made, nor even the high politics that Connor has essayed and largely survived. While the ending is fully in keeping with the sense of local value characteristic of the Welsh industrial novel, the book has arrived at that position in a complex and well-argued way.

That seriousness of analysis and impact may itself be a function of gender: Heinemann, as both intellectual and woman, stands outside the heroics of industrial male fiction and sees clearly the competition and the compromise of male careerism. The result is strikingly like the serious feminist thrillers of Sara Paretsky, where a commitment to criticize the masculinist structures of crime fiction brings with it the capacity to unveil political corruption in civic life in a way that male authors like Raymond Chandler offered but never delivered, so bemused were they with female threats.

In gender position, tone and genre, there is no continuity between Heinemann's work and that of Gallie, in spite of the fact that they are close contemporaries. But nor is there continuity between Gallie and Roberts, though again there are overlaps of culture and even location. These three women writers, operating from different bases and with different methodologies, have all produced potent alternatives to the traditional ways of telling the Welsh industrial story, alternatives which include not only gender politics but also a range of forces and values wider than the simple and male-imagined opposition of worker and capitalist. As Gallie indicates in the quotation used for the title of this chapter, a true account may be one that does not deal in simple certainties and rapid movements. Roberts, Gallie and Heinemann find, in just those 'uncertainties and hesitations', both a sense of 'truth' beyond the conventional accounts of the industrial experience and also a quality and weight that suggest they and their fictions have been overlooked for too long among the more celebrated male writers of Welsh industrial fiction.

Notes

[1] J. Aaron, 'Introduction', *The View across the Valley* (Dinas Powys, 1999), x–xi.

[2] Kathleen Freeman's 'The Coward' has a somewhat distant context of quarrying, and Rhian Roberts's 'The Pattern' is located in a mining town: both are

stories about human relationships, and interestingly both use a male narrator;
Dilys Rowe's 'The View across the Valley' is about a woman deliberately leaving a
steel-making town.

[3] K. Gramich, 'Introduction', *Queen of the Rushes* (Dinas Powys, 1998), 5.

[4] *Traed Mewn Cyffion* (Aberystwyth, 1936); *Feet in Chains*, trans. J. I. Jones
(Denbigh, 1979). Page references are in the text.

[5] Job 13: 26.

[6] *Chwalfa* (Aberystwyth, 1943); *Out of their Night*, trans. Richard Ruck
(Aberystwyth, 1950).

[7] In 'The comforts and discomforts of home', *Planet*, 107 (1994), 75–82, see 75.

[8] *The Welsh Extremist*, 2nd edition (Talybont, 1991), 74.

[9] Jones, 'The comforts', 79.

[10] 'Y Condemnedig', *Baner ac Amserau Cymru*, 29 (1931), 3; trans. Joseph P.
Clancy as 'The Condemned', in Alun Richards (ed.), *The Second Penguin Book of
Welsh Stories* (London, 1993), 10–18.

[11] *Kate Roberts* (Cardiff, 1974), 19.

[12] See Meic Stephens (ed.), *The Oxford Companion to the Literature of Wales*
(Oxford, 1986), 529.

[13] Gallie's career is discussed by Angela Fish in 'Flight-deck of experience', *New
Welsh Review*, 18 (1992), 60–4, and also in the foreword by Angela V. John to the
reprinted edition of *Travels with a Duchess* (Dinas Powys, 1996), pp. v–xi.

[14] London, 1959. Page references are inserted in the text.

[15] See *The Oxford Companion to the Literature of Wales*, 208.

[16] 'The novelist and community: Menna Gallie', *Anglo-Welsh Review*, 14, 34
(1964), 52–63, see 54.

[17] Stephens, 'The novelist and community', 53.

[18] Aberystwyth, 1953; trans. Waldo Williams as *The Old Farmhouse* (London,
1961).

[19] London, 1962; reprinted by Honno with an illuminating Introduction by Jane
Aaron, Dinas Powys, 2000. Page references are from the 1962 edition and are
inserted in the text.

[20] Stephens, 'The novelist and community', 58.

[21] Ibid., 54–5.

[22] *Britain's Coal* (London, 1944).

[23] 'The end of socialist realism: Margot Heinemann's *The Adventurers*', in
David Margolies and Maroula Joannou (eds.), *Heart of the Heartless World:
Essays in Cultural Resistance in Memory of Margot Heinemann* (London, 1995),
195–215.

[24] London, 1960. Page references are inserted in the text.

[25] *Literature, Politics and Culture in Postwar Britain* (Oxford, 1989), 258.

[26] Ibid., 267.

[27] Croft, 'The end of socialist realism', 215 n. 26.

[28] Ibid., 214 n. 24.

[29] See *The Historical Novel*, trans. H. and S. Mitchell (London, 1969 [1962]), 37.

14

'Work as if you Live in the Early Days of a Better Nation': Scottish Fiction and the Experience of Industry

IAN A. BELL

'It was nearly all derelict buildings down at the docks, most of them shells but some boarded up.'[1] Living now in the recently created post-industrial world, it seems an appropriate moment to review the ways in which imaginative writers have up until this point dealt with the role of industry in British culture. Although most novels and short stories remain confined to the depiction of various distinctly bourgeois individualist activities, attention can also be drawn to those few moments when industry and the workplace became unusually prominent in writing, as with the Welsh mining novels of the 1930s or the north of England factory novels of the 1950s and 1960s. However, it does not take long to realize that the record is far from perfect, and that there are very significant gaps in the literary representation of British working life. This general statement is made more serious by the ways in which particular areas have their own specific difficulties. In attempting to chart the representation of industry and industrial activities in Scottish fiction, as I am about to do, I immediately encounter a curious and vexing problem of chronology, a kind of slippage between historical reality and its representation.

In Scotland, literary fiction and heavy industry seem somehow to have got out of step with each other at some point. Simply put, Scottish fiction has been most visible and instrumental at those historical moments when Scottish industry has been a less buoyant or stable feature of the culture. In the emergent period of Scott, Galt and Stevenson during the nineteenth century, the massive growth in heavy industry which was already beginning to affect the central Lowlands had not been fully recognized or assimilated by Scottish authors or by their public. Then the period of the so-called 'Scottish Renaissance' in the 1920s and 1930s – the next major development in literature in Scotland – coincided with the great inter-war depression, when the very future of industry throughout the whole of Britain was uncertain. And, finally, the tremendous revitalization of writing in Scotland since around 1980 has happened alongside the radical process of deindustrialization, charted with differing kinds of intensity by writers like Alasdair Gray, James Kelman, Jeff Torrington and Alan Warner. So by a complex and interactive historical process, Scottish authors from the nineteenth century onwards have largely avoided the need to represent some of the central features of contemporary Scottish social and economic life, their episodic and selective commentary overlooking both the initial rapid expansion and the more gradual but eventually terminal decline of heavy industry in twentieth-century Scotland. Any reader who relied on imaginative Scottish writing alone for an account of nineteenth- and twentieth-century Scottish history would be, to say the least, patchily informed.

Although often overlooked in the past, such failures of the literary imagination are now more widely recognized. Indeed, in a well-known passage from Alasdair Gray's *Lanark: A Life in Four Books* (1981), that great manifesto for a reinvigorated Scottish fiction, the serious and damaging consequences of artists' sins of omission are made obvious:

> 'Glasgow is a magnificent city,' said McAlpin. 'Why do we hardly ever notice that?' 'Because nobody imagines living there,' said Thaw. McAlpin lit a cigarette and said, 'If you want to explain that I'll certainly listen.' 'Then think of Florence, Paris, London, New York. Nobody visiting them for the first time is a stranger because he's already visited them in paintings, novels, history books and films. But if a city hasn't been used by an artist not even the inhabitants live there imaginatively. What is Glasgow to most of us? A house, the place we work, a football park or golf course, some pubs and connecting streets. That's all. No, I'm wrong, there's also the cinema and library. And when our imagination needs exercise we use these to visit London, Paris, Rome under the Caesars, the American West at the turn of the century, anywhere but here and now. Imaginatively, Glasgow exists as a music-hall song and a few bad novels. That's all we've given to the outside world. It's all we've given to ourselves.'[2]

If imaginative writing is to be accurate, compendious and author-itative, if it is to serve as a reliable and provocative commentary on the central features of our social being, the 'here and now' in question obviously has to include a full rendering of the industrial experience, of 'the place we work'. But according to Alasdair Gray (or at least according to the authorially endorsed character through whom he speaks), the sustained misrepresentation of a major industrial city like Glasgow, built on commerce and manufacture, supported by the daily labour of unrecorded thousands, shows that this task has been lamentably overlooked and underperformed by writers, leaving the entire culture bereft of ways of imaging itself, and of remembering itself.

Although the broad sweep of this idea is very seductive, a note of caution may be necessary here. While Gray's assertion may indeed have been the case at the moment of the narrative in the 1950s – and may still have been arguable at the time of the book's publica-tion in 1981 – it is surely no longer an easily tenable position. Over the last twenty years, there has been an extraordinary outpouring of contending 'imaginings' of life in Scotland, paying fresh and serious attention to a great many previously overlooked sectors of society and areas of human activity. Alongside its more traditional attachment to the recreational lives of the middle classes, petit-bourgeois merchants, razor kings and the philosophical captain of a Clyde puffer, recent Scottish fiction has also dealt with the lives of individuals as they are defined by their employment: soldiers, fishermen, shopkeepers, policemen, criminals, schoolteachers, a cinema usherette, a supermarket employee, a supervisor of security installations, a public health inspector, and (famously) the bus conductor. The range of characters and experiences presented in more recent fiction is certainly an impressive one, and the sense of a real yearning on behalf of authors and readers to give voices to the previously silenced is unmistakable. But for all the ackowledge-ment of the varieties of 'the place we work', there remains very little real or sustained engagement with the particular impact of industry on the lives of Scots, past and present.

And, perhaps surprisingly, this is really nothing new. Although Scotland was for a long time an extensively industrialized nation, prominent internationally in its output from the heavy manufac-turing and engineering industries, that central feature of the culture was rarely the focus of its artistic intelligence. More often than not operating within the broad forms of historical narrative and romance established by the major and persistent influences of Sir Walter Scott and Robert Louis Stevenson, Scottish authors in the early part of the twentieth century traditionally seemed reluctant to confront the economic and social realities of their contemporary culture, preferring more sentimental alternatives.

Now that we live in a rapidly deindustrialized society, in the early days of the post-industrial nation, it is as though the whole growth, success and eventual failure of heavy industry in Scotland has gone largely unrecorded in our imaginative literature. In Gray's terms, it is not one of the things we have given to the outside world. And it is not one of the things we have given to ourselves.

An obvious cause for this silence has been the ambivalence with which Scottish writers have recorded the principal venue for industry, the industrial city. The overwhelming rural and small-town bias in earlier Scottish writing has often been remarked upon by commentators. Writing in 1888, J. M. Robertson was among the first to identify the problem: 'What tolerable Scotch fiction we have tends to deal only fragmentarily with rural lives and never with the collective life of our larger towns.'[3] This brief reflection was undeniably accurate at the time, its emphasis on the 'collective' nature of urban life very suggestive, and increasingly impassioned versions of the same sentiment surface as a constant complaint in accounts of Scottish writing throughout this century. In his splendidly titled *Literature and Oatmeal* (1935), William Power claimed: 'Though Scotland had been severely industrialised . . . and though Glasgow was one of the largest of British cities, it was still assumed, for literary purposes, that the majority of Scots people lived in rustic villages.'[4] And even as recently as 1956, the novelist and critic George Blake could make virtually the same point, in very strong and indignant terms:

> In the meantime, Scotland had been most miserably industrialised . . . The time came when fully two-thirds of the population of Scotland was immured within the narrow Clyde-Forth belt. In other words, the essential life of the Scottish people was thus narrowly and sordidly confined. So we ask what the contemporary Scottish writers had to say about this almost melodramatic state of affairs . . . Was there nobody in Scotland to tell the truth about what was happening? And to our question we get a dusty answer. The representative Scottish writers of the period went on – and on – representing their coevals as either bucolic philosophers or eagle-plumed gallants in the heather . . .[5]

Writing forty years before its release, Blake here makes an uncanny (if unwitting) prophecy of the success of the film *Braveheart*.

Power and Blake and the others are writing polemically, of course, and no doubt they are deliberately generalizing rather too much in order to make a point. They speak the truth, I believe, but perhaps not the whole truth. On closer inspection, a number of fictional accounts of industrial activity in Scotland can be discovered, although they are often ambivalent in attitude and difficult to interpret. Even in writing which seems to be overtly committed to urban experience as the defining feature of modern existence, the representation of industry is complex and uncertain of its direction. In *Grey Granite*, the final volume of Lewis Grassic Gibbon's monumental trilogy, *A Scots Quair* (1932–4), there is a genuine attempt to get inside urban factory life. Near the end of the novel, the politically committed Ewan Tavendale has taken up a low-skill industrial job in Duncairn, working on the shop floor in the brutalizing environment of Gowans and Gloag:

> Gowans and Gloag made metal containers. Bolts and girders and metal trestles, fine castings for sections of engine casings, a thousand men working in great rattling sheds built to hold the labour of three times the number in a rattle and roar of prosperity. Ewan Tavendale would think of that now and then, Gowans had flourished just after the War, high wages and bonuses dished out to all, pap for the proletariats. Wonder what they did with the high money then? – Spent it on the usual keelie things, dogs and horse-racing and sleeping with whores, poor devils – it had nothing to do with him.[6]

This is a very odd perception indeed. Not only does it suggest a sudden and recent decline in industrial activity – 'a thousand men working in great rattling sheds built to hold the labour of three times the number' – it also withholds sympathy for those still involved. The whole description is focalized through the perception of Ewan, who retains the apparently unique capacity to reflect on the situation, but there is also some authorial interference. By the deliberate omission of the pronoun – 'Wonder what they did with the high money then?' – we must remain uncertain as to whose perception this is, offered with what authority. Does the dismissive sneer at 'the usual keelie things' emanate from Ewan's own puritanical streak, or from the author's lack of engagement with urban working-class lives? Or is it a direct rhetorical challenge to readers, soundly chastising the imaginative failure of the existing urban proletariat?

The text itself offers no clear answers to these questions, preferring to flaunt the brutalizing effects of the factory on those who work there, in order to create sympathy for the radically un-representative and alienated figure of Ewan himself, rather than for his 'keelie' workmates. Once again, the dilemmas of the liberal and sensitive marginalized individual – a motif so central to the whole project of the novel as a literary form at this time – are given priority over the collective nature of urban and industrial experi-ence. Although the book ends with Ewan heading south to embark on a solitary life of political activism, the collective experience of the workplace remains drastically under-recorded by the author, and the narrative concludes with an elegiac return to a rural environment.

In another central 'realist' text of the 1930s, George Blake's *The Shipbuilders* (1935), a comparable sense of the debilitating effects of the Depression is recognizable. Although the book strives to render something of the flavour of industrial experience at all levels, it is prevented from a fully realized account by the sense of crisis it expresses. At one point, Leslie Pagan, owner of a Clyde shipyard, takes a trip down the river on a newly launched ocean liner, built in his own yard. Seeing the great ship *Estremadura* as the only important remaining commission in any of the yards, he reads the scene passing before him as a relic of better days:

> It was in a sense a procession that he witnessed, the high, tragic pageant of the Clyde. Yard after yard passed by, the berths empty, the grass growing about the sinking keel-blocks. He remembered how, in the brave days, there would be scores of ships ready for the launching along this reach, their sterns hanging over the tide, and how the men at work on them on high stagings would turn from the job and tug off their caps and cheer the new ship setting out to sea. And now only the gaunt, dumb poles and groups of men, workless, watching in silence the mocking passage of the vessel. It was bitter to know that they knew – that almost every man among them was an artist in one of the arts that go to the building of a ship; that every feature of the *Estremadura* would come under an expert and loving scrutiny, that her passing would remind them of the joy of work and tell them how many among them would never work again.[7]

Pagan's lofty and deeply pessimistic perception of the decline of the shipping industry is confirmed in the novel by the parallel narrative of the worker Danny Shields. The two men are linked by personal acquaintance, having served together in the trenches during the Great War, and though socially far apart, they are further paired by sharing in the decline of industry. Shields is a riveter in Pagan's yard, but loses his job early on in the novel. Instead of dealing with the day-to-day business of industry, the book then concentrates on the full range of working-class recreational activities, featuring a zesty combination of gambling, drinking and anti-Semitism. As Danny goes on to rebuild his life, he finds no avenues back into industry, and instead reinvents himself as a door-to-door supplier of firewood.

The distanced, always uneasy, perception of industrial life found in both Gibbon and Blake is a recurrent feature of Scottish writing at this difficult and volatile time, with both writers clearly thinking that 'the brave days' are gone. But why should it be so? I have so far hidden behind the unexamined notion that there are complex historical processes at work here – and there are, even though to say that is only an act of labelling rather than the beginning of a proper explanation – but to clarify the quiddity of the Scottish presentation, I want to suggest that there may be three discernible reasons for the lack of a more complete and nuanced representation.

As has already been suggested, the first factor may be found in the conventionalized representations of the country and the city which remain deeply embedded in preceding and contemporary British writing. As a feature primarily of the urban experience in Scotland (unlike in Wales, for example, where the south Wales mining valleys remained as much smaller knowable communities), industry will enter its texts on terms of reference arrived at more generally elsewhere. The way in which any literature will be able to portray industry will necessarily be dependent on the ways it has previously imagined urban experience. As Raymond Williams puts it in *The Country and the City* (1973):

On the actual settlements, which in the real history have been astonishingly varied, powerful feelings have gathered and have been generalized. On the country has gathered the idea of a natural way of life: of peace, innocence, and simple virtue. On the city has gathered

the idea of an achieved centre: of learning, communication, light.
Powerful hostile associations have also developed: on the city as a place
of noise, worldliness and ambition; on the country as a place of
backwardness, ignorance, limitation.[8]

Williams offers a more abstract and schematic account of the
problem identified earlier by Robertson, Power and Blake. In this
formulation, no writer ever starts out with a completely blank
sheet of paper: writing always has to inherit 'gatherings', pre-
conceptions and associations from the past, and it always has to
negotiate with them. A Scottish writer describing rural life may
choose to emphasize the positive associations (as in 'kailyard'
writing) or the negative (in, say, *Gillespie* or *The House with Green
Shutters*). Any writer newly embarking on such a project will
inherit these associative representations, as indeed Gibbon himself
does in the first volume of *A Scots Quair*, and may set them in
dialogue. Scottish literature affords an extensive array of depic-
tions of the country, and writers have much to negotiate with.
However, writers embarking on urban narratives have much less
support, and without this intertextual penumbra their accounts are
inevitably thinner and less densely allusive.

For Scottish authors at this period of the 1930s, there are very
few appropriate positive precedents for a representation of city life
or industry, because so few writers seem to have imagined living
there. The city as formulated in earlier Scottish writing remains the
city of dreadful night, as any reading of Edwin Muir or Hugh
MacDiarmid will confirm. The problems encountered by Lewis
Grassic Gibbon in *Grey Granite* are symptomatic of this silence,
and it may even be argued that the absence of a positive rendering
of urban life was a powerful force in the dwindling of the Scottish
Renaissance after the mid-1930s, and in its failure to replenish itself
or to attract a wider metropolitan audience.

Not until Alasdair Gray threw out the challenge to imagine
Glasgow anew in 1981 did a more confident urban voice emerge,
uttered by Gray himself, as well as James Kelman, Tom Leonard,
Agnes Owens, Alan Spence and many others. But as far as industry
went, perhaps it was already too late, for by that time the major
shipbuilding and steel industries had been reduced to mere
remnants of their earlier incarnations. Writing, it seems, may
always be retrospective, better at remembering than at confronting,

for reasons arising from its social location and function. Forming part of the superstructure of any society, literature may always be reactive and sometimes slow to respond to stealthy and concealed changes in the base. As Walter Benjamin put it in 'The work of art in the age of mechanical reproduction': 'The transformation of the superstructure which takes place far more slowly than that of the substructure, has taken more than half a century to manifest in all areas of culture the change in conditions of production . . .'[9] If we accept Benjamin's observation, then imaginative writing is always poorly equipped to address the 'here and now', better at nostalgia than at contemporary analysis. Again, this is a provocative suggestion, but it seems applicable to the situation of Scottish writers. In short, when there was industry in Scotland, no one wrote about it. And when they wrote about it, there was no longer any industry.

A final factor is identified, if rather flamboyantly, by Jack Mitchell, as the essentially collaborative nature of writing alleged to be 'working class':

> One of the 'achievements' of decadent bourgeois literature in the 20th century has been the pseudo-working-class novel, usually the work of middle-class or declassed authors. Scotland has had more than its fair share of them. This type of book has the full support of the Establishment's commercial machine. As a result they . . . have been widely identified with the 'Scottish working-class novel' as such. This has conveniently obscured the fact that there is another more genuine tradition of working-class novel writing in Scotland.[10]

This account of the pseudo-working-class novel sounds plausible, and Mitchell singles out George Blake as a prominent example. It may be true that both Blake and Gibbon fall into the categories of the 'declassed', and that few genuinely working-class writers, informed by the experience of industry, could be found, however hard we looked. None the less, Mitchell's claim for some 'other more genuine tradition' is very hard to substantiate, and it is the more pessimistic part of his statement that rings true.

So the case has been put forward. Scottish writing cannot truly confront the urban, or the contemporary, and its authors have little genuine experience of the industrial environment. But that is not the end of the story. The interesting thing is that those features which most seriously disable the presentation of industrialized society in Scotland actually serve to enable the presentation of post-industrial society. With the erosion of strict class divisions (or at least, the erosion of the loyalties they once generated), with the visible decline in civic prosperity and with the earlier days of industry now suitable for elegiac treatment, a new post-industrial wrtiting has become possible.

Many writers are involved in this project, including Gray and Kelman, but it has reached far beyond any literary coterie and addressed a wider public. The following passage from Irvine Welsh's massively popular *Trainspotting* (1991) shows the new range of tone:

> We go fir a pish in the auld Central Station at the Fit ay the Walk, now a barren, desolate hangar, which is soon tae be demolioshed and replaced by a supermarket and swimming centre. Somehow, that makes us sad, even though ah wis eywis too young tae mind ay trains ever being there. Some size ay a station this wis. Git a train tae anywhair fae here, at oane time, or so they sais, ah sais, watching ma steaming pish splash oantae the cauld stane. *If it still hud fuckin trains, ah'd be oan one oot ay this fuckin dive, Begbie said. It wis uncharacteristic for him tae talk aboot Leith in that way. He tended tae romanticise the place.*
>
> An auld drunkard, whom Begbie had been looking at, lurched up tae us, wine boatil in his hand. Loads ay them used this place tae bevvy and crash in.
> – What yis up tae lads? Trainspottin, eh? He sais, laughin uncontrollably at his own fuckin wit. [11]

The 'auld drunkard' turns out to be Begbie's father, and the whole episode dramatizes a collapse in the social fabric. For these characters, 'a house, the place we work' – Gray's touchstones – have all been transformed into functionless and almost entirely useless places. The site of major industrial activity has become 'a barren, desolate hangar'; the industrial workforce is represented by an 'auld drunkard'. Throughout this book, Welsh's characters live lives without shape or purpose, narrated without any encompassing or totalizing authorial attitude. The fact that this site of industrial activity – remembered warmly in an unfocused sort of way – is to be turned into a supermarket reinforces the novel's move from the industrial society to a consumerist culture, and the casual way in which the author offers his forlorn cultural pessimism becomes deeply disquieting.

Not all accounts of the post-industrial world, however, are as bereft of real compassion as Welsh makes himself out to be. Both

James Kelman, in many short stories and most powerfully in *How Late It Was, How Late* (1994), and Alan Warner, in *The Sopranos* (1998), make more humane cases for living after the industries have closed down or gone elsewhere. Neither writer is facile or casually optimistic, but in each a sense of humanity can be seen behind the bitter or anarchic narrative.

In each case, there seems to be a conflict in the texts between remembering a way of life that has gone, and being uncertain about what is to follow. The blind narrator of Kelman's novel seems devoid of purpose, assailed by the culture in which he lives, and deeply unsure of what to do next. The schoolgirl choristers in Warner's much more exuberant novel approach the city with a winning mixture of innocence and knowingness. Both books attempt to confront urban life, however, as it now is, at a moment of decisive change, when nothing will be the same ever again.

That sense of an ending and a simultaneous beginning can now be found in many texts. The days of building ships and trains may be over, but the days of building a new culture are only just starting. In Ian Rankin's novel *Dead Souls* (1999), the venue for a new creation is described:

> Later that night, he found himself in Cowgate again, further to the east this time, past the mothballed mortuary, walking towards the building site on Holyrood. Behind it, he could make out a couple of the Greenfield tower-blocks, and behind those Salisbury Crags. The sun had set, but it wasn't quite dark. The twilight could last an age at this time of year. Demolition work had stopped for the day. He couldn't be sure where everything would go, but he knew there'd be a newspaper building, a theme park, and the Parliament building. They'd all be ready for the twenty-first century, or so the predictions went. Taking Scotland into the new millennium. Rebus tried to raise within himself a tiny cheer of hope, but found it stifled by his old cynicism.[12]

In writing a detective novel, Ian Rankin has inevitably been probing into the past, looking for explanations and origins. But he ends the narrative at a point of rebuilding, radically unsure about whether the past can be overcome. As his character sees it, the 'tiny cheer' is silenced by 'the old cynicism'. But other writers seek a more optimistic position. The old industries may have gone, but in the new post-industrial world the writer himself (or herself) has emerged as a more potent cultural force, agitational and imaginative, seeking to define identities and create a sense of purpose. As Alasdair Gray said, in a slogan embossed on the cover of *Poor Things*: WORK AS IF YOU LIVE IN THE EARLY DAYS OF A BETTER NATION.[13]

Notes

[1] James Kelman, 'Joe laughed', *The Good Times* (London, 1998), 1.

[2] Alasdair Gray, *Lanark: A Life in Four Books* (Edinburgh, 1981), 243.

[3] J. M. Robertson, quoted in Moira Burgess, *Imagine a City: Glasgow in Fiction* (Argyll, 1998), 26.

[4] William Power, *Literature and Oatmeal* (1935), quoted in Burgess, *Imagine a City*, 26.

[5] George Blake, *Annals of Scotland, 1895–1955* (London, 1956), quoted in Burgess, *Imagine a City*, 26–7.

[6] Lewis Grassic Gibbon, *A Scots Quair* (London, 1934), 372.

[7] George Blake, *The Shipbuilders* (London, 1935), 118.

[8] Raymond Williams, *The Country and the City* (London, 1973), 9.

[9] Walter Benjamin, 'The work of art in the age of mechanical reproduction', in *Illuminations* (London, 1970), 219–20.

[10] Jack Mitchell, 'The struggle for the working-class novel in Scotland', quoted in Burgess, *Imagine a City*, 112–13.

[11] Irvine Welsh, *Trainspotting* (London, 1991), 308–9.

[12] Ian Rankin, *Dead Souls* (London, 1999), 405.

[13] Alasdair Gray, *Poor Things* (London, 1992).

15

People Like That: the Fiction of Agnes Owens

INGRID VON ROSENBERG

Agnes Owens presents the rare case of a female working-class writer. Even in the 1930s and in the late 1950s, the two periods when working-class writing was blooming, there were very few women among the authors. One of the reasons was probably that the key industries, providing most of the manual work, were still male-dominated: shipbuilding, mining, machine-tool and car production, for example. While working men, through a lifelong involvement in such industries, could build a sense of identity or even pride through work, women rarely had the opportunity to do so. For them, if they kept working at all after marriage, work was little more than a means to earn money, to supplement, often in a variety of jobs, the family income.

With the decline of heavy industry and the concomitant rise in unemployment since the 1970s, with the growth of industries based on modern technology and the increasing importance of the service sector, the work (or redundancy) experiences of men and women have become less differentiated. But to this day, despite feminism's urging of women from all strata to articulate their positions, the female working-class writer remains an exception.

Before she joined, in her fifties, a writing class in Alexandria, West Dumbartonshire, run by tutors from the University of Glasgow, Agnes Owens's life was not markedly different from that of other working women of her generation (she was born in 1926). 'I suppose you could say my life was a struggle, as it is with most men and women of the working class even in years of good employment . . . I always worked when possible at anything I could find, i.e. in shop, office or factory.'[1] Out of economic necessity she continued, for example, to work as a cleaner even after she was a published writer in the 1980s. Owens's life was also typical for one of her class, sex and generation in that she married early and had a large family to look after, four children from her first marriage, and more from her second.

There is a distinct Scottishness about Agnes Owens's work, shaping her choice of character and setting and colouring her style and use of language. By the critics she has been recognized as 'part of a Golden Age in Scottish literature'.[2] So far Agnes Owens has published five books: the novels *Gentlemen of the West* (1984), *Like Birds in the Wilderness* (1987), *A Working Mother* (1994) and *For the Love of Willie* (1998); and a collection of stories, *People Like That* (1996). She also published a collection of stories jointly with James Kelman and Alasdair Gray, *Lean Tales* (1985). Alasdair Gray, experienced in the world of literature and the book market, has supported her with friendship, advice and practical help, contributing, for example, the jacket drawings for *People Like That* and *A Working Mother*, and even acting as her agent.

With her background it seems small wonder that Owens, at the beginning of her literary career, should have taken up patterns of earlier working-class writing, which were, however, predominantly male. Her first two novels, though following different narrative traditions, form a sequence. Both are told as first-person narratives in the voice of a twenty-two-year-old 'brickie', a bricklayer from west Scotland. The language is simple and interspersed with the occasional Scottish word such as 'broo' (Labour Exchange) or 'bevvy' (beverages), while most of the dialogues are written in a mild version of Scots which, however, never presents any serious obstacles to the understanding of a broader readership.[3] The time of action of both novels is the Thatcher years, when intensifying economic decline hit Scotland particularly badly and the laws protecting workers' rights were scrapped: 'There's nae protection onywhere nooadays', says the 'ganger' on a building site to the hero when the latter mentions the Employment Protection Act of 1974.[4] It is significant that, with the exception of the young hero and his workmates, who manage to find jobs, though with interruptions, and people working in pubs or other services, the majority of the protagonists are permanently unemployed. A prominent group are some elderly tramps, ironically termed

'Gentlemen of the West', who while away their time drinking in pubs or, if money is short, under the bridges. Already these two earliest of Owens's books are less concerned with the experience of work than with the lack of it or the fear of losing it. If Owens, when choosing the building industry for her hero's context, was thinking of making a link back to one of the great classics of working-class literature, Robert Tressell's *The Ragged Trousered Philanthropists*, her approach is – in response to a fundamentally changed historical situation – totally different. While Tressell, writing in the early 1900s, had no doubts about the necessity of work as such and was merely concerned with the unjust organization of it in capitalist society, Agnes Owens's characters, by contrast, have to come to terms with a world in which work itself has become a scarcity, not merely for cyclical, but for structural reasons. While nobody in Owens's books reflects theoretically on this great change in the articulate manner of Tressell's hero Frank Owen, the consequences are registered in the bewildered psychological state of many of her characters.

Owens's strength does not lie in broad epic descriptions nor in in-depth studies of the individual psyche, but rather in the brief poignant episode. The short story comes naturally to her as a narrative form, and her longer fiction tends to be either extended novellas, such as her last two novels, or of an episodic structure, such as her first two. The episodes of her very first novel *Gentlemen of the West*, which draws on the rogue and hooligan tradition of English literature, place in the centre either the hero, Mac, or one of his much older drinking companions. Some of the stories are harmless jokes like, for instance, the story of an inexpert burglary undertaken by Mac and a friend which ends with their arrest, reminiscent of the mishap of Sillitoe's long-distance runner. A particularly comic story is the one of Mac's chance meeting with a German, in which the British stereotype of the militarist Hun is deconstructed. Other episodes, however, have a more serious note to them, signalling the mental degradation of the people and foreshadowing the grim tales Owens will tell in her later work. There is, above all, the story of Paddy McDonald's death. Paddy is one of the old tramps, unemployed and an alcoholic, who lives in a ramshackle cottage on the outskirts of town, which is nevertheless a favourite meeting-place of his cronies because of its warm atmosphere. One Christmas morning Paddy is found almost frozen stiff outside the local pub, and it turns out someone has burnt down his house and killed his pigeons, 'maybe the cat as well'.[5] Though Paddy is found by his friends, only Mac is willing to help and even he does so with a grudge: 'I was dying to get away but it was difficult to leave a potential corpse, especially at this time of the year.'[6] Paddy then dies in the pub where Mac has brought him, ignoring the protest of the landlord. On the whole, however, in this first of Owens's novels, human relations are still fairly intact, especially family ties. Though there is much bickering between Mac and his mother, who brought him up alone, there is warmth underneath. When Mac, unable to find any more employment in his home town, decides to go north to where the North Sea oil promises better opportunities, both feel genuine regret:

> 'I'll miss you,' was all she said. 'I'll miss you as well.' It was true. Right then I felt I would genuinely miss her. After all we had been together for twenty-two years. I put my arm round her cold shoulder, 'Don't worry, I'll be OK.'[7]

In her second novel *Like Birds in the Wilderness*, which describes Mac's experiences in the north, Owens uses the picaresque model to replace the rather loose structure of *Gentlemen of the West*. When the novel opens, Mac lives in a doss-house, surrounded by a colourful group of characters all living on the margin of society, and works under hard conditions on a building site. With the first cuts he loses his job and moves even further north in search of employment, accompanied by his girlfriend. In an old newspaper he has read about a planned new settlement, which, however, turns out to be a scam. This journey north is an interesting reversal of the journey south to London as a lively centre of economic activity promising not only gainful, but interesting work, so familiar a topos for heroes in novels of the 1950s and 1960s: Keith Waterhouses's Billy Liar, John Wain's Charles Lumley, Kingsley Amis's Lucky Jim, Alan Sillitoe's Frank Dawley and many others followed this route. But the lure of Scotland's north proves illusory, so that Mac at the end returns home to accept work as a caravan driver for the once despised ragman, who – a model disciple of Thatcher's enterprise ideology – has become a successful businessman.

Like Birds in the Wilderness gives a less convincing reflection of the situation of the Scottish working class than the first part of the sequence, partly perhaps because Owens, possibly in order to give more coherence to her narrative, drew on two further literary traditions: the romance and the adventure story. The love story between Mac and the office girl Nancy is of the conventional bitter-sweet type, ending with separation, and the adventure story is confused. It circles round Mac's repeated encounters with two suspicious characters, possibly police informers, whom he comes across on his journey again and again under weird circumstances. One small episode does nevertheless deserve special mention. Through the workings of these two, Mac at one stage finds himself in a mental home after a night of heavy drinking. This scene heralds many subsequent ones in Owens's work in which lunatic asylums are favourite locations, no doubt symbolizing the state of society.

Critics have uttered mild surprise that Owens as an elderly woman should have chosen a young and extremely masculine hero for her first two novels, apparently following the example of such successful working-class writers of the 1950s and 1960s as Alan Sillitoe and Sid Chaplin. Even her mentor Alasdair Gray seemed to wonder about this aspect of her work. In an article 'Thoughts suggested by Agnes Owens's *Gentlemen of the West* and an appreciation of it', he wrote that 'no talented male author' in the 1980s could still cheerfully embody himself in 'an unambitious bricklayer',[8] labouring with his hands. Their situation was so depressing that any male with guts and imagination would rather want to write of someone breaking out. He concluded with the suggestion: '*Gentlemen of the West* could only be written by someone who knew and liked building workers, and, without approving the harsh and violent parts of their lives, found a certain release in imagining them. It had to be written by a mother.'[9]

Whether such criticism had any effect on Owens or not is hard to say. In any case she gradually shifted to a more interesting – because more contemporary and original – sort of writing, including a wider variety of topics and protagonists. The majority of the protagonists now became female, though the social setting of the later fiction remained working-class, or in some cases lower middle-class. The locale is often recognizably the run-down or even derelict parts of towns in the depressed areas, particularly the Glasgow of the 1980s. Yet, apart from the drab streets and shabby interiors of Glasgow's poor quarters, there are also places of action that could be anywhere in the industrialized northern hemisphere: a golf course, a park, a train, a station, a hotel, a meeting hall, a beach. Two stories are even located in the south of France and one in South America. The view is thus widening from the concentration on a particular depressed area to visions of a more general decay: Glasgow has become a cipher for post-industrial society. In this Owens goes along with (or was perhaps encouraged to follow by?) some of her Scottish male colleagues, notably Alasdair Gray and James Kelman.

Owens's use of language also undergoes a change. All attempts at a jokey tone have been dropped. Her characteristic combination of simple, straightforward narrative with extensive dialogue, some-times in Standard English, sometimes in mild dialect, remains, however, and serves her new purpose of general applicability very well. Moreover, her narrative has become economical to the point of being laconic and, with the exception of some of her earliest stories, is almost totally lacking in authorial commentary: her stories are indeed 'lean tales' whose meaning cannot easily be pinned down. This is also because the social realism has given way to a writing in which the borderlines between the real and the imagined are blurred. As in much of contemporary fiction, the world takes on inexplicable, frightening and sometimes even surrealist features. In the story 'Fellow Travellers' from *Lean Tales*, for instance, in which a young woman makes a temporary escape from her possessive mother by catching the next train, it is not clear whether her fellow travellers, an elderly couple and a middle-aged man, are really hostile or whether she is imagining it. And in a story called 'A Change of Face' it remains unexplained why an ugly woman who undergoes plastic surgery should wake up with the face of her room mate, a whore, who happens to disappear at the same time.

But the most impressive example is the story 'The Lighthouse' from *People Like That*. This, of course, has its ironical intertextual reference point in Virginia Woolf's novel *To the Lighthouse*, which established a meaningful pattern of human relationships. Megan, a ten-year-old girl, is left on the beach to look after her three-year-old brother Bobby. Being bored, she bullies the reluctant little boy to follow her to the lighthouse in the distance. When they eventually climb a dune for a better view, they arrive at a golf course, where they meet a man who tells them to beware the flying balls.

Thinking of her parents' warning of strangers, Megan pulls her brother away and they resume their walk. Soon, however, they start quarrelling, and Megan marches furiously off on her own. When she finally arrives at the lighthouse, she is not only disappointed but suddenly frightened. Hurrying back, she sees her brother digging in the sand, oblivious of the man from the golf course standing close behind him. Shouting and running towards him, Megan stumbles over a rock and splits her head open. The man bows down to check whether she is still alive:

> When her eyes flickered he put his hand over her mouth and nose and held it there for a considerable time. After that he turned to Bobby saying, 'We'll have to get an ambulance. You can come with me.' Bobby said he didn't want to get an ambulance. He wanted to go back to the other beach. 'All right', said the man, taking him by the hand and dragging him towards the sand dunes with Bobby protesting all the way. His cries died down when they vanished over the top.[10]

It is impossible to fix a particular meaning to this disturbing story. Is it meant as a cautionary tale? Is it a psychological story about a sister–brother relationship? Is it a pervert's story? Is Megan's death accidental, deserved punishment for her negligence, or a pointless crime? Even Bobby's fate is open – will he have to die too or will he 'only' be raped? Only one thing seems certain: that there is violence in this world and that the reasons are dark.

While direct political comment is hardly ever an issue in Owens's work, in her stories she, even more strictly than before, focuses on the human effects of the social, political and economic circumstances. Most of the main characters are people who were not fit or clever enough to leave Glasgow in the darkening depression to find jobs in the south; they are the people who stayed behind, the sad inhabitants of the post-industrial city. Work no longer yields an identity in this world. Most of Owens's Glaswegian 'people like that' are not only temporarily unemployed but have drifted to, or been driven to, the margins of society, are drug addicts, alcoholics or mental cases, many of them women, though there are some who are better off in the financial sense.

One group of her stories centres on chance encounters between such people, who meet as strangers. The outcome is invariably depressing: take 'Bus Queue' in *Lean Tales*. The people at a

suburban bus stop on a particularly chilly evening fail to realize the
danger a boy is in. He is harassed by members of a rival youth
gang, who eventually stab him to death while the bus is driving off.
'The boy was dismissed from their thoughts. They were glad to be
out of the cold and on their way.'[11] The common denominator of
such stories is clear: human solidarity among strangers does not
work any more under the circumstances of post-industrial society,
though the people do not necessarily intend evil.

Even more depressing than the tales of chance meetings are those
that deal with core relationships – parents and children, sisters,
couples – which form the bigger share of the stories. In contrast to
Mac's relationship with mother and girlfriend in the early novels,
relationships which were still basically intact, close bonds in the
stories prove brittle, cold and unreliable, sometimes to the point of
betrayal and even murder (though there are some comical versions
too, like, for instance 'The Silver Cup' about mutual mistrust
between father and son). The woman protagonist of the story 'The
Castle' from *People Like That* masterminds her sister's death
during a holiday in France in order to have their inheritance to
herself. And in 'The Marigold Field', from the same volume, a
woman finds good reason to suspect her father of having tried to
drown her little brother. 'The Warehouse' from *People Like That* is
a particularly sad story, in which a middle-aged homeless woman,
deserted by her lover for a young girl, accidentally sets fire to
herself in a deserted shed, falling asleep with a burning cigarette in
a state of utter drunkenness. With such stories and images Owens
very effectively deconstructs the myth of the family as a warm
haven of solidarity and love, a bulwark against a hostile outside
world.

Many of the stories are very aptly wrapped in a cold and wet,
often also dark, atmosphere skilfully sketched with a few words:
'The hut was so dark and dreary that I wished I had never come.
Hardboard covered the windows to keep intruders out. I asked my
husband if we should light a fire . . . "My feet are freezing." '[12] The
main defence against the general feeling of chill is alcohol – cheap
sickly sweet wine which, to increase the sense of misery, is often
bought from the off-licence and swilled down in draughty corners
rather than enjoyed in the communal warmth of a pub.

Not all of Owens's characters, however, are meekly resigned to
the deplorable state of the world. Some, particularly women, put

up a brave resistance. There is a mother who – in the good old working-class tradition of defying 'them' – eloquently defends her lout of a son against the headmistress of the school, though she is determined to punish him herself later for bullying fellow pupils. There is Léonie, the heroine of one of the two French stories in *People Like That*, who leaves a brutal husband and goes to live with an aunt. And there is, above all, Arabella in the story of the same title in *Lean Tales*, a wonderfully crazy old hag living on prostitution and by selling obscure health potions, who gets rid of an unfortunate sanitary inspector in her own way.

Though she is less successful in her single-handed fight against the world, the most interesting of Owens's female characters, however, is Betty, the heroine and first-person narrator of her third novel *A Working Mother* (1994). If it is difficult in many of Owens's stories to decide whether the protagonists are either more wicked or more the victims, this is particularly true of Betty. She tells her story – as becomes clear only at the end – in a mental home to a fellow patient, who sometimes follows the narrative greedily, sometimes drops off to sleep. In a moment of exasperation with her inattentiveness Betty shouts at her: 'Supposing I told you I made the whole thing up? Only some of it is true . . . When you're in here everything gets too jumbled up, it's hard to know the truth.'[13] The reader is not only left to draw his or her own conclusions from the chain of events, but the story itself is explicitly steeped in doubt, with Betty being established as the constructor of her own story. As a mental case and an alcoholic, she is a particularly unreliable narrator.

Betty tells of her stunted life in a tiny suburban house in Glasgow and her unhappy marriage to Adam, an unemployed ex-soldier, their two children Rae (aged eight) and Robert (aged ten) and Adam's friend Brendan, Betty's lover. And she tells of her new job as a typist, which she has taken on to top up the meagre family income; she tells of her colleague Mai, a young single mother, of her boss, seventy-year-old Mr Robson, a lawyer, who in his leisure time is engaged in a private research on 'human behaviour in animals', and of Mrs Rossi, her adviser at the labour exchange, who likes to tell fortunes. In Betty's presentation, all these people are crazy or deranged: Adam is said to suffer from the after-effects of (unrevealed) war experiences, Brendan is immature and childlike, Mr Robson lures her to his house to satisfy obscure sexual needs (he asks her to undress in front of a mirror fixed to a screen behind which he disappears uttering grunting noises) and Mai seems to be a nymphomaniac. But as the narrative goes on, more and more hints are dropped that tell quite another story and present Betty not at all as a self-effacing mother, but as a scheming, if not deranged, personality. The children rightly complain about neglect, unsuspecting Mai gets sacked because Betty told lies about her and, worst of all, Betty manipulates Brendan to murder Mr Robson. The clearest hint at a second layer of truth is a note Mr Robson wrote about Betty which she comes across after his death:

> It would appear that this subject is a reckless young woman who will readily enter into a situation without any thought of consequences. Given certain factors she could be a danger to society. Without any qualms she sits on the other side of the screen with an air of expectation which would be frightening if it were not so interesting.[14]

In the end, all her scheming gets Betty nowhere: Brendan is in prison, Mai and Adam live together, forming a new family with the children, while Betty abandons herself to drink and mental collapse.

What, then, is the point of the novel? The deceptively simply told story, with its cleverly woven double layer of truths, proves another one of Owens's attempts at deconstructing the myth of the loving family, in this case the cliché of the self-sacrificing mother: it crumbles under the pressures of modern society. Betty is neither selfless nor even loving. Especially interesting is that Owens here, in so firmly setting the action in a working-class milieu, explicitly attacks the cliché of the warm solidarity of the working-class family, centring, as Richard Hoggart once put it nostalgically, on the mother as the pivot of the home. Under the conditions of postmodern society even this stronghold does not hold anymore – if it has not always been a construction. Additionally, the feminist ideal of emancipation by gainful work is deconstructed and revealed as a myth. Getting out of the house and swapping roles as breadwinner with Adam does not liberate Betty or add meaning to her existence in any way. Her life remains as lonely and chaotic as before. So the book, a particularly elaborate version of the topic of frustrated close relationships, does indeed tell a most depressing story. Owens has come a long way from her rather traditional beginnings, bespeaking idealistic trust in the stamina of the working class bravely to withstand any social pressures. What saves the novel from gloomy sentimentality is a marked streak of the grotesque and black humour, already heralded in some short stories and here reminiscent of Fay Weldon's she-devil or Hilary Mantel's Evelyn Axon, particularly in the Robson and Rossi scenes.

Owens's most recent novel, *For the Love of Willie* (1998), follows a similar cunning narrative structure insofar as, again, the full meaning is revealed only by an unexpected and shocking twist at the very end. The narrative situation is also comparable. The story is again told by a woman – this time Peggy, aged fifty – in a mental home to a fellow inmate. The time frame, however, is wider, juxtaposing the present as the time of narration and the war years as the time of action. Again a female myth is deconstructed: this time the myth of innocence ruthlessly seduced by the socially superior male employer. In contrast to *A Working Mother*, however, the circumstances of narration in the new novel alert the reader from the very beginning against any naïve acceptance of the story (which is interspersed with the hospital scenes) at its face value.[15] In not telling Peggy's story in the first person as she told Betty's, but in the third, she makes ironic use of the most conventional 'frame of mind' style of popular novels of the Mills and Boon type – which are all her only listener reads. Peggy's narration includes brief descriptions of the weather, of clothes, people's looks and the interior of houses, as well as insights into the heroine's thoughts and feelings, expressed in the most commonplace manner: 'At that moment she thought she had never loved him so much.'[16] Or 'He handed her a bit of toffee and she felt she was floating on air.'[17]

During the war Peggy, aged sixteen, is made pregnant by smart, womanizing Willie Ropers, manager of the village shop, for whom she does the paper round. The story avoids no cliché: Willie, quickly tired of the girl, suggests abortion or adoption, in unison with her mother. So far Peggy – in her own version of the story – appears as the classic victim in the tradition of Pamela, Tess and uncounted others, though there are some incidents that will not quite fit the image of the pure girl. Thus Peggy knows about Willie's sick wife and finds her attractive and kind, and she is herself not faithful to Willie. In the home for expectant mothers, where her mother hides her for the birth, the story takes the decisive turn: Peggy kills her child in order to avoid adoption, a murder for which she is then put into the mental home where the reader finds her writing her story thirty years later. No author's comment on Peggy's state of mind prepares the reader for the deed. We just read that Peggy handed over the quiet baby to the adopting young couple, and only then comes the shock, a chilling insight into Peggy's state of mind: 'And only now that she was safely on the tram did she allow herself the luxury of wondering how long it would take the couple to discover the baby was dead.'[18] The murder of a baby is treated as just a practical joke. Peggy's earlier resolve to keep the baby has proved a hollow pose which easily collapses when her mother slaps her in the face. Peggy is no Esther Waters, bravely taking up the challenge of single motherhood, nor has she as good reasons as Sethe in Toni Morrison's novel *Beloved*, who killed her daughter to save her from slavery.

For the Love of Willie is another text in which Owens reveals the degradation of human relationships, even the closest of them. In her last two novels Owens particularly focuses on demythologizing the role of women who, since the eighteenth century, had been ideologically elevated to the position of 'angels in the home' or 'priestesses of the hearth', as they were described in the famous epithets of Patmore and Ruskin. Owens's women are no longer providers of comfort in a hostile world, but so weak or so wicked that they are reduced to mental cases, and the asylum seems the proper place for them. Ever since Wollstonecraft's *The Wrongs of Woman*, mental asylums have been used in literature as places symbolizing the unjust limitations imposed on women by society, but here the asylum seems appropriate because the madness of society has infected these women's heads and hearts, turning them from innocent victims into culprits themselves. *For the Love of Willie* does, however, offer a glimpse of hope at the end. When the hospital has to close down because of cuts in the National Health Service, Peggy is transferred to a flat she will have to share with an old and rather dotty woman, released from another asylum. Rather than jumping from the high-rise as she had planned, Peggy decides to look after this woman.

Summing up, I would say that Agnes Owens, by applying a feminist perspective as well as postmodern narrative techniques, has ventured on an exciting new type of working-class writing – though her messages are by no means always cheering.

Notes

[1] Agnes Owens, 'Marching to the Highlands and into the Unknown', in *People Like That* (London, 1996), 175.

[2] Laura Cumming, 'The mother of invention' (review of *A Working Mother*), *Guardian* (10 May 1994).

[3] Here is an example: ' "Sorry, aboot that, Paddy," spluttered Splash. "I'll get ye anither drink". "Yae, well watch it then," said Paddy. He added, "I never thought tae see the day when an animal wid put a man aff his drink – here, whit the hell ist that?" ' Agnes Owens, *Gentlemen of the West* (Edinburgh, 1984), 65.

[4] Agnes Owens, *Like Birds in the Wilderness* (London, 1987), 10.

[5] Owens, *Gentlemen*, 96.

[6] Ibid., 92.

[7] Ibid., 126.

[8] Alasdair Gray, 'Thoughts suggested by Agnes Owens's *Gentlemen of the West*, and an appreciation of it', *Edinburgh Review*, 71 (1985), 31.

[9] Ibid., 32.

[10] Owens, *People*, 9.

[11] James Kelman, Agnes Owens, Alasdair Gray, *Lean Tales* (London, 1987 [1985]), 120.

[12] Owens, *People*, 139.

[13] Agnes Owens, *A Working Mother* (London, 1994), 149.

[14] Ibid., 133.

[15] Agnes Owens, *For the Love of Willie* (London, 1998). The hospital scenes offer a bitterly satirical picture of the loveless atmosphere and the inexpert treatment in a NHS mental home where the nurses drug the patients in case of any sign of independent thinking.

[16] Owens, *Willie*, 31.

[17] Ibid., 5.

[18] Ibid., 16.

Index